IMAGES
of America
ASHLAND

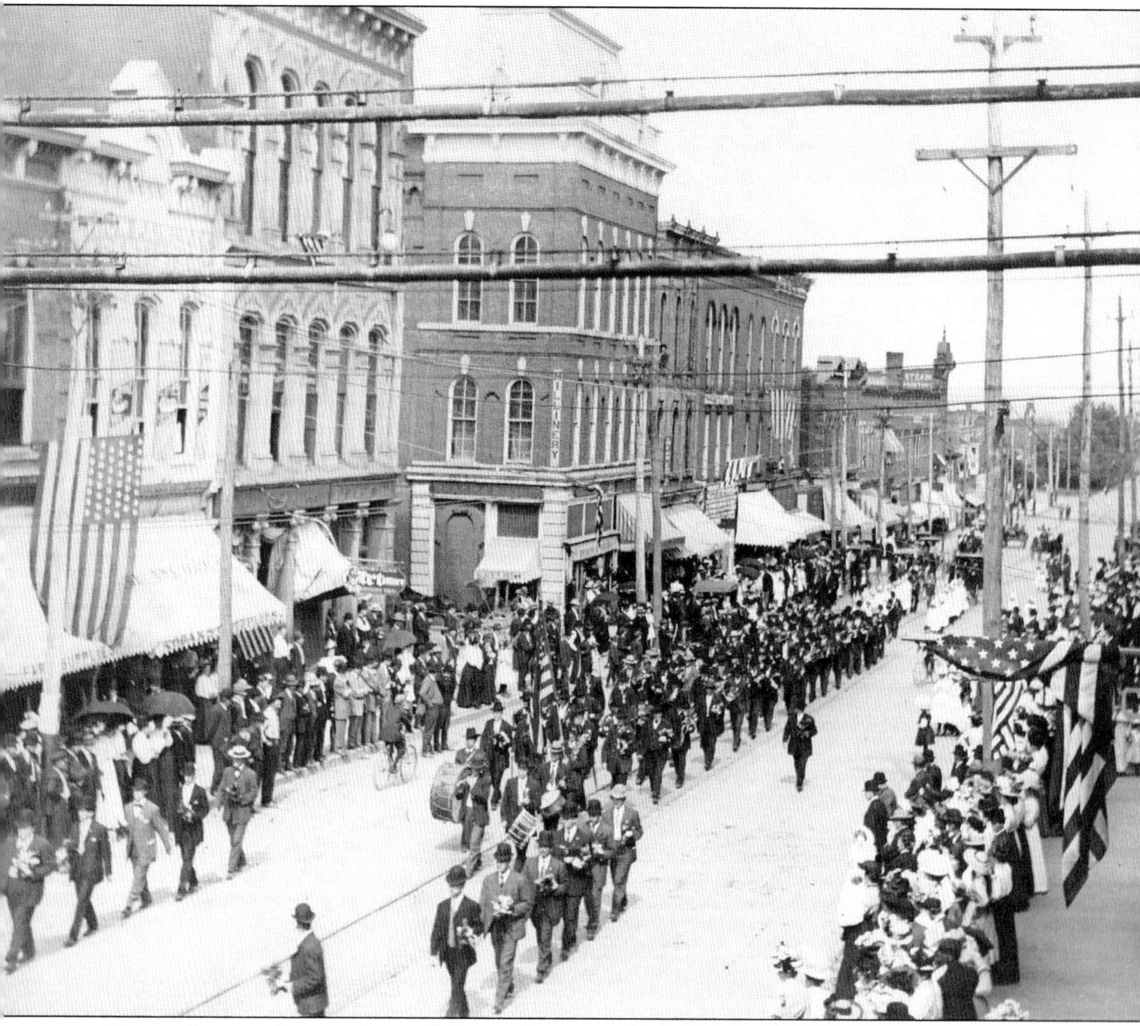

Remembering the sacrifices of those who came before us took place as early as 1868, when Decoration Day was first observed at Arlington Cemetery by placing flowers at the graves of Civil War soldiers. The citizens of Ashland are shown above, parading Main Street to the cemetery in remembrance of their own hometown fallen heroes. This photograph of American flags flying high, men carrying flowers, ladies with colorful hats, and children keeping stride behind the band was taken on Decoration Day in 1909. Through the years, Decoration Day became known as Memorial Day. It is still observed today as not only a day to remember the veterans of this great nation, but as a time to remember and honor all who came before us, especially our own hometown men, women, and children. (Ashland County Historical Society collection.)

On the Cover: At the fire station on the corner of Second and Orange Streets is William Greenamyer, the driver of the fire department's horse-drawn ladder wagon. Pictured in 1912, Greenamyer is ready for business with his trusty fireman's dog, along with a neighborhood boy, Paul Shank, posing in back of the wagon, and the station's team of horses, Frank and Bill. Frank and Bill faithfully served the city for nearly 16 years until the first motorized fire truck was purchased in 1919. (Ashland County Historical Society collection.)

IMAGES
of America

ASHLAND

Christine H. Box on behalf of
the Ashland County Historical Society

ARCADIA
PUBLISHING

ISBN 978-0-7385-8266-5

Published by Arcadia Publishing
Charleston, South Carolina

Printed in the United States of America

Library of Congress Control Number: 2011928804

For all general information, please contact Arcadia Publishing:
Telephone 843-853-2070
Fax 843-853-0044
E-mail sales@arcadiapublishing.com
For customer service and orders:
Toll-Free 1-888-313-2665

Visit us on the Internet at www.arcadiapublishing.com

To Betty for your endless devotion to the history of Ashland

Contents

ACKNOWLEDGMENTS

The Ashland County Historical Society was founded in 1981. Since that time, many hands have come together, giving countless hours to provide an invaluable resource about past generations of this community. It is my wish to thank all that have given endlessly to the preservation of local history. Because of you, the historical society's archives, research library, and collection of photographs have provided immense support to the writing of this book. The pages within cannot begin to hold the amount of history that this community embraces. The direction of this book was led by the images made available in the museum collection. It became evident upon the start of this paperback pictorial that much of the town's illustrative history is missing within the Ashland County Historical Society's archives. There is so much more to tell and share; therefore, to the Ashland community, I ask for you to please remember to provide your photographs, memorabilia, and stories with the historical society, as it seeks to maintain the history of this great city. Remembering the past for future generations is the most important gift that we can give to those who follow in our footsteps.

To the outstanding staff, volunteers, and trustees of the historical society, I give my most sincere gratitude for your daily assistance, research, understanding, and encouragement during the days preceding this publication. To Spectrum Photo and Digital Services, thank you for your tireless advice and the outstanding, professional image scanning for this assignment. I also give appreciation and gratefulness to those that have shared their own research information and photographs for use in these pages. This venture could not have been completed without each and every one of you. Lastly, to my family, thank you for your love, support, and understanding during this lengthy project.

Unless otherwise noted, the photographs on the following pages appear courtesy of the Ashland County Historical Society.

INTRODUCTION

Ashland, Ohio, had settlers within its boundaries as early as 1811, but it was in 1815 that William Montgomery established the village, first known as Uniontown, named after Montgomery's hometown in Pennsylvania. Prior to that time, mound builders erected mounds while Native Americans roamed this unsettled area of the state. Beginning on a single street of dust and mud with 14 family cabins strung along its edge, the one-lane settlement began to develop. By 1822, the town had grown to include a blacksmith shop, a shoemaker, a tannery, a tavern, three distilleries, a general store, and one physician. It was at this time that a petition was made for a post office. Though upon this request, it was discovered that there was more than one Uniontown in Ohio, and the village was given the new name of Ashland, named after Henry Clay's estate in Kentucky. From that point on, the growing community had its own identity, growing strong through the years. It became the county seat in 1846 with 1,300 residents, 5 churches, 16 stores, 2 newspapers, and a private academy for both boys and girls.

From the beginning days of this modest village, growth came about quickly with an increase in population, as well as events, occasions, and inventions falling on the heels of one another. By 1915, the 100th anniversary of the town, Ashland was a force of industry. Busting at the seams with inventions, local manufacturers became world leaders in their field, turning Ashland into the hub of industry in Ohio. When the introduction of the railroad made its way to the manufacturing corridor of the community, pumps, animal remedies, balloons, and auto jacks found their way around the globe. Known for the popular Myers Pump, as well as for being the balloon capital of the world with more than 70 percent of the world's balloons manufactured here, Ashland was on the map. The local industry of today has seen many changes, adapting to the economic transformation of the times with a new generation leading the way.

It is important to remember that industry was not the only special part of this town's history. Most notably, it was the people of Ashland that formed a caring society, connecting with each other through years of growth, prosperity, hard times, and change. The years past have shaped a compassionate community that was, is, and will always be an exceptional place to live and raise a family. With that in mind, a favorite town slogan, "Ashland, Someplace Special," could not be more appropriate for this small town situated in the heart of Ohio.

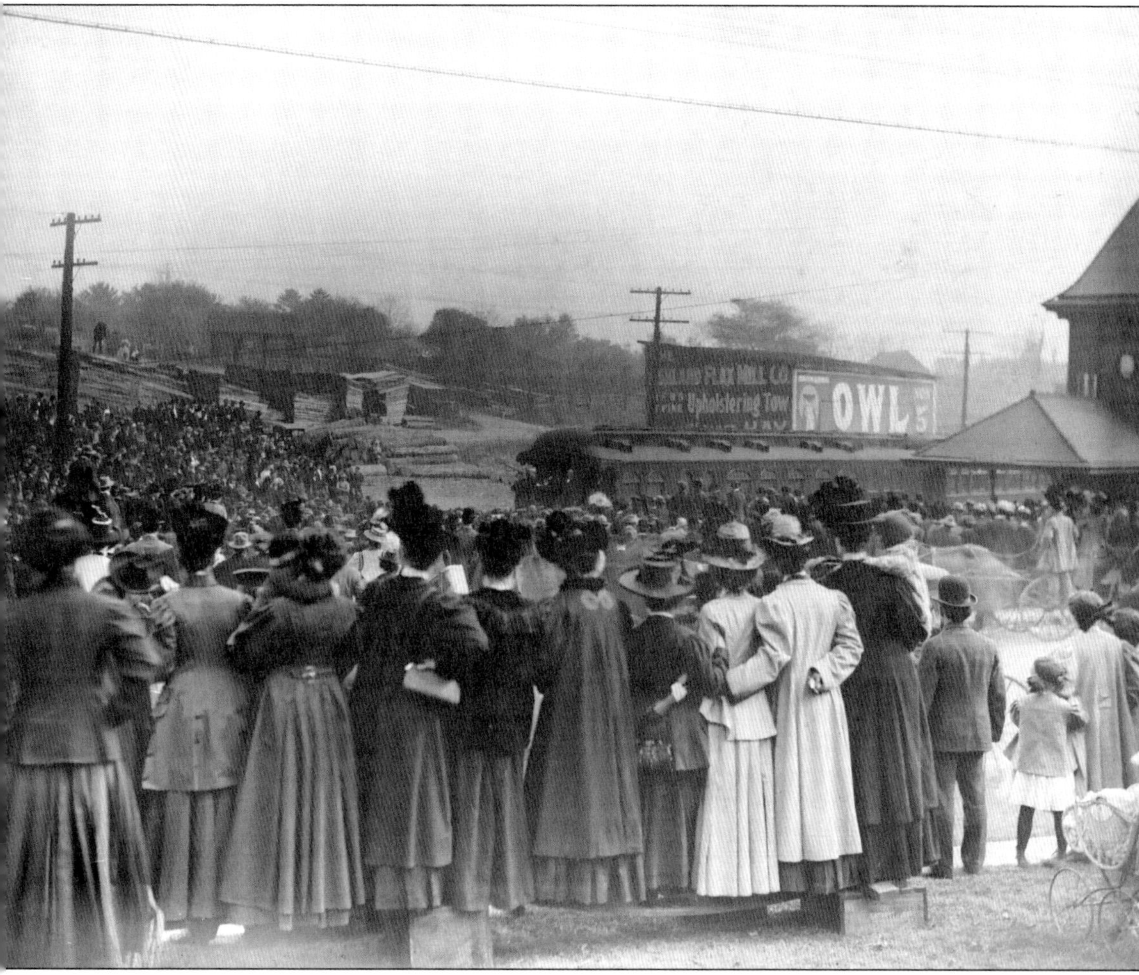

Before the days of airplanes and driving the highways, travelers used the rails to make their way across the country. The railroad was Ashland's link to the nation, and this link brought the above presidential candidate to the town. On his third run for the presidency, Democrat William Jennings Bryan made a whistle-stop speech at the Erie Railway depot in 1908. Witnessed by thousands, Bryan campaigned from the back of a train while pausing at the Erie depot for a 15-minute speech. A Democratic town at the time, the city carried Bryan, though he was defeated for the presidency by Republican William H. Taft in the 1908 election.

One

Friends of the Community

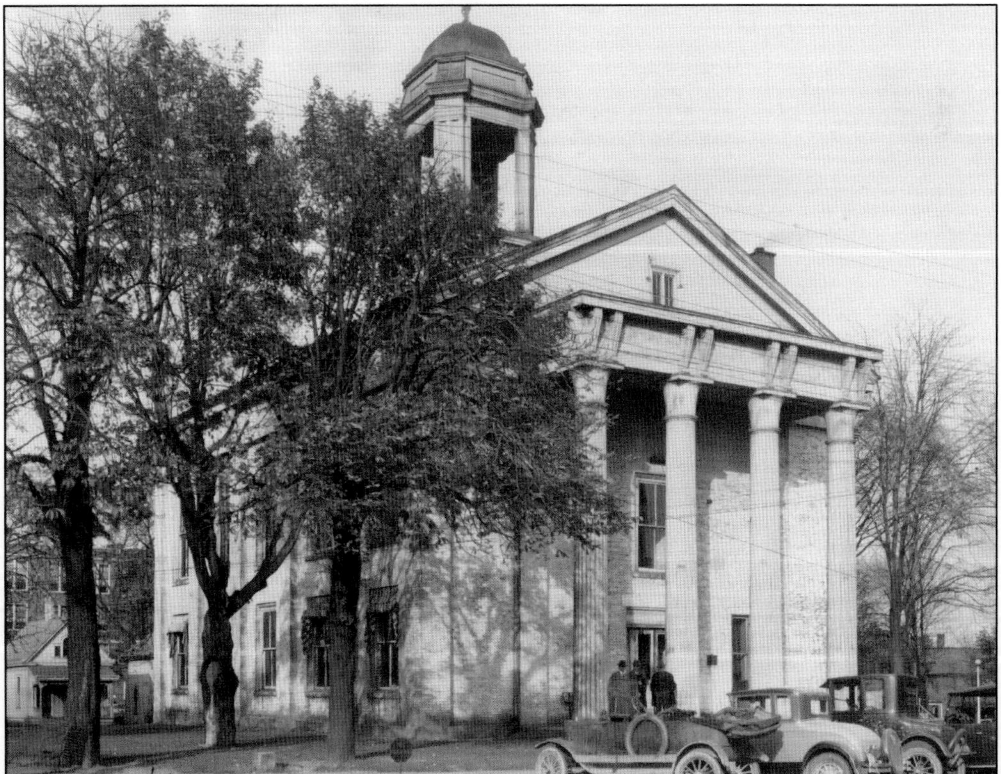

Ashland County came into being in 1846. Seven years later came the construction of the white-pillared courthouse, as pictured above. Located at the corner of Second and Cottage Streets, this house of government was completed in 1853 at a cost of $20,000. Located on the first floor of the new courthouse were the treasurer, auditor, recorder, clerk of courts, and probate judge offices. The second floor housed the county commissioner's office, common pleas judge chambers, and courtroom. Outside privies were attached. This courthouse proudly served the people until growth of the community forced its replacement in 1928.

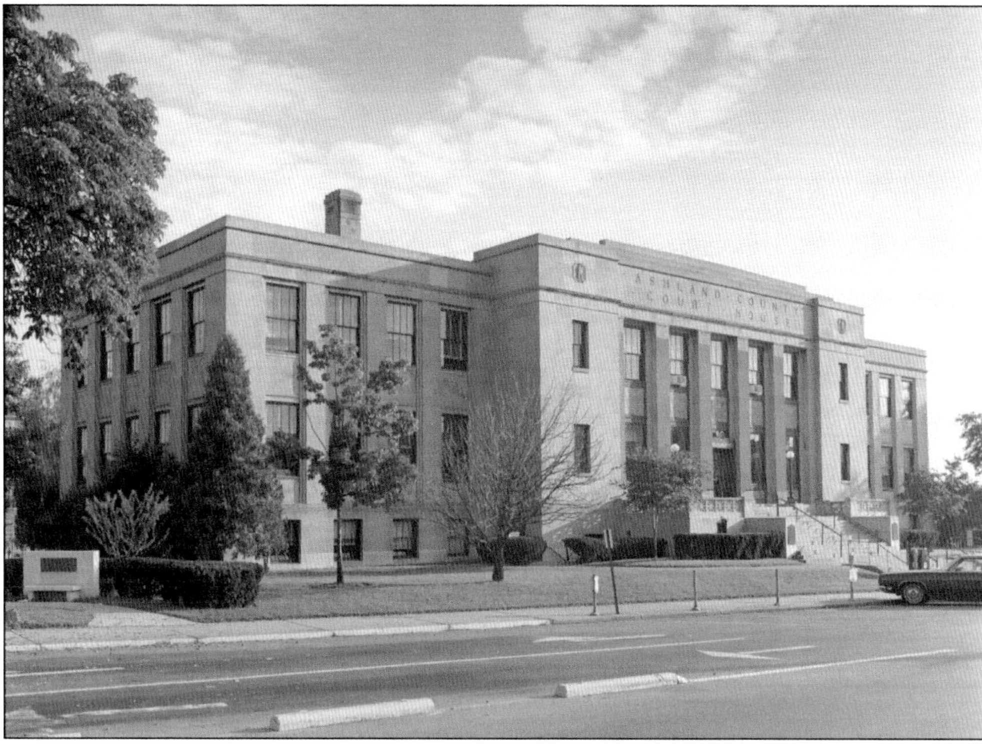

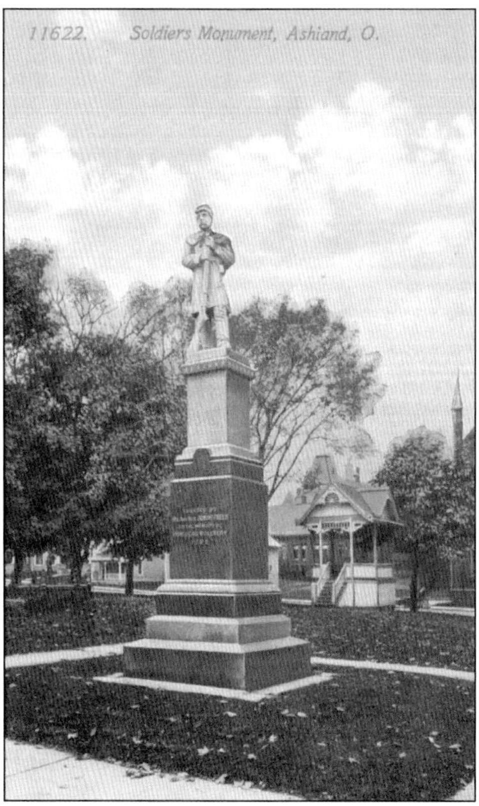

By 1928, with the increase in the county's population, the first courthouse was no longer sufficient for conducting county business. Over the objection of many, the decision was made for it to be replaced by a larger, more modern courthouse, pictured above, at the same location. That new $315,000 courthouse was dedicated on September 2, 1929, and continues to serve the community today. (Barb Queer collection.)

This Soldiers Monument stands proudly on the courthouse lawn in honor of the Union soldiers of the Civil War. Mary A. Freer, wife of merchant and banker Jonas Freer, gave the monument to the town in 1888. Former president Rutherford B. Hayes spoke at the November 15 dedication, praising Freer for her patriotism. The monument faithfully looks over the citizens of Ashland today on the Second and Church Streets corner.

This Victorian home was built in 1886 on land sold to the city for $2,500. It was one of the finest residences in town, standing on the corners of Second, Cottage, and Main Streets, an area referred to as Jail Hill. Known for its projecting bays, busy roofline, and imposing tower, this mansion, built to signify importance, was the Ashland County Jail and home to the sheriff and his family. Over time, the old jail, as it became known, did not meet the needs of the judicial system. Amongst controversy, the community voted to raze the building. On November 8, 1977, the old jail was brought down, leaving room on the corner of Cottage and Main Streets for widening to ease traffic flow through town. The picture below shows an unidentified sheriff on the jail steps with his family.

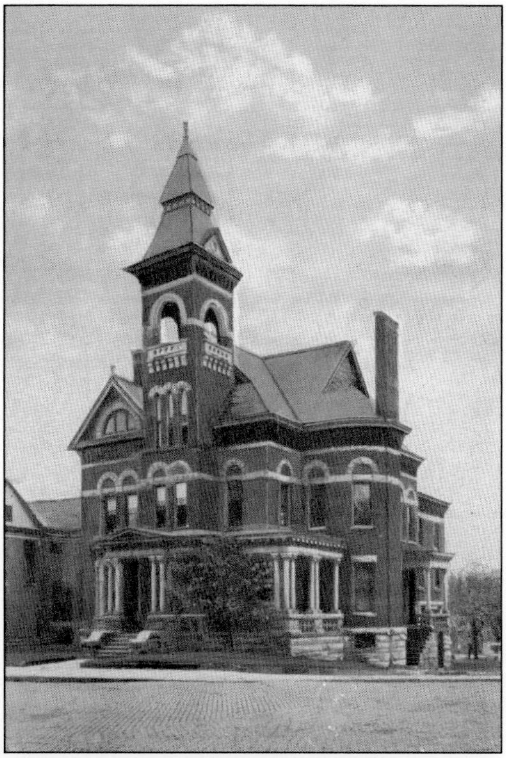

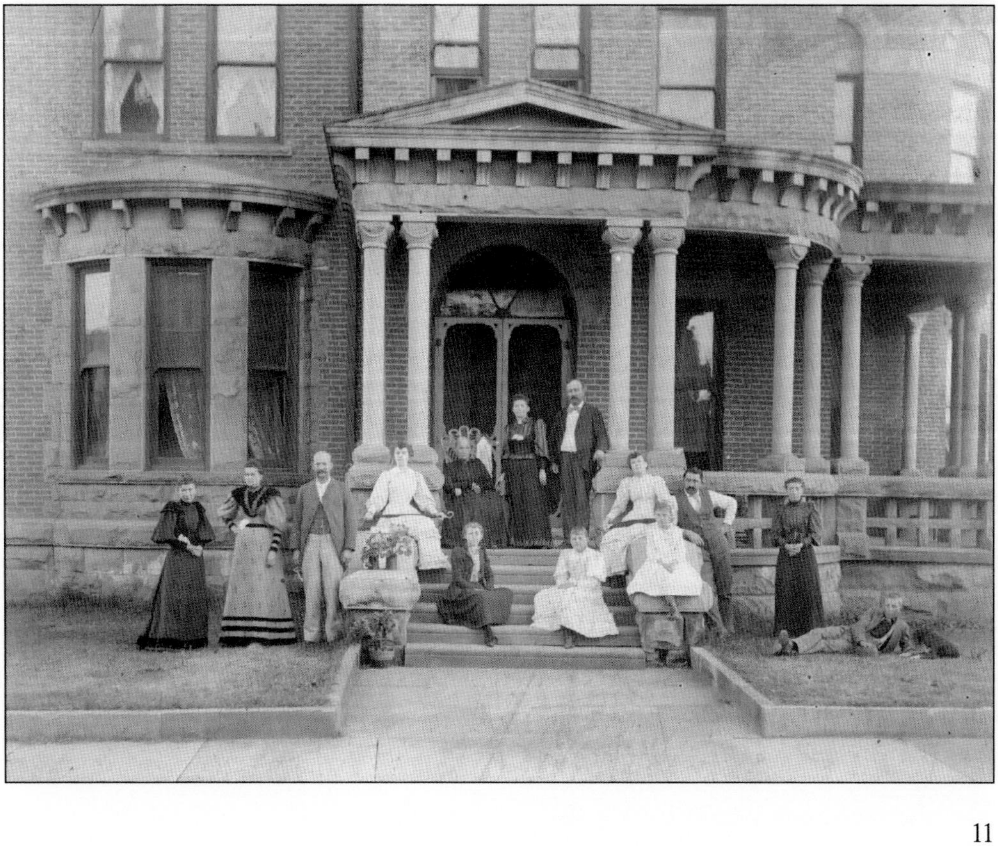

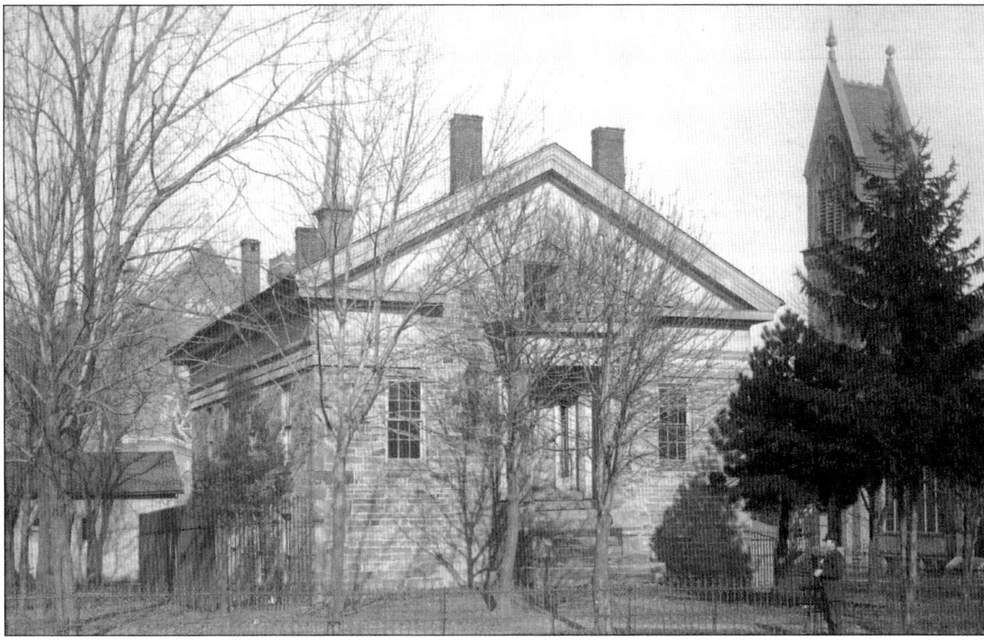

George Andrew Horn, 24, and William Henry Gribben, 28, were housed for more than a year in the town's first jail on Second Street, accused of the murder of Henry Williams of Polk, Ohio. On May 16, 1884, Horn and Gribben were hanged on the lawn between the courthouse and jail. The yard was enclosed, and only the most prominent of Ashland's citizen were issued tickets, pictured below, to witness the 9:00 a.m. hanging. The ticket allowed witnesses to sit on benches and, thus, be "assistants to the execution." Outside the enclosure, an angry mob of 6,000 was controlled by the Ohio Militia, which had been summoned to stand guard. This became the last public hanging in the state of Ohio, as there was much controversy and rioting surrounding such events.

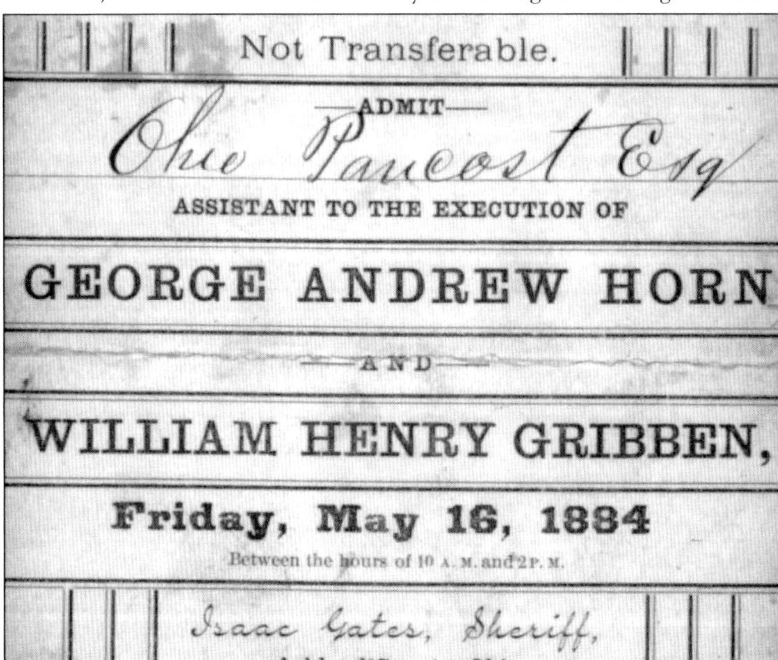

Not Transferable.

—ADMIT—

Ohio Pancost Esq

ASSISTANT TO THE EXECUTION OF

GEORGE ANDREW HORN

—AND—

WILLIAM HENRY GRIBBEN,

Friday, May 16, 1884

Between the hours of 10 A. M. and 2 P. M.

Isaac Gates, Sheriff,

Ashland County, Ohio.

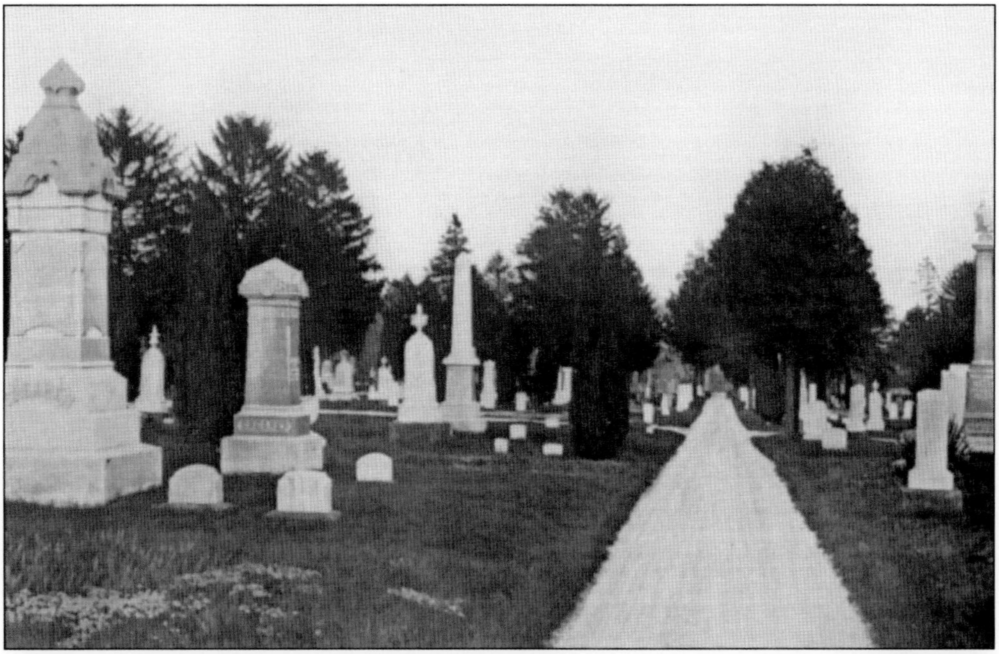

In 1856, a group of leading citizens formed a cemetery association under the laws of the State of Ohio. Then, with the purchase of 10 acres for $819.50 from Lorin Andrews, a cemetery was developed at 523 Main Street. Years later, more acreage was purchased to assure that space would be available for future citizens. Additionally, a home was built for the cemetery superintendent to the left of the entrance.

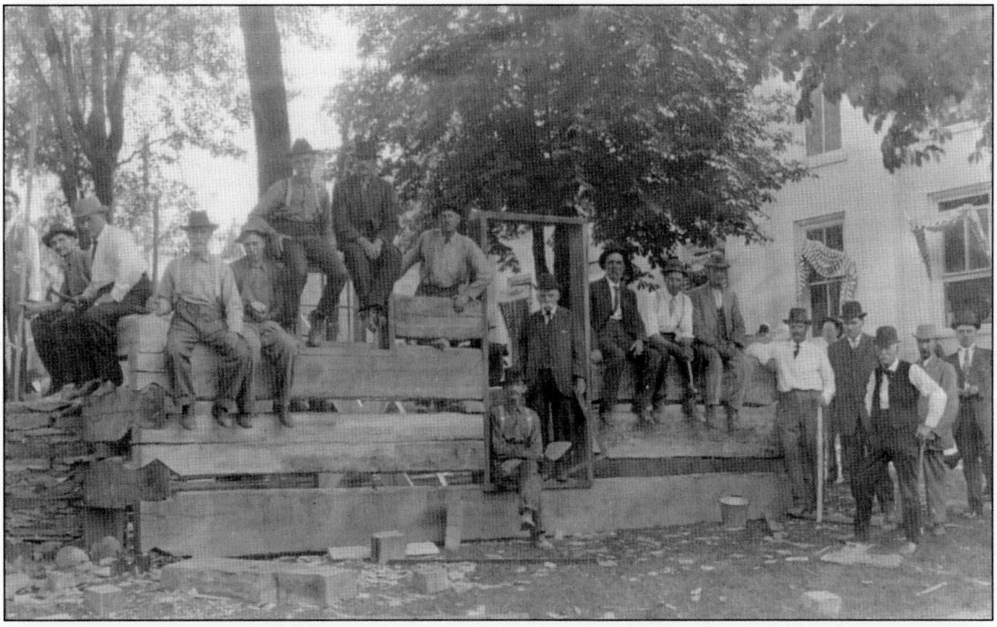

In celebration of the 100-year anniversary of the town, the Carter cabin was reconstructed in the courthouse park in 1915. In 1815, the Daniel Carter family was the first settlers in Montgomery Township on the Loudonville Road (State Route 60). The above group of hardworking men used original logs from the Carter cabin to construct the pioneer cabin in the park.

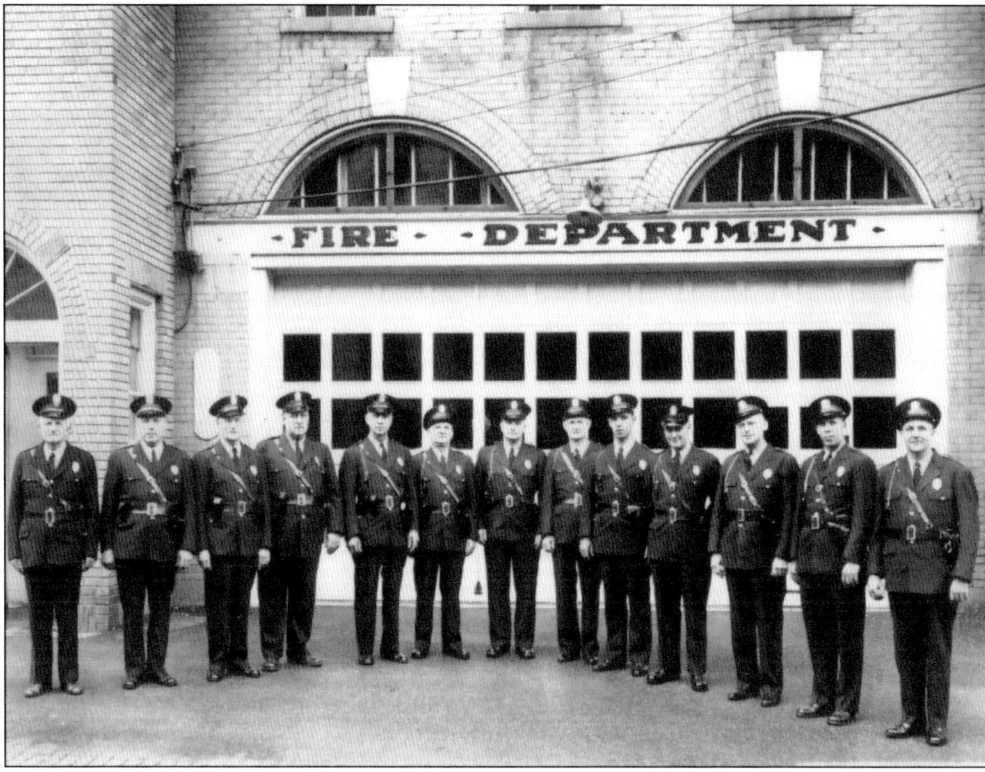

Early records state that in 1844, Marshal Abe Swineford kept peace in the streets. The growth of the town forced the need for more protection in the community, and by 1911, the town boasted a police chief and three officers. Nine men patrolled the town in 1940, and the police department combined locations with the fire department on Second Street. The force is pictured above in 1942 with Chief Miles McCarty, second from left, in front of the fire and police building. In 1956, town growth moved the peacekeepers to the Municipal Building on Claremont Avenue. They were moved again in 2000 to the Justice Center on East Main Street, with 30 officers protecting streets under Chief William Miracle's command. Pictured below are officers preparing to destruct confiscated alcohol by court order in 1947. (Both, Ashland Police Department collection.)

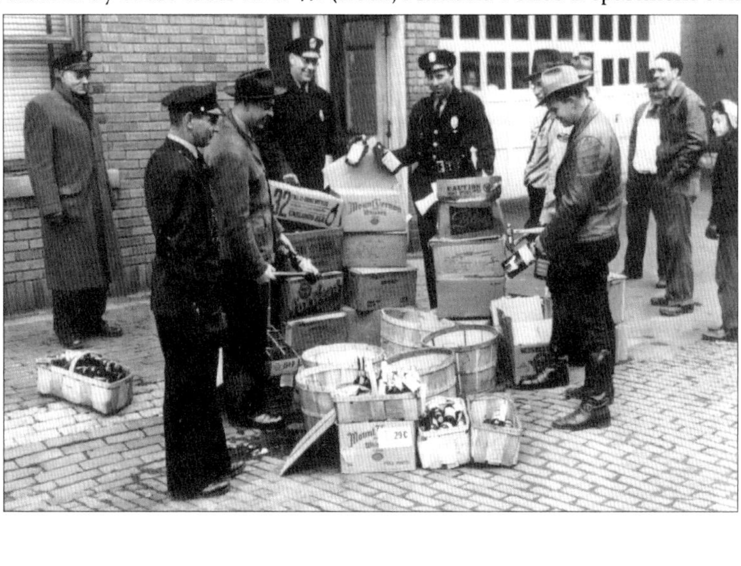

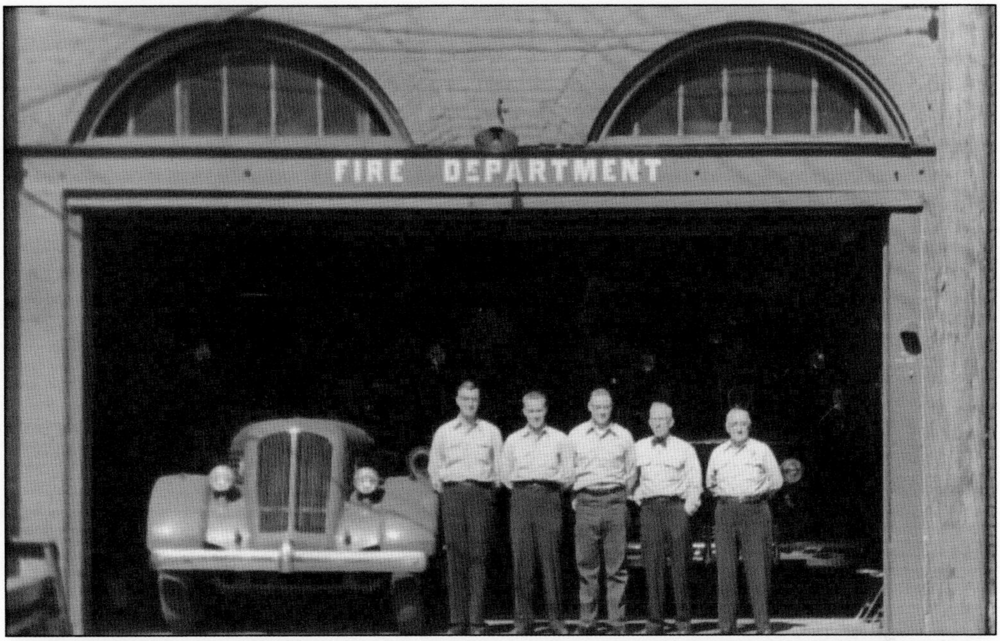

As early as 1853, the town had a volunteer fire unit. By 1882, the Citizens Relief Fire Company was organized with William Stubbs as volunteer chief, assisted by P.A. Myers. In the late 1880s, the first station was built, located at the corner of Second and Orange Streets. In later years, the municipal offices, police department, and the city jail were housed on the west end. Standing at attention above in the mid-1950s are, from left to right, firemen Paul Soles Jr., Bob Willis, Harold Keener, Roby Tobias, and Chief Paul Soles Sr. In 1903, the department purchased its first ladder wagon, pictured below with volunteer chief Henry J. Shultz (white coat), driver E.B. Hettinger, driving horses Frank and Bill, and four others. The station was relocated to 274 Cleveland Avenue in December 1970. (Above, Ashland Fire Department collection.)

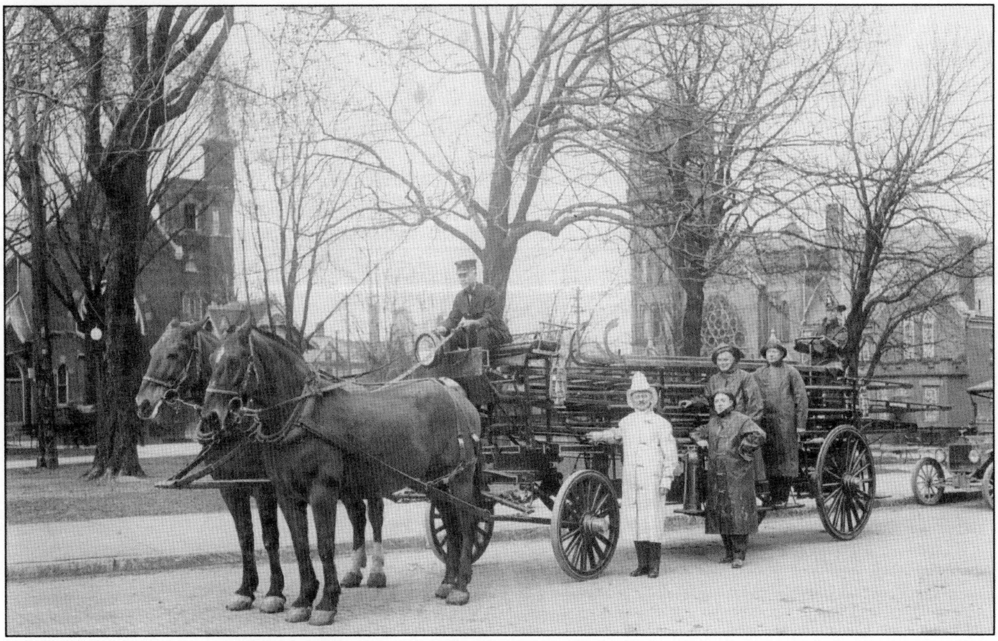

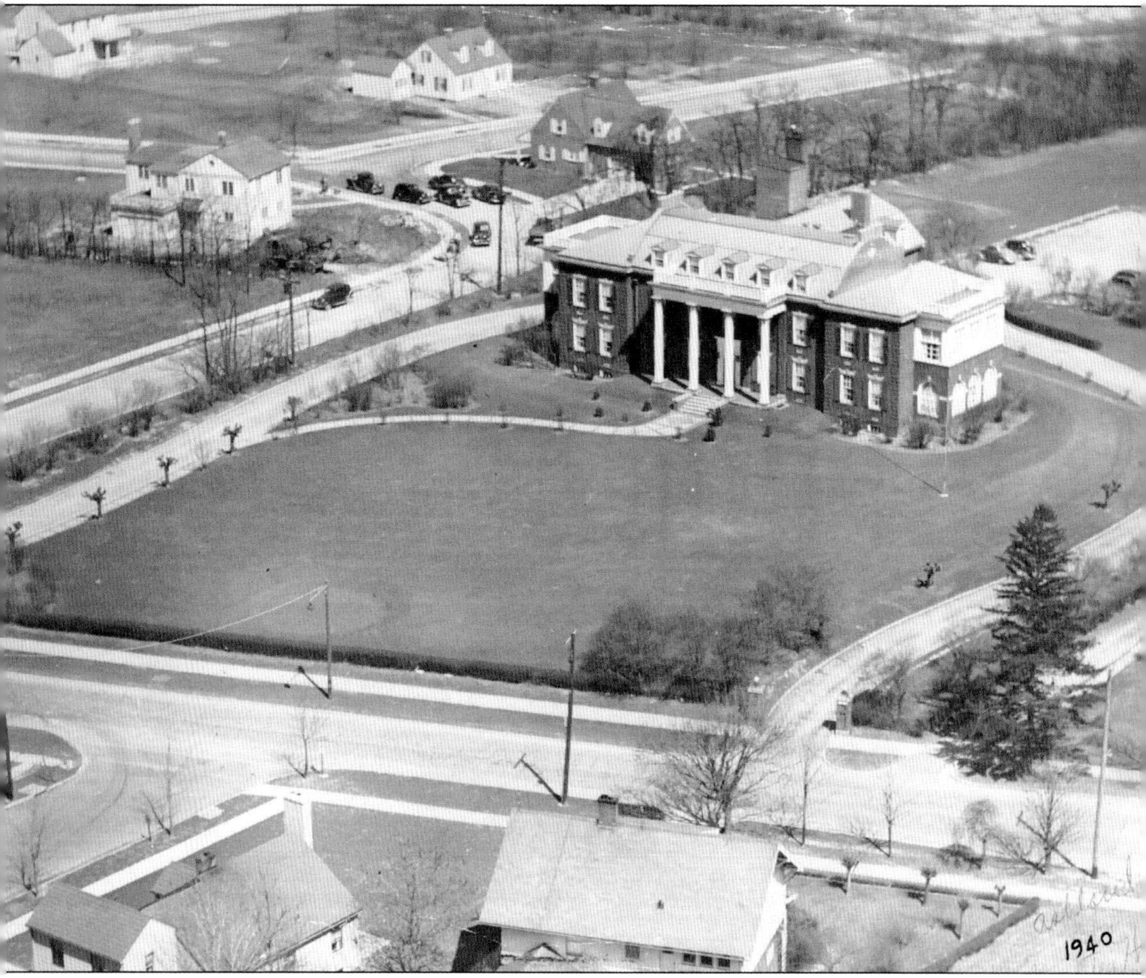

The community was blessed with its first hospital through the generosity of Jesse Lewis Clark. After attending the Lutheran Church one Sunday in 1911, Clark pondered the morning lesson of being a Good Samaritan. It was at that time that Clark realized that no sick person should ever be refused care, rich and poor alike. Clark conceived the plan and provided the resources for the construction of Samaritan Hospital, the first in the community, situated atop a gentle four-acre slope overlooking the country, shown above in 1940. The 27-bed facility was dedicated on May 28, 1912, along with a training school for nurses. This program continued until it was phased out in 1974. In addition to patient charges of $1 per day or $2 for a private room, an endowment fund was created to support hospital expenses.

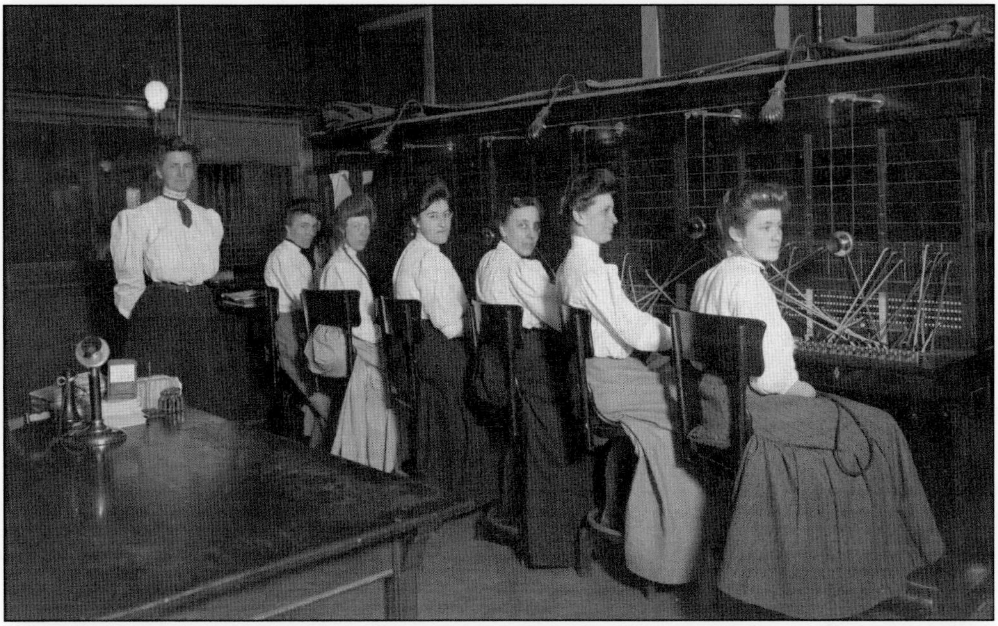

The Peoples Telephone Company, established in 1886, was the first telephone exchange in town. In 1899, with 30 telephones in the city, Peoples was purchased by the Star Telephone Company, under the direction of Howard Grabill and several partners. The above 1905 photograph shows Star switchboard operators in the Guth Building at the corner of Church and Second Streets, which served as its headquarters until 1952. The photograph below shows a larger team of operators in 1952, an indication of the growth and popularity of the telephone network. Northern Ohio Telephone purchased Star in 1953, moving operations to 128 Main Street. Northern Ohio was purchased by General Telephone Company in 1975, eventually becoming GTE North from 1988 to 2000. The company moved its headquarters in 1994 to 1534 SR 511 South. Verizon Communications took control in 2000 and was sold to Frontier Communications in 2010.

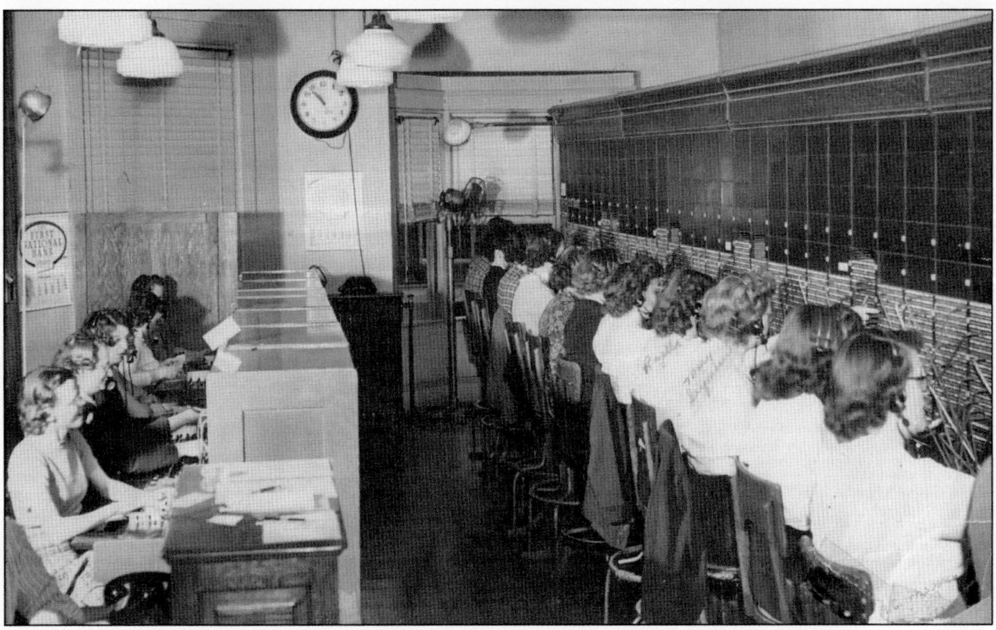

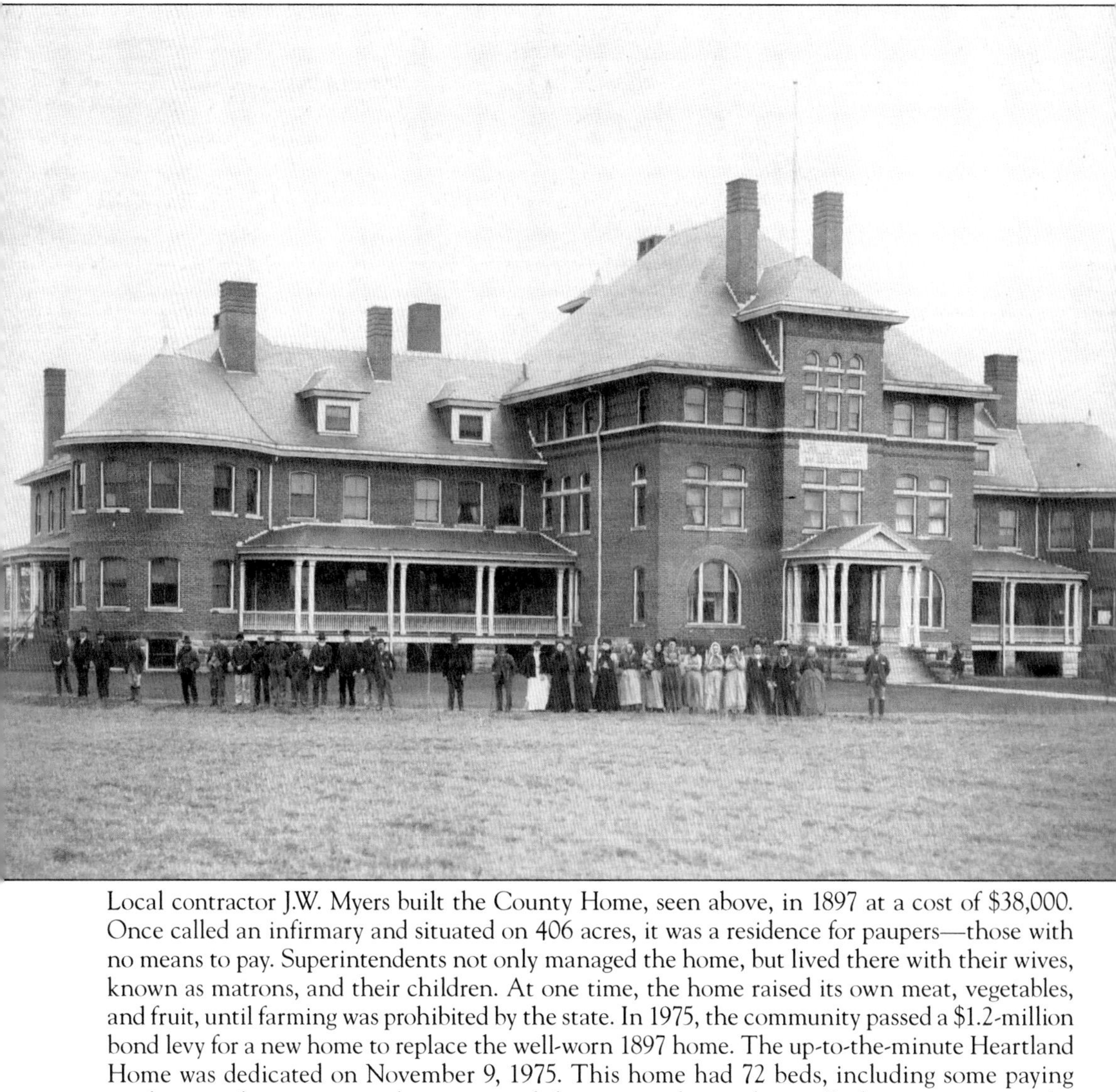

Local contractor J.W. Myers built the County Home, seen above, in 1897 at a cost of $38,000. Once called an infirmary and situated on 406 acres, it was a residence for paupers—those with no means to pay. Superintendents not only managed the home, but lived there with their wives, known as matrons, and their children. At one time, the home raised its own meat, vegetables, and fruit, until farming was prohibited by the state. In 1975, the community passed a $1.2-million bond levy for a new home to replace the well-worn 1897 home. The up-to-the-minute Heartland Home was dedicated on November 9, 1975. This home had 72 beds, including some paying residents, and over time, no longer carried the stigma of a poorhouse. Budget restraints on the county caused its closing by county commissioners in 2009.

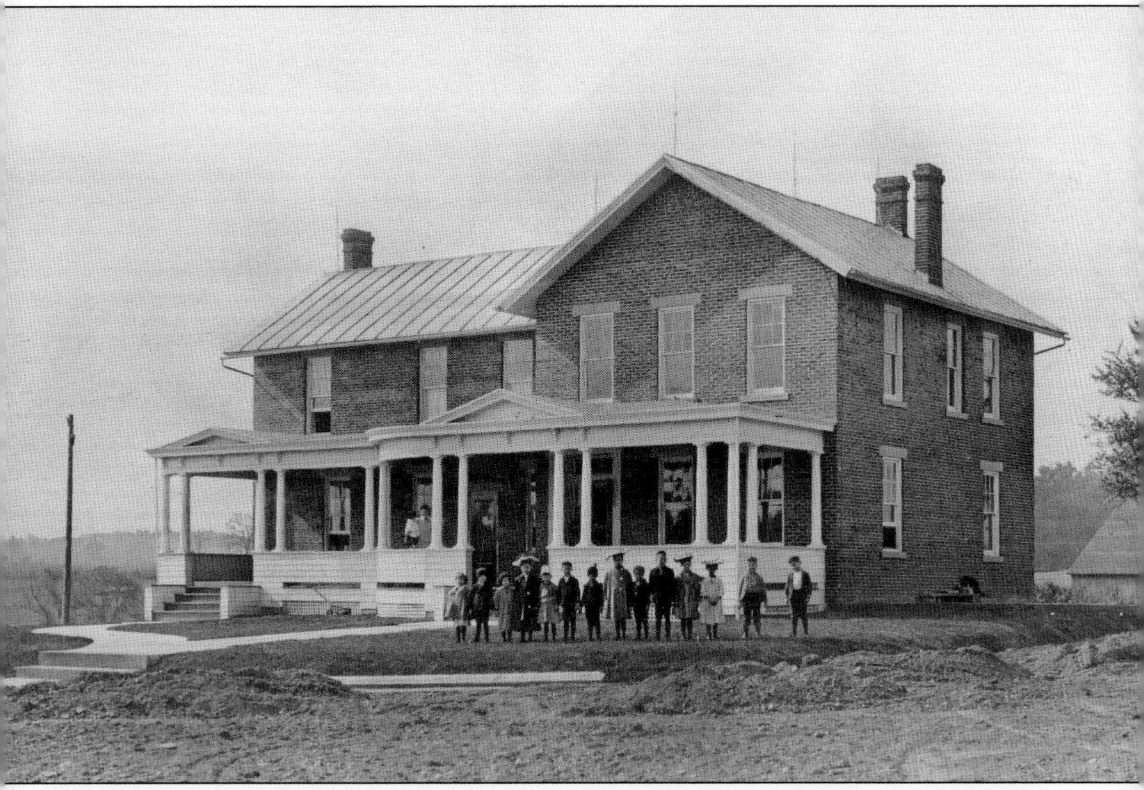

Children held a special place in the heart of Mary Freer. Having no children of her own, she raised nine orphans, including historian Will Duff, in her home at the southeast corner of Center and Walnut Streets. Upon her death, Mary, wife of merchant and banker Jonas Freer, willed 94 acres, including a farmhouse and barn on Hayesville Road (Center Street), to the county commissioners for an orphanage. The farmhouse was converted to house 19 children, and upon its dedication on October 17, 1907, fourteen orphans had a new home, as pictured above. Nearly 1,000 children over the course of 80-plus years lived in the children's home. Additions and changes were made to the home in 1934 and again in 1952. Mr. and Mrs. L.C. Chamberland were the first hired to manage the operation, which included the farming of the land and raising the cattle. The children assisted in their own care, helping with household chores, and running the farm. In 1989, the home became the office building for various agencies that continue to serve the children of the county.

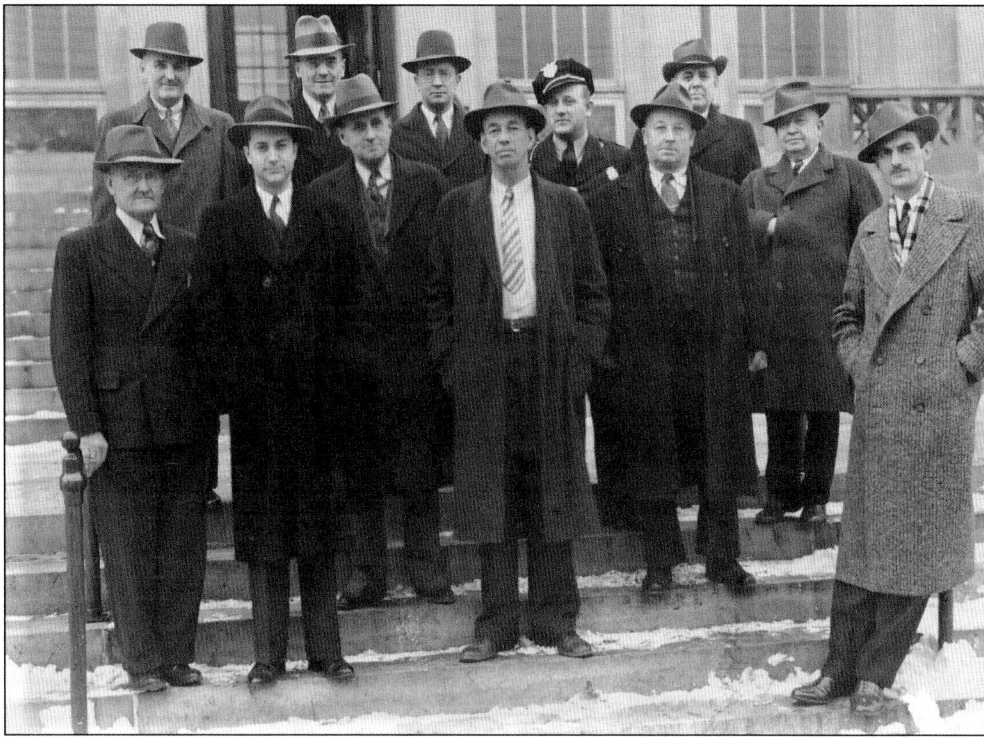

The 1941 elected city officials posing are, from left to right, (first row) L.G. Shenberger, engineer; A.R. Siverling, prosecuting attorney; T.J. Stence, H.F. Wallett, and C.I. Harmon, commissioners; S.H. Boffenmeyer, probate judge; and K.K. Kick, treasurer; (second row): R.H. Maffett, recorder; F.E. Wicks, auditor; C.A. McBride, clerk of courts; L.D. Hammond, sheriff; and H.E. Culbertson, common pleas judge.

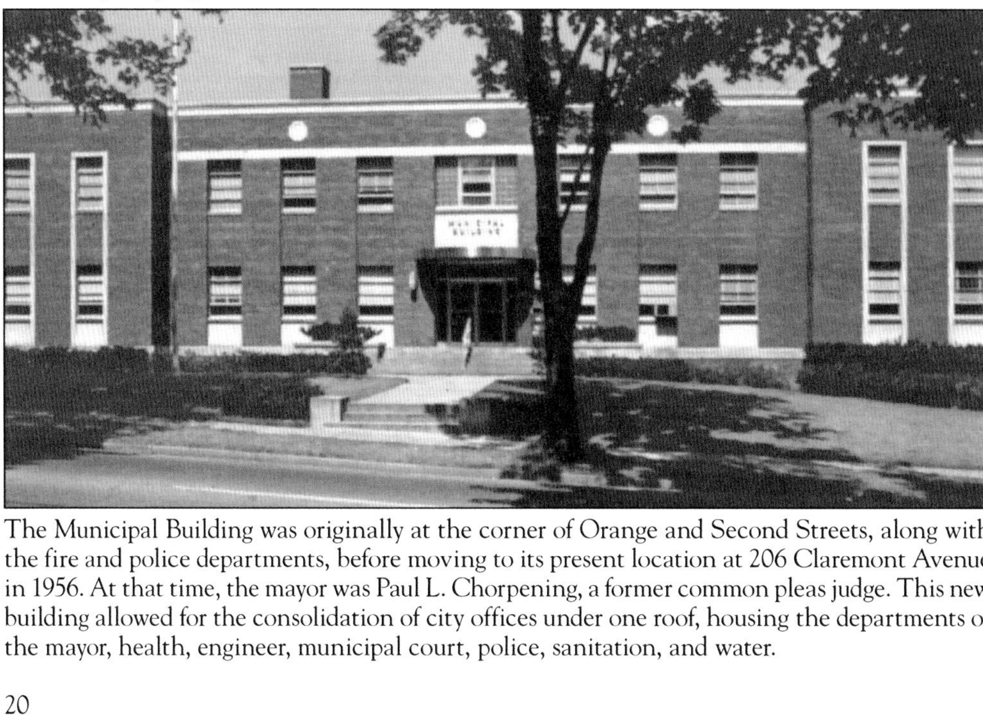

The Municipal Building was originally at the corner of Orange and Second Streets, along with the fire and police departments, before moving to its present location at 206 Claremont Avenue in 1956. At that time, the mayor was Paul L. Chorpening, a former common pleas judge. This new building allowed for the consolidation of city offices under one roof, housing the departments of the mayor, health, engineer, municipal court, police, sanitation, and water.

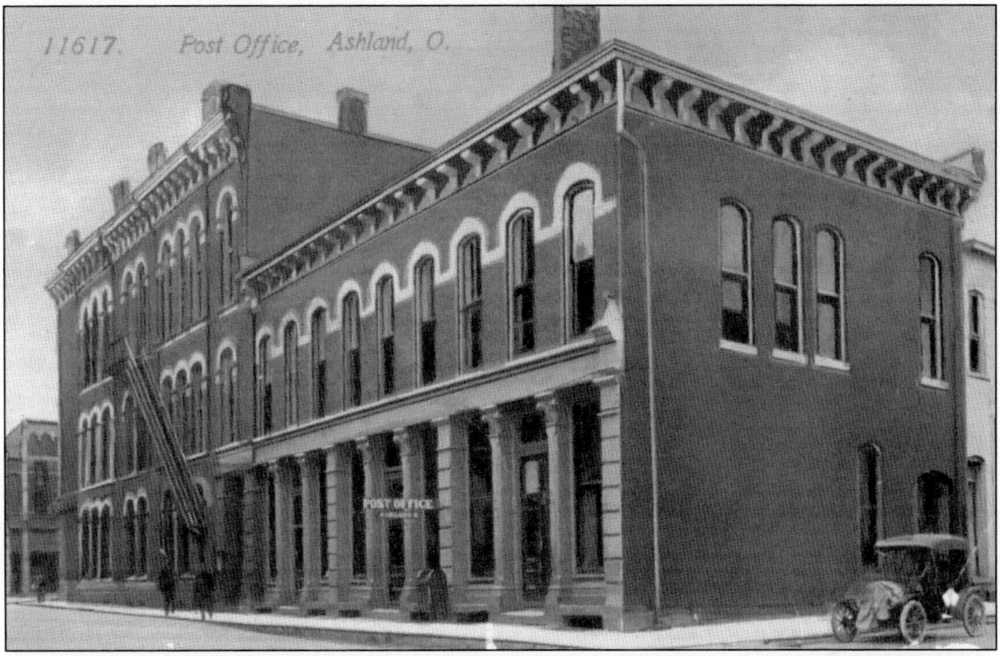

Arriving in town from Sandusky, Ohio, in 1821, Francis Graham opened a mercantile business and soon realized the need for a post office. Upon this request to district congressman Judge Sloan, Graham discovered that Ohio already had one Uniontown; therefore, the new name of Ashland was chosen, named after Henry Clay's estate in Kentucky. Becoming the first postmaster, Graham conducted postal business first in his home, then at various locations on Main Street before finally settling on Orange Street in 1874 behind the First National Bank building, as shown above. By 1915, local postal receipts totaled $110,000 per year, the largest for its size in the United States. With increased demand for service, a new $100,000 post office, below, was built in 1917 on the northwest corner of Cottage, Main, and Sandusky Streets. It was relocated to 530 Claremont Avenue in 1968.

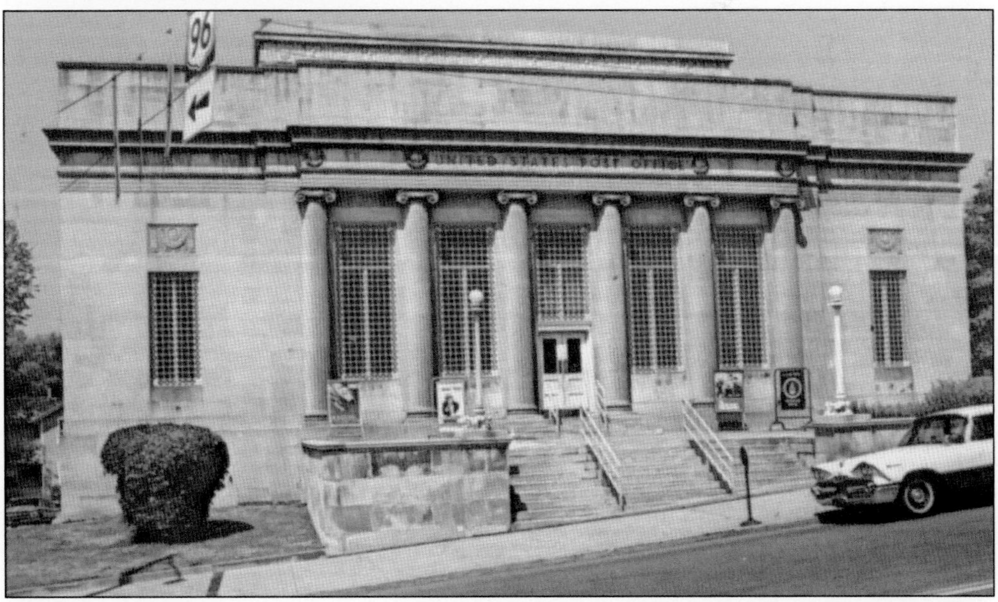

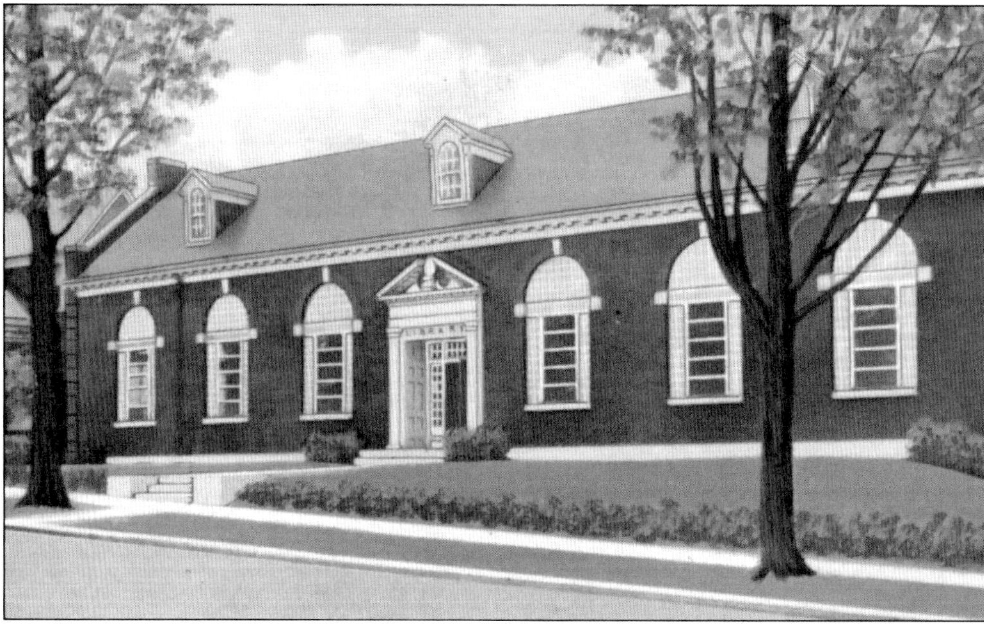

A library service was established in the Sunday school room of the Lutheran church in 1892, followed by a library association that formed the following year. By 1900, there were 1,145 books for borrowing and a public reading room, both located on the second floor of the Opera House building. Mrs. E.C. Arthur was the first librarian, earning $120 a year. Through the decades, the library flourished, increased services, and prepared for expansion with the passing of a $125,000 bond issue in 1944 to build a new library at 224 Claremont Avenue in 1951. Thirty years later, library usage was demanding an expansion to fulfill the needs of the community again. In 1982, with the passage of another bond issue, the library expansion began to unfold, followed by a rededication service in 1987. The bookmobile used in 1972 is pictured below. (Below, Ashland Public Library collection.)

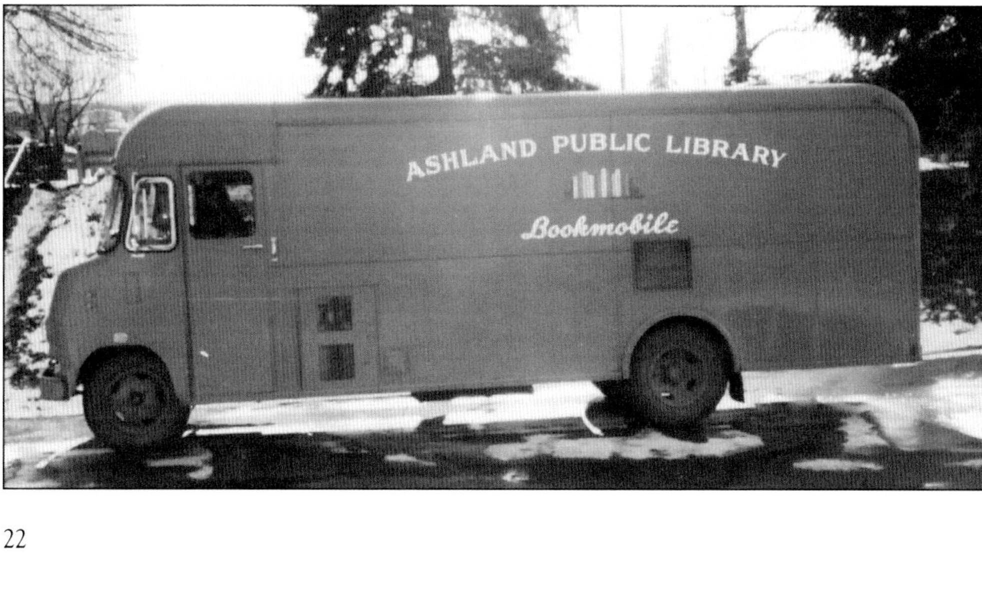

Two

The Main Endeavors

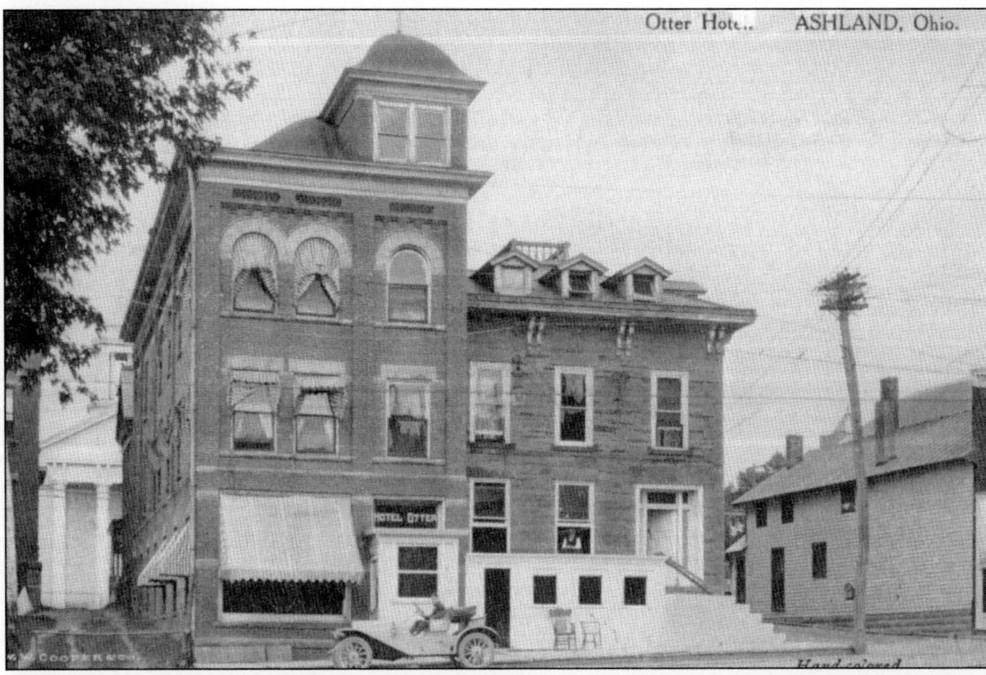

"Good Home Cooking" and plenty of it was the motto of the Hotel Otter dining room. Established in 1899 by William "Billy" Otter and located at 132 Main Street, Otter's rooms were amongst the finest in the state with hot and cold water, a bathtub in the bridal suite, and hack service to the train depot. The Otter was razed in 1959 to make way for First Federal Savings and Loan.

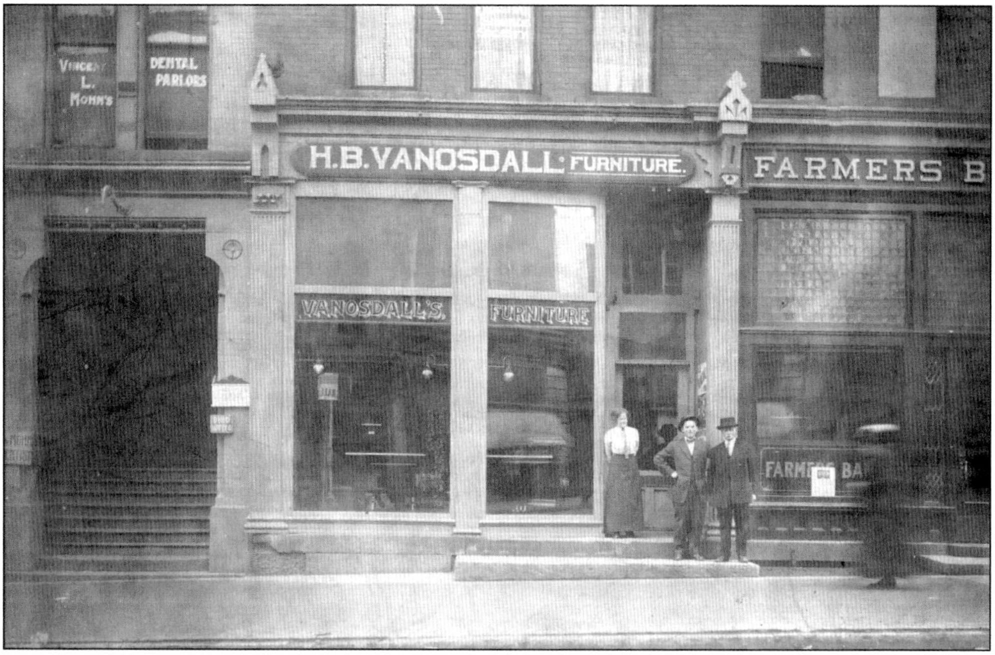

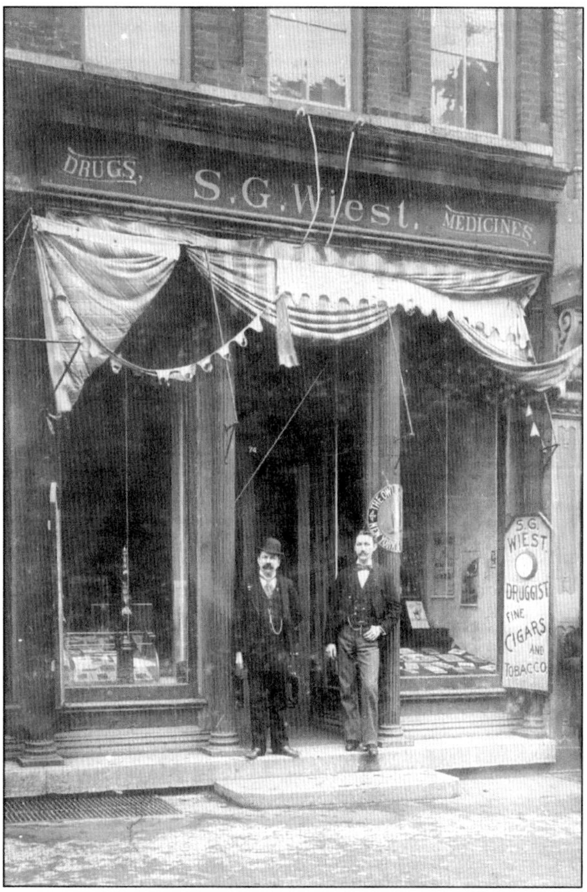

Harry B. and Henry N. Vanosdall, two of eight brothers, were "Makers of Happy Homes," according to their furniture store slogan. In 1899, Vanosdall Furniture opened for business at 13 Main Street, shown above. The brothers relocated to 129 South Street in 1917, and in 1920 changed locations to 128 East Main Street. For nearly 100 years, the Vanosdall name was associated with furniture, serving the community until closing its doors in 1995.

Established in 1872, druggist Samuel G. Wiest took care of the medical needs of the town for more than 30 years. Wiest was known for compounding popular syrup of white pine and tar, as well as for selling the finest cigars in town. In 1913, Wiest sold his store, located at 6 Main Street. Through the years, the location remained a drugstore with different owners until 1975.

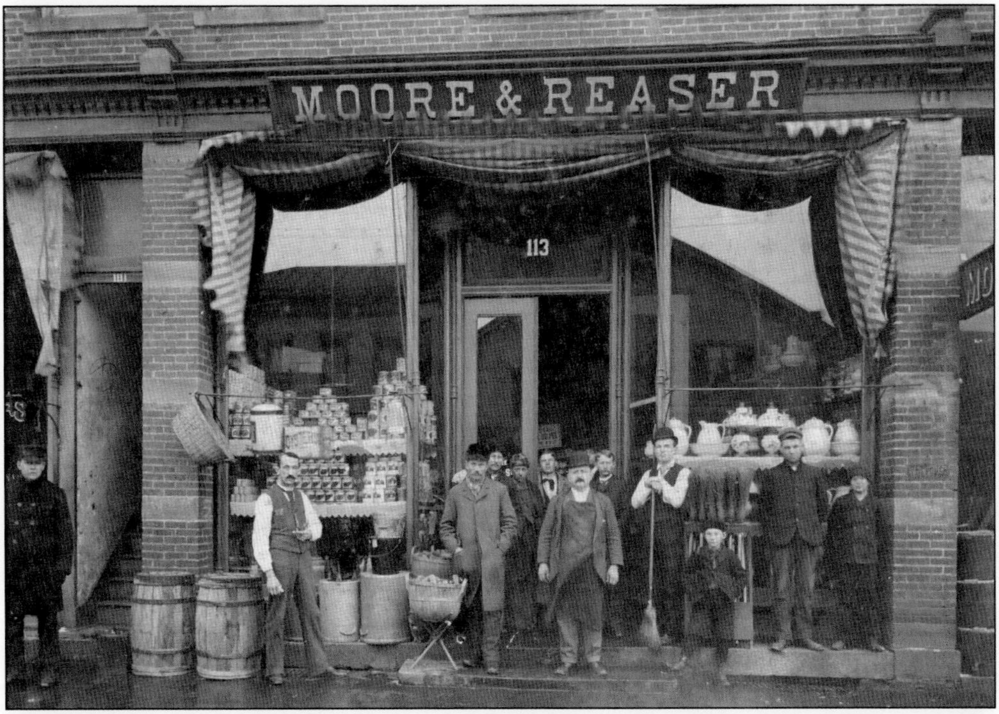

Wholesale and retail grocers W.C. Moore and J.T. Reaser operated the above store at 113 Main Street in 1895. In 1906, Moore started his own business at 143 Main Street with his son M.K. Moore joining him in 1917. W.C. Moore and Son were known for fresh and fancy groceries, fruits, and vegetables.

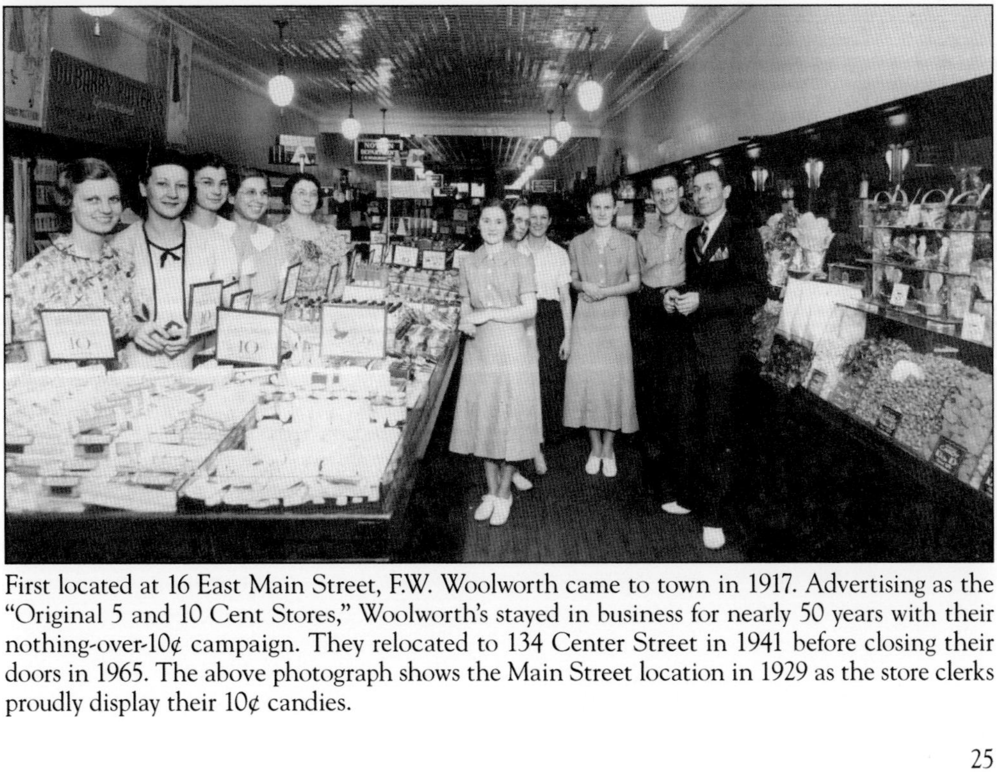

First located at 16 East Main Street, F.W. Woolworth came to town in 1917. Advertising as the "Original 5 and 10 Cent Stores," Woolworth's stayed in business for nearly 50 years with their nothing-over-10¢ campaign. They relocated to 134 Center Street in 1941 before closing their doors in 1965. The above photograph shows the Main Street location in 1929 as the store clerks proudly display their 10¢ candies.

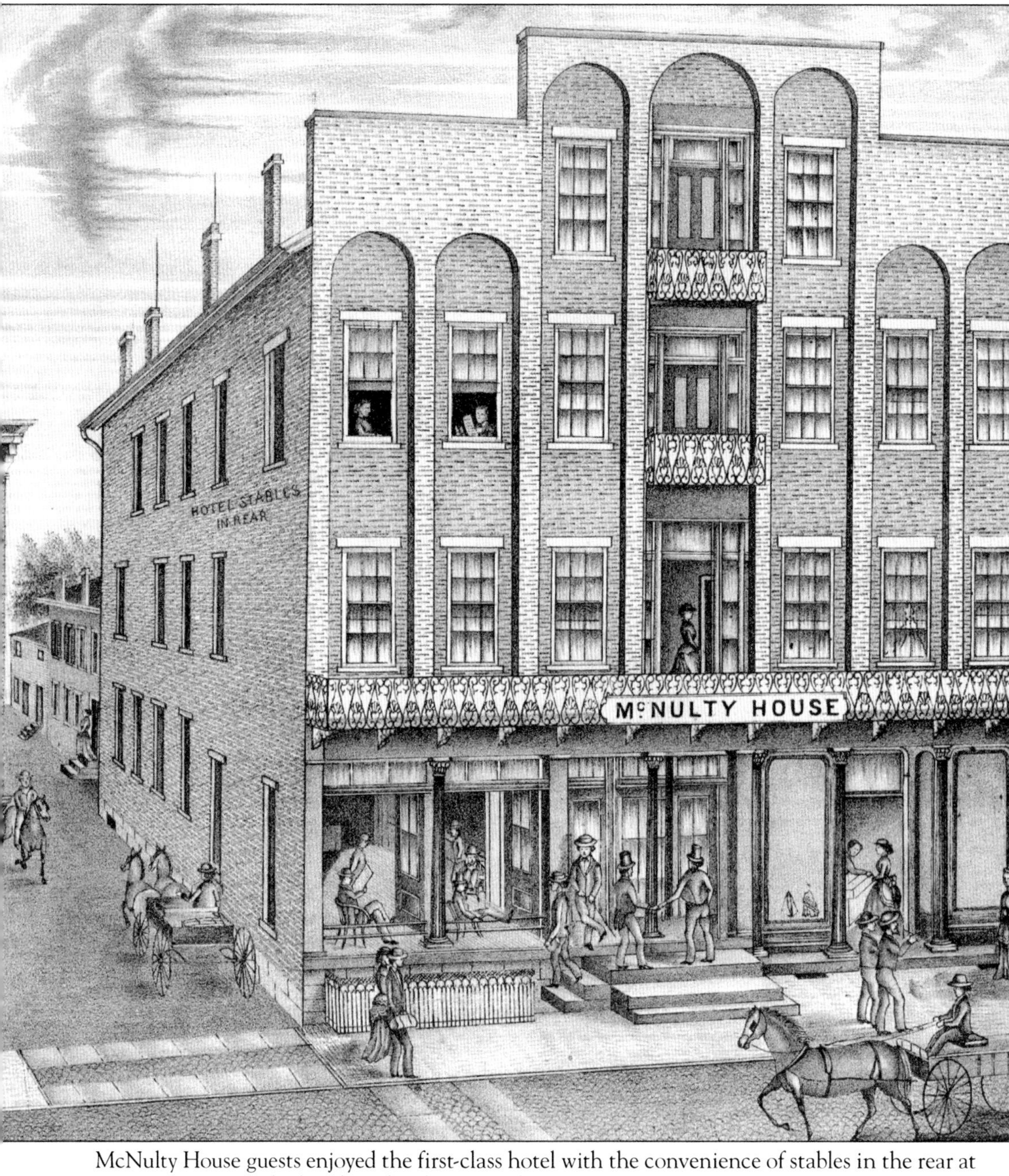

McNulty House guests enjoyed the first-class hotel with the convenience of stables in the rear at 105 Main Street. The hotel, under the ownership of William McNulty, was a popular overnight stop in town from 1859 to 1890. The upper outside doors led to balconies, where bands were heard performing concerts on Saturday nights. In 1913, George M. Gilbert and Alpha B. Rogers purchased the McNulty House, moving their furniture business from 14 Orange Street into this freshly remodeled location. A funeral home and chapel were additionally incorporated into the store, but space restrictions forced its relocation to 308 Claremont Avenue in 1939. Four generations saw the need to expand business several times through the years, with the Rogers family at the helm for its 100th birthday in 1965. Gilbert's ultimately changed hands and closed in 2008.

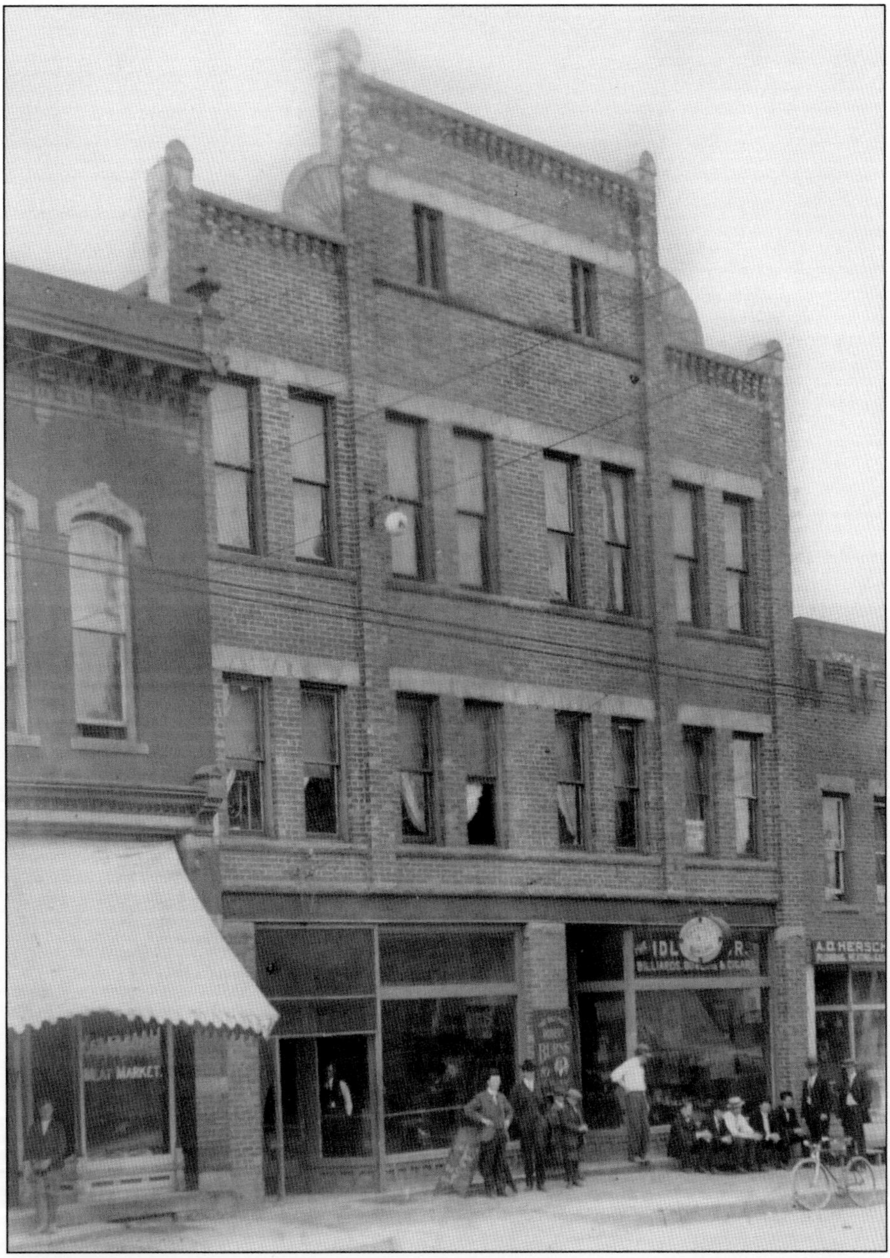

At 151 Main Street, situated across the street from the Otter, was the Mason-Brubaker Block, built in 1901 by realtors Calvin Mason and David Brubaker at a cost of $15,000, making it one of the most costly properties on the street. Over the years, this block was home to the Idol Hour (an establishment of billiards, bowling, and cigars), the Arlington Hotel, the City Market, and the Grand Theatre. Locke Mason operated his law office here, which eventually became the law office of grandson Josiah L. Mason; it also housed granddaughter Margaret Mason Strub's insurance agency. The second floor contained rooms for the Arlington Hotel, later to become a rooming house, while the third floor of the block was owned by Knights of Pythias, where meetings, gala dinners, and dances were held, drawing crowds of the town's finest citizens. The picture above shows the Idol Hour with a gang of patrons on the Mason-Brubaker Block.

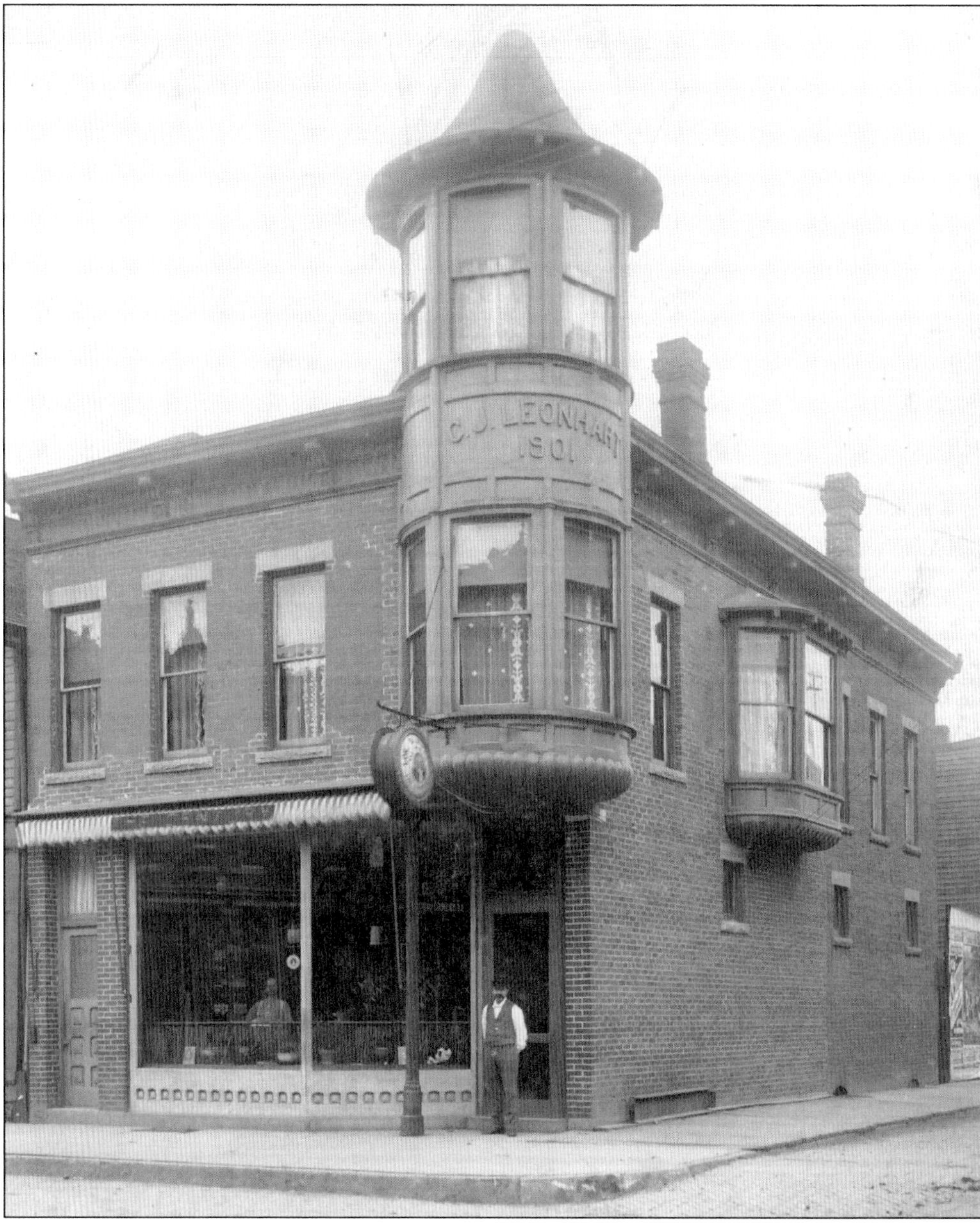

George Leonhart constructed this 1901 building on the northwest corner of Main and Church Streets. The Leonhart family, as was the case with many store owners, lived in the upstairs of their building, enjoying the bird's-eye view of the town's central thoroughfare of Main Street from their second-floor home. Leonhart ran the Elk's Cafe around the corner on Church Street, while the Century Department Store, shown above, occupied the building facing Main Street. Beginning in 1905, Ashland Bank and Savings held business here for 30 years before relocating to 26 Main Street. For a short time thereafter, the Main Street storefront was occupied by Edwards' Food Store. This was followed by the Korner Food Market in 1941, under the ownership of W.R. Willits and Archie Carter, before becoming the law office of Howard Lutz in 1956. When Lutz became partners with Bill Oxley in 1959, the two purchased the corner building for their partnership offices.

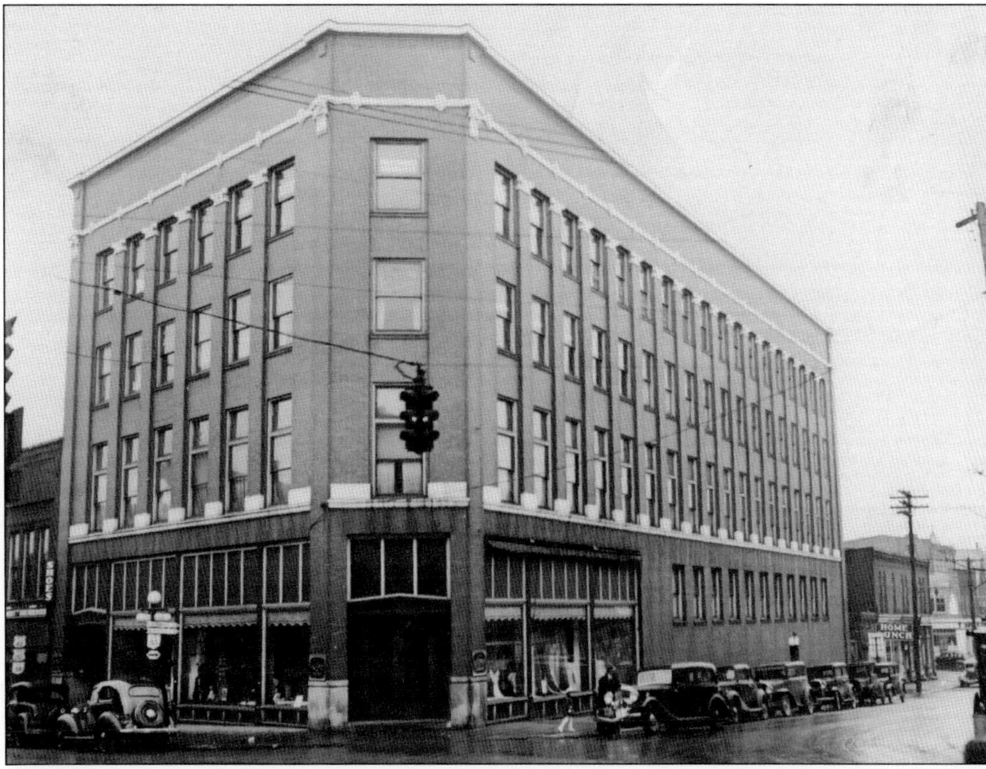

Located in the handsome Myers building at the southeast corner of Main and Center Streets, the Home Company opened its doors on May 17, 1910, with the consolidation of two dry goods establishments in town: the Shinn, Stockwell, and Company store and the Beach and Brown store. Occupying three of the building's five floors, the store utilized 30,000 square feet, selling numerous items, such as men's and women's clothing, infant wear, linens, draperies, rugs, and carpet. At that time, it was doubtful that another town in Ohio the size of Ashland could boast of a retail establishment equal to the Home Company. The store also enjoyed the modern convenience of a customer and freight elevator, restrooms, and a cable cash-carrying system that transported money to the cashier's office that overlooked the main floor.

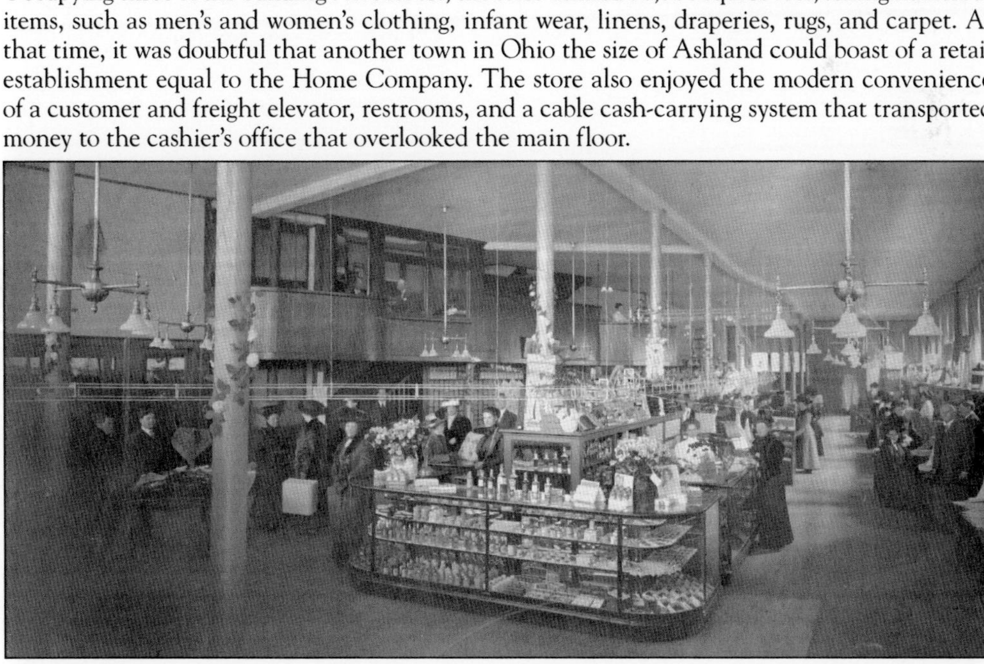

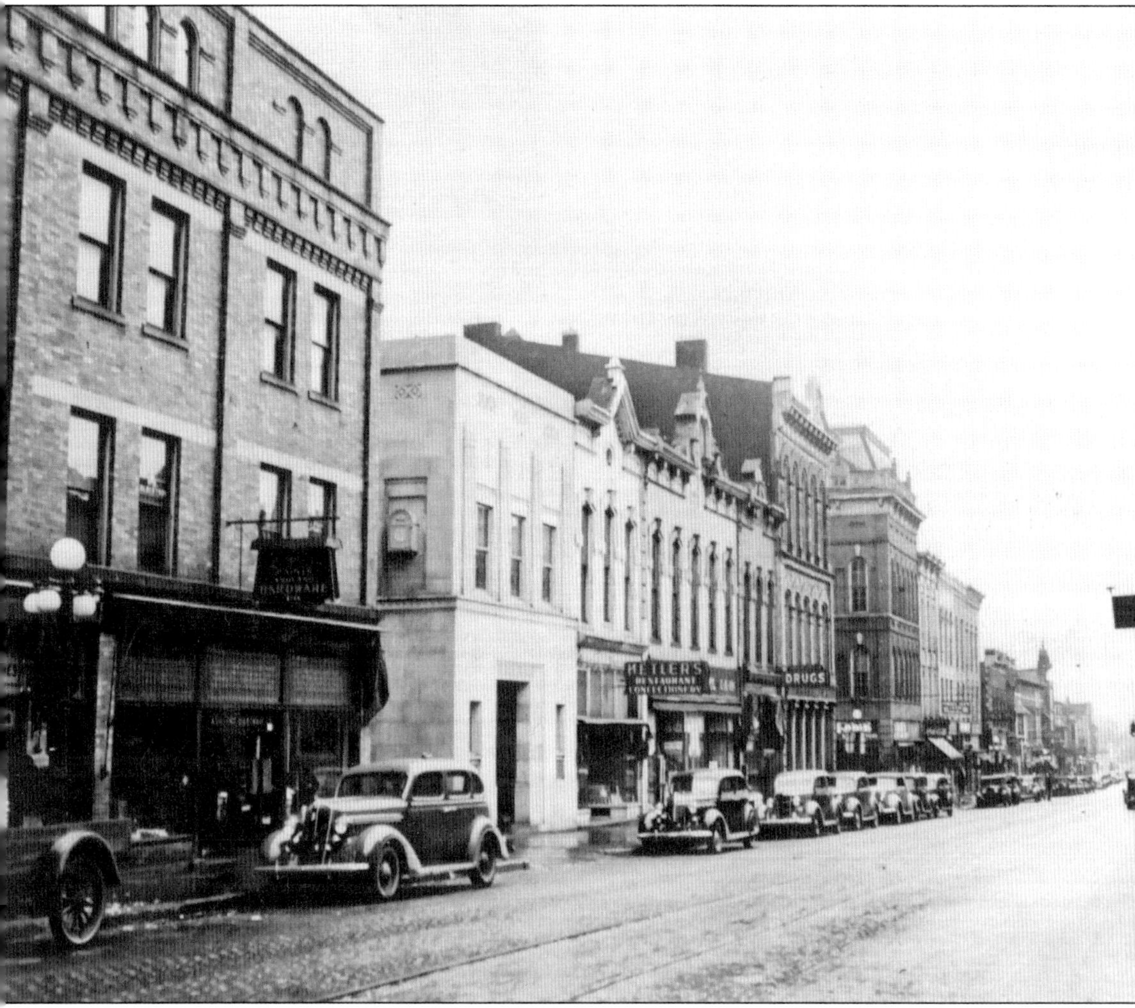

A Main Street of brick, lined with cars and interurban tracks, can be seen in front of the Ashland Bank and Savings, located to the left of Hetler's Restaurant and Confectionery, shown above. The bank, founded in 1905, was one of the fastest growing financial institutions in town by 1915, with I.H. Good as the first president. Ultimately outgrowing its original location on Main Street at the northwest corner of Church Street, the bank moved to 24 Main Street in 1935 and merged with Banc One Corporation in 1979. Hetler's, the home of "Just Good Food," opened its doors at 22 Main Street in 1928. With a first-floor restaurant and a second-floor banquet room, all under the ownership of Earl H. Hetler, the local eatery was known to host the Lion and Rotary Club meetings for many years until the business was sold in 1939. This location then changed hands several times; it became the S.S. Kresge store in 1951, followed by the Jupiter Department Store, and eventually became the Department of Liquor Control in 1984.

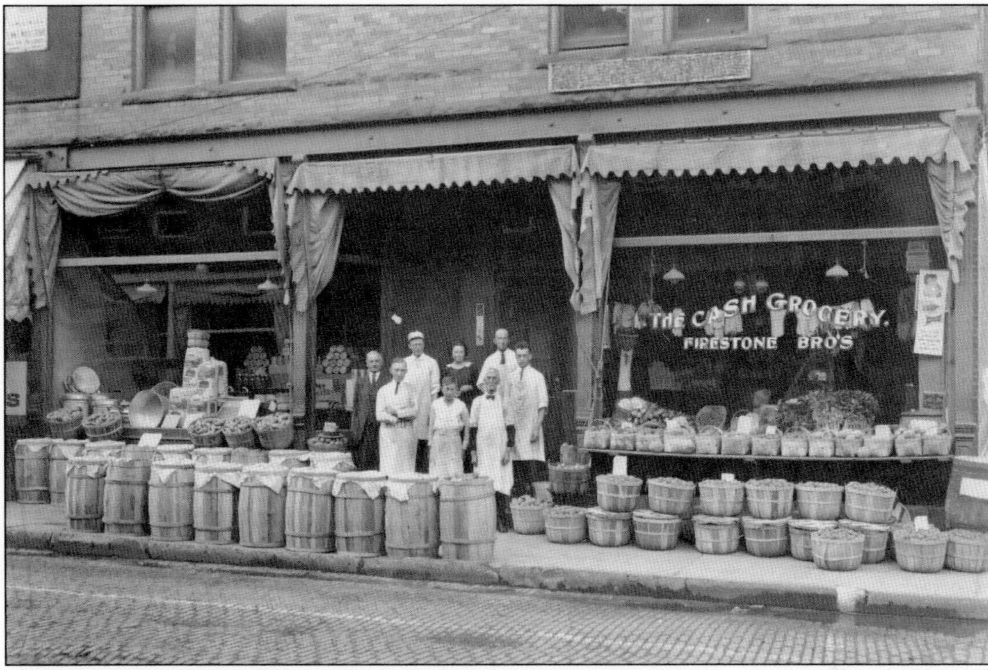

Three years before the 100th anniversary of the town, the first cash grocers, the Firestone Brothers, shown above selling apples and sweet potatoes, opened in 1912 on the corner of Orange and Third Streets. Accepting only cash for goods, owners O.D. Firestone and his brother Clark, once employing eight clerks, locked their doors in 1932 when competition from the Kroger Grocery and Baking Company forced their closure. Opening in approximately 1926, the grocery below, one of three Kroger stores in the city, was located at 252 Union Street between Second and Third Streets. All three stores would eventually consolidate and relocate three times before settling in at 2310 Claremont Avenue near the State Route 42 bypass. It was here that Kroger's remained in business from 1969 to 1984, providing nearly 60 years of service to the community.

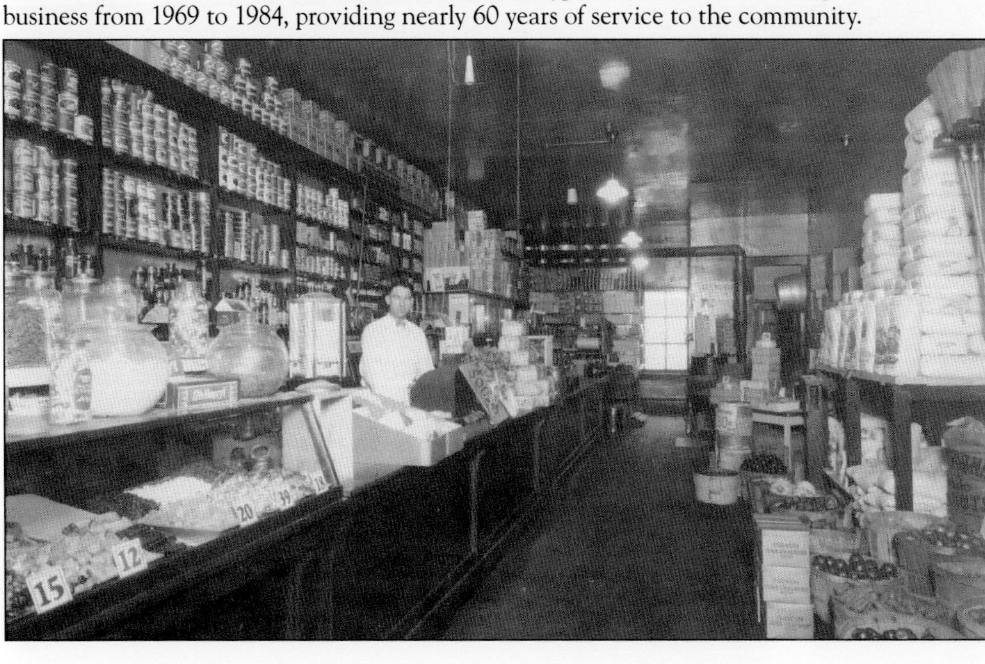

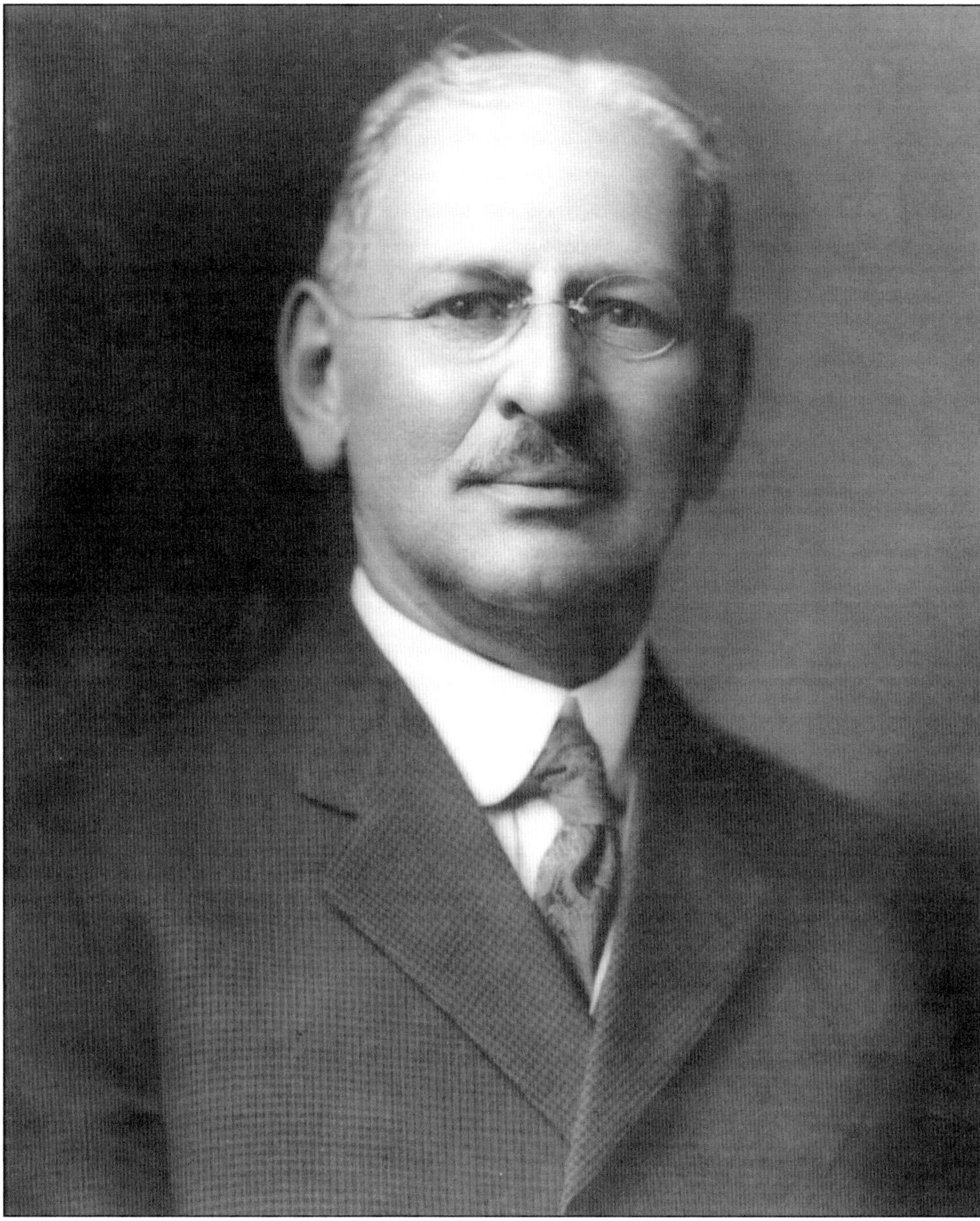

When the train Nathan Strauss was working on broke down in town, he became friends with Jacob Cahn, who gave Strauss a job at Cahn's clothing store. Striking a lasting friendship with Cahn, Strauss never left town, moving his family here from Kentucky. He first became a partner before buying the men's store in 1909. While operating the store, Strauss was an active civic leader in the community, helping to organize the first chamber of commerce and forming the volunteer fire department with P.A. Myers. Strauss became a volunteer fire chief in 1921, only one year before his death. The Strauss and Company Clothing store was located at 43 Main Street for 78 years before moving to 47 Main Street in 1962. Strauss was proud of the quality clothing line sold to his customers over the years, with locally owned Cresco products topping the list. Through the years, four generations operated the clothing store before closing its doors in 1991.

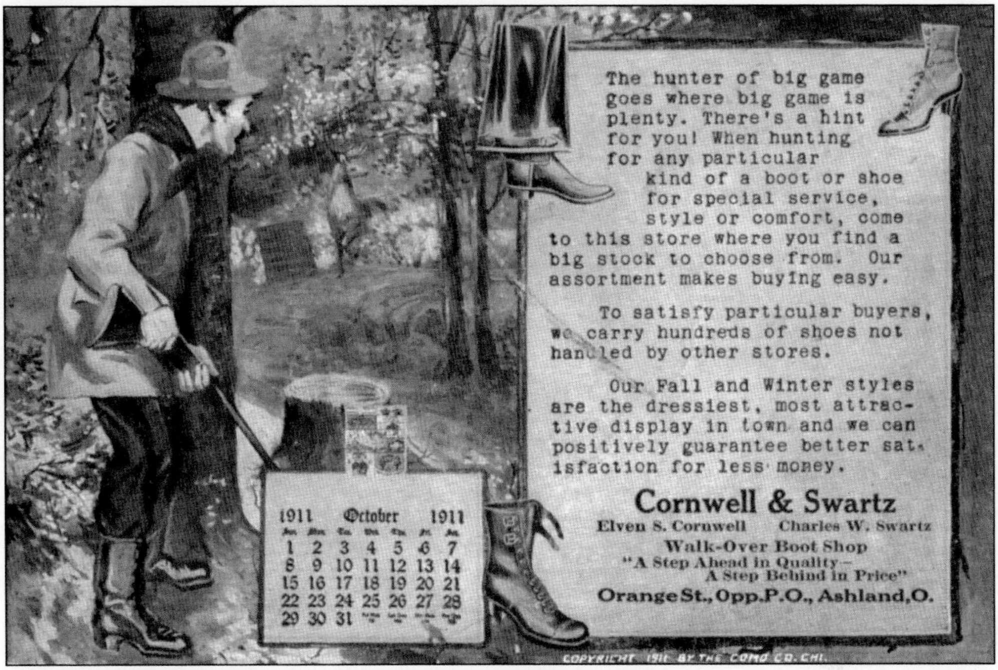

Located on busy Orange Street between Main and Second Streets was the Cornwell and Swartz shoe store. Owners Elven Cornwell and Charlie Swartz marketed their vast assortment of shoes with the 1911 store postcard pictured above. Opening in 1911, Cornwell claimed that Orange Street challenged Main Street as the leading thoroughfare in town. In 1918, Cornwell relocated to 115 Main Street when that thoroughfare won the battle. Cornwell remained in business at that location until 1965.

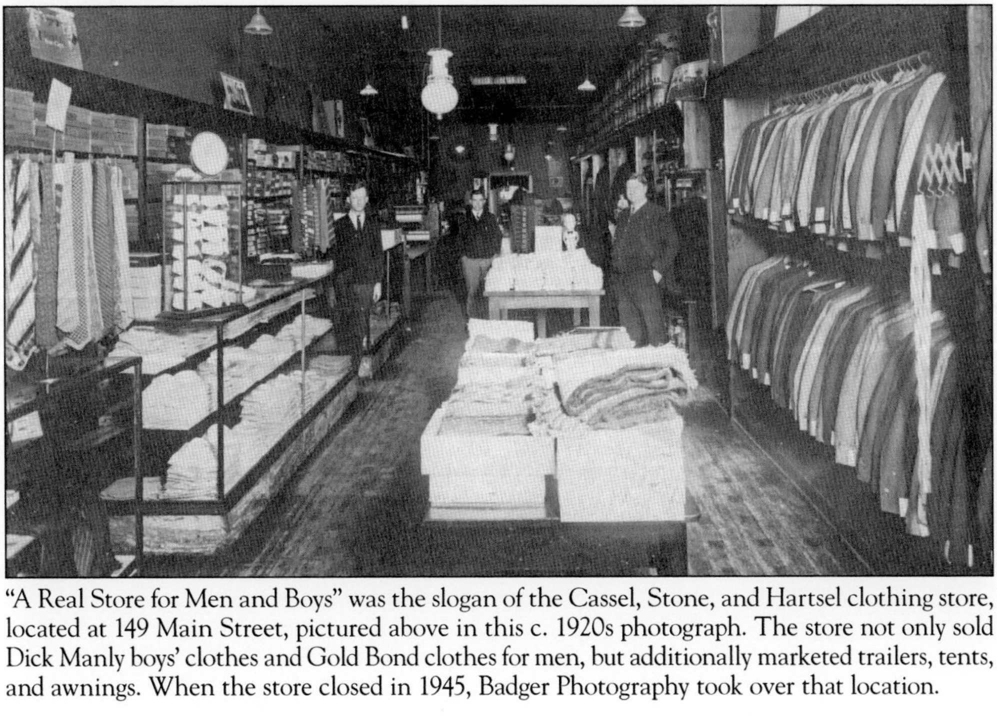

"A Real Store for Men and Boys" was the slogan of the Cassel, Stone, and Hartsel clothing store, located at 149 Main Street, pictured above in this c. 1920s photograph. The store not only sold Dick Manly boys' clothes and Gold Bond clothes for men, but additionally marketed trailers, tents, and awnings. When the store closed in 1945, Badger Photography took over that location.

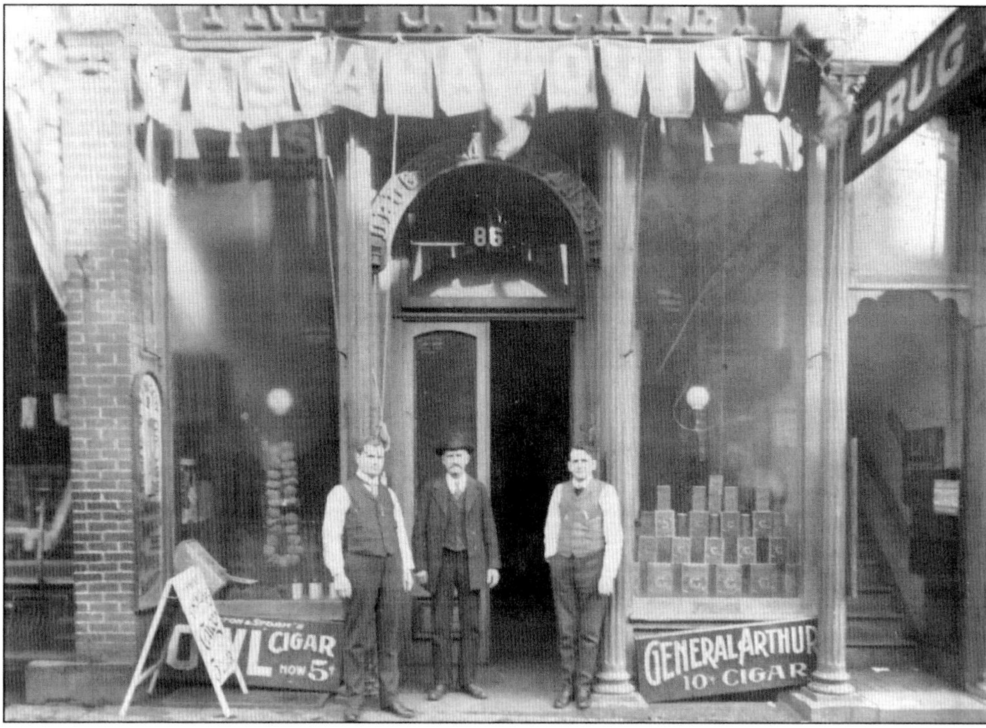

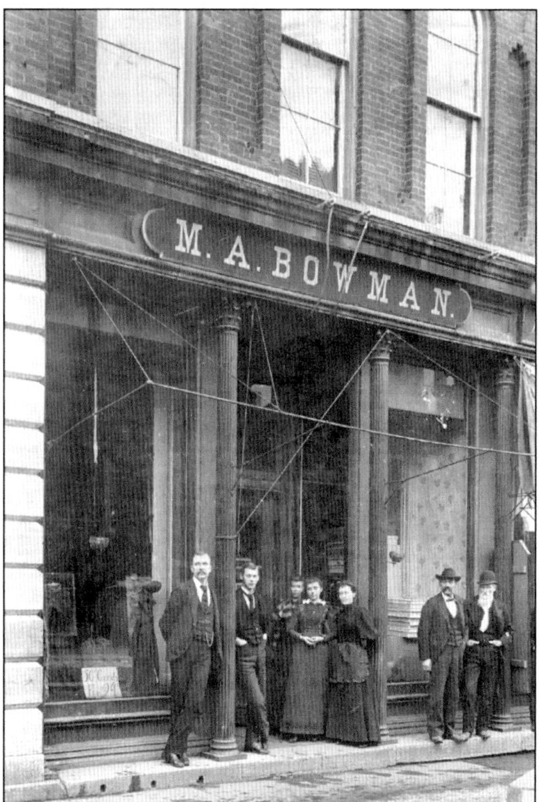

Bockley Brothers Drug Store, located at 18 Main Street, was owned by F.J. "Fred" Bockley and brother W.L. Bockley. Fred Bockley, above left, one of the town's leading druggists, formerly operated a store at 86 Main Street, while W.L. Bockley worked as a clerk for competitor druggist, S.G. Wiest. The two joined forces in 1911 and served the community for nearly 10 years.

In 1888, Marcellus A. Bowman opened a dry goods store on the corner of Main and Orange Streets. Four years later, when Emery Brown joined the store, seen here second to the left, the name was changed to Bowman and Brown, with Bowman's interests eventually turning to the Reliable Match Company. Joined by William Beach in 1908, the new Beach and Brown store joined enterprises with Shinn and Stockwell in 1910, forming the Home Company.

In January 1864, meeting the increased demand for banking facilities and the anticipated growth of the town, stockholders Hulbert Luther, Jacob Crall, and associates organized the First National Bank with Luther serving as bank president until 1870. Construction for Ashland's first banking institution then began in 1873. This Italianate-style bank, located at the corner of Main and Orange Streets, was eventually razed in 1979.

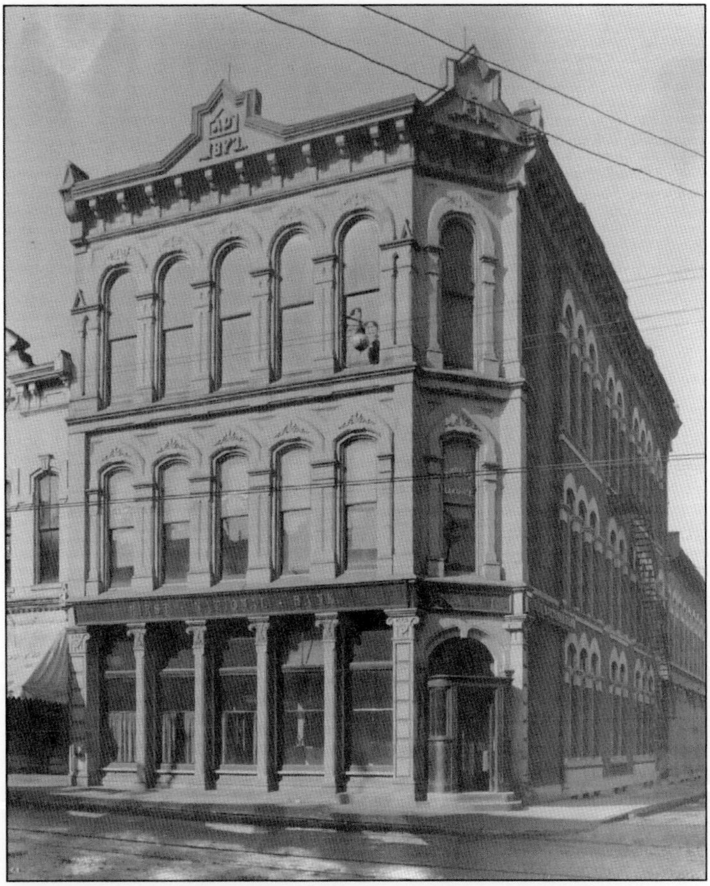

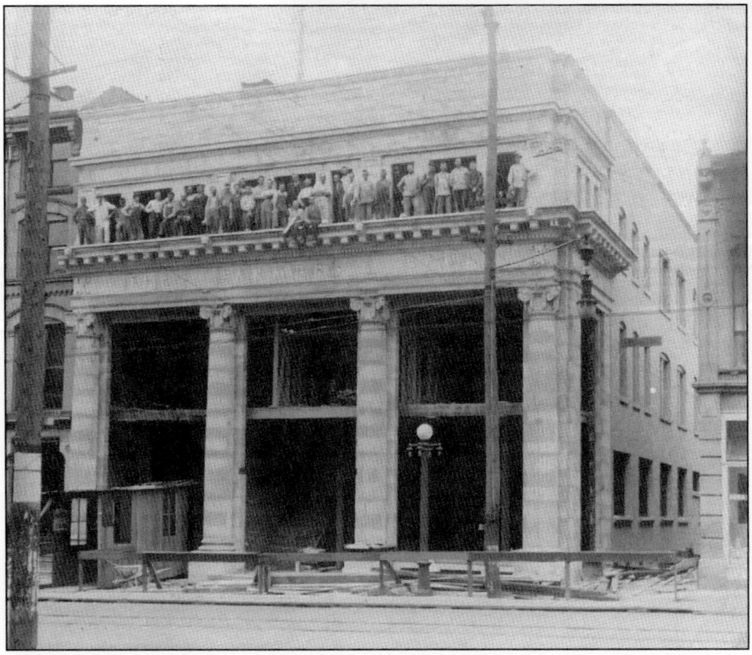

Before banks were established, storekeepers acted as bankers to their farmer customers. Such was the case of the Farmers Bank, which began in the Jonas and Randolph Freer general merchandise store at the corner of Center and Walnut Streets. The Freer brothers relocated to Main Street in 1874, where the bank stands today as Huntington National Bank. In this 1917 image, the bank is being remodeled.

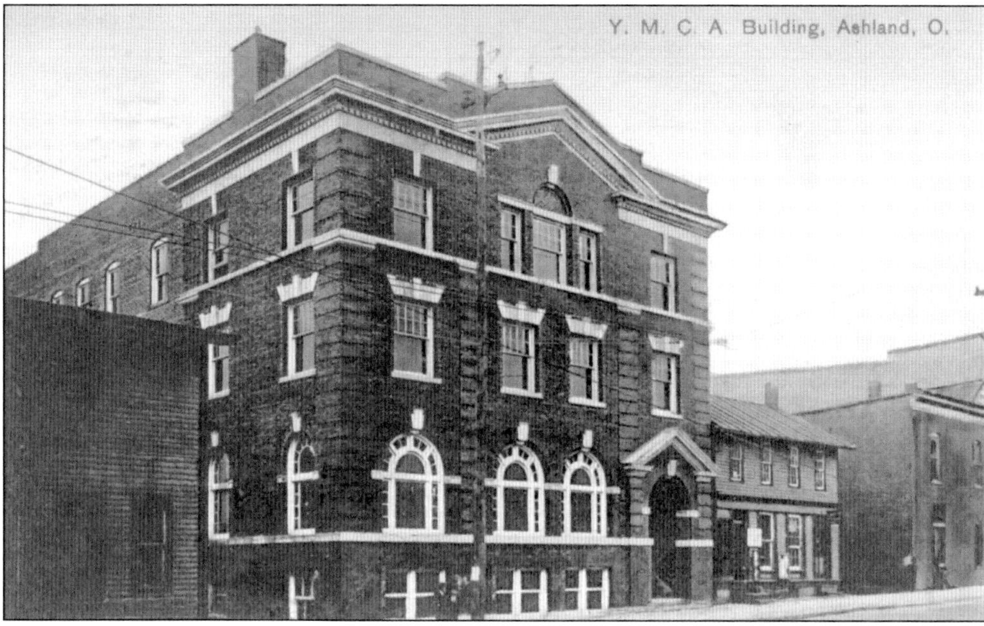

In 1907, when the city of 6,000 voted the town dry, 17 saloons were put out of business, forcing young men to look for something constructive to do. With this in mind, the thought of a YMCA in town took shape, with nearly $18,000 raised within 10 days toward its construction. At a cost of nearly $40,000, the realization of that dream came true with the dedication of the facility on June 14, 1909. Located on 101 East Main Street, the four-story YMCA, above, housed a gymnasium, two bowling alleys, billiard room, swimming pool, lockers, assembly room, kitchen, and a dormitory with 30 sleeping rooms. The lower level housed Clem Denbow's barbershop, shown standing in photograph below on the right. The 10¢ shaves and 5¢ haircuts kept Denbow busy. (Below, Joe Denbow collection.)

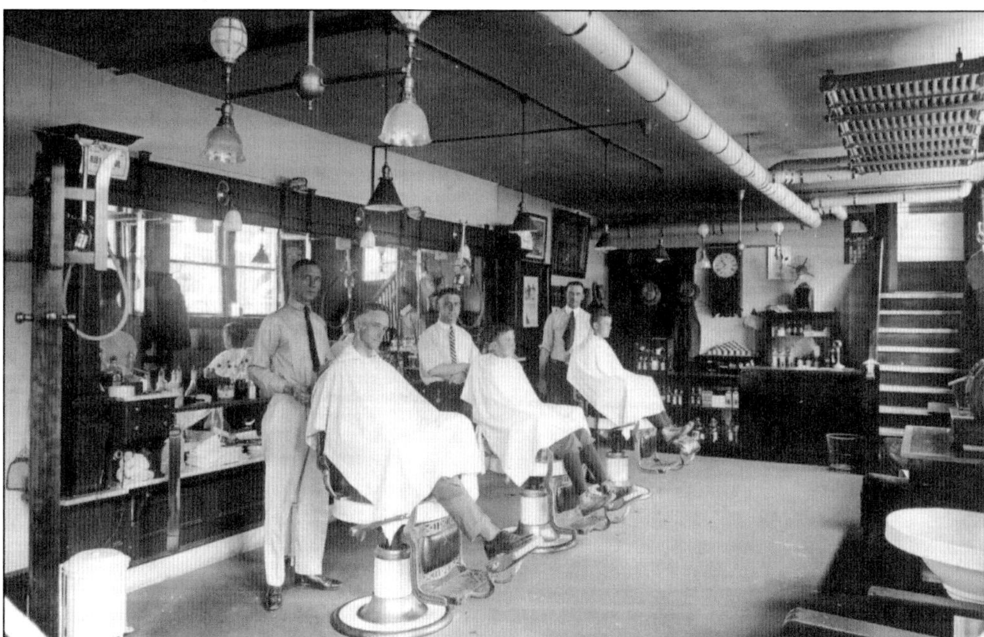

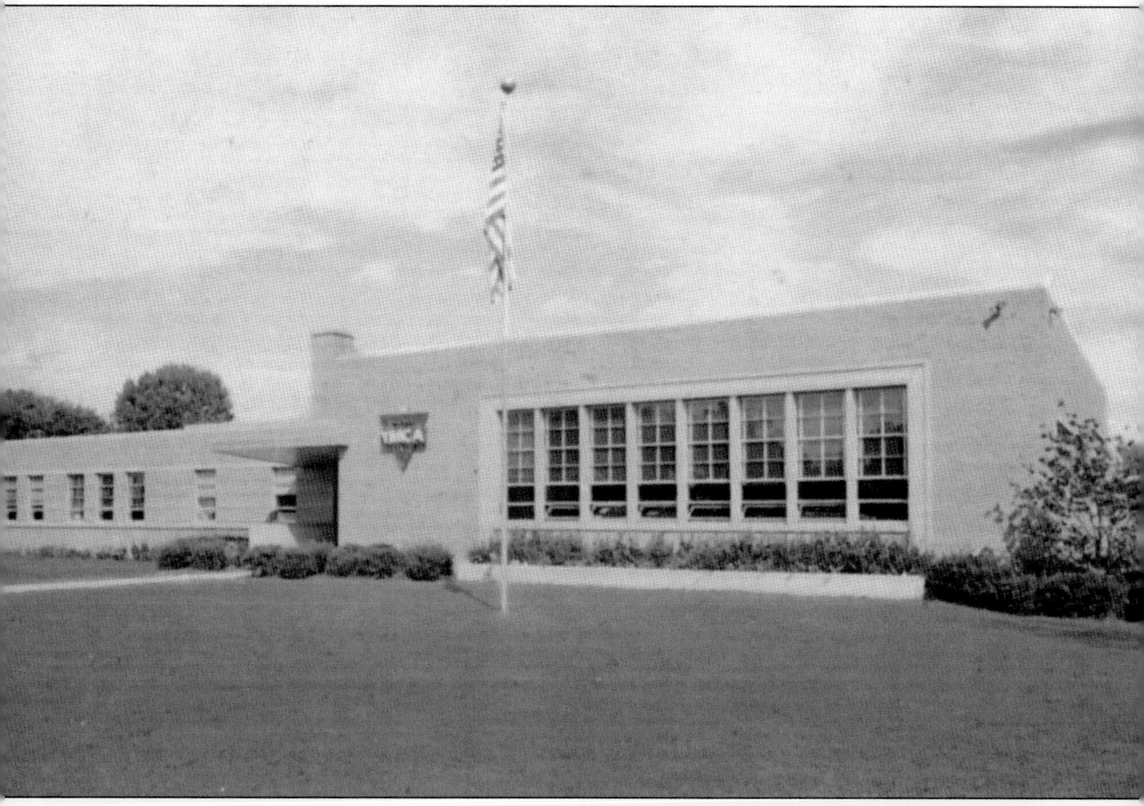

Reaching nearly 1,100 members by the mid-1950s, the YMCA at 101 East Main Street had outgrown its four walls. To keep up with its growing popularity, a fund drive took place for the construction of a new YMCA at 207 Miller Street on the site of Myers Field. In 1929, industrialist P.A. Myers gifted the city a parcel of land valued at $55,000. It was this location on Miller Street that would become home to the new YMCA. The cornerstone, which encased a record of the popular sheet music of the day, was laid on July 14, 1956, and on January 13, 1957, the new building was dedicated. Construction costs for this one-story building was $477,000. Myers Field boasted a new facility on the west end and an athletic field complete with a field house and dressing rooms on the east end. For many years, the field was home to high school football, baseball, track, and tennis.

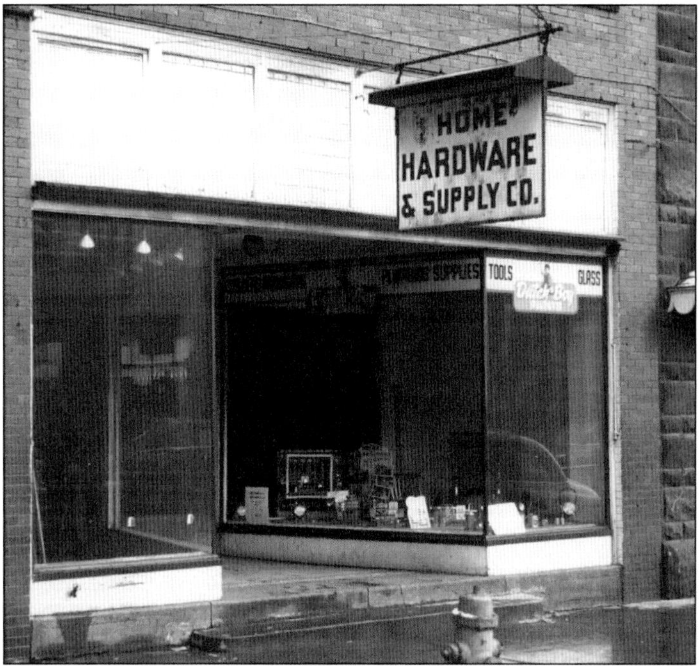

Established in 1926, Home Hardware, under the ownership of Henry Gebhart, was located at 235 Orange Street. Growing and expanding through the years, the store, pictured here at 74 East Main Street, relocated four times from its original location and finally settled at 140 Center Street, where it stands today. Ultimately, ownership changed through the years from Gebhart and David Downie to Gaylord Miller and Downie, to Miller and his wife, Beulah, in 1954. (Home Hardware collection.)

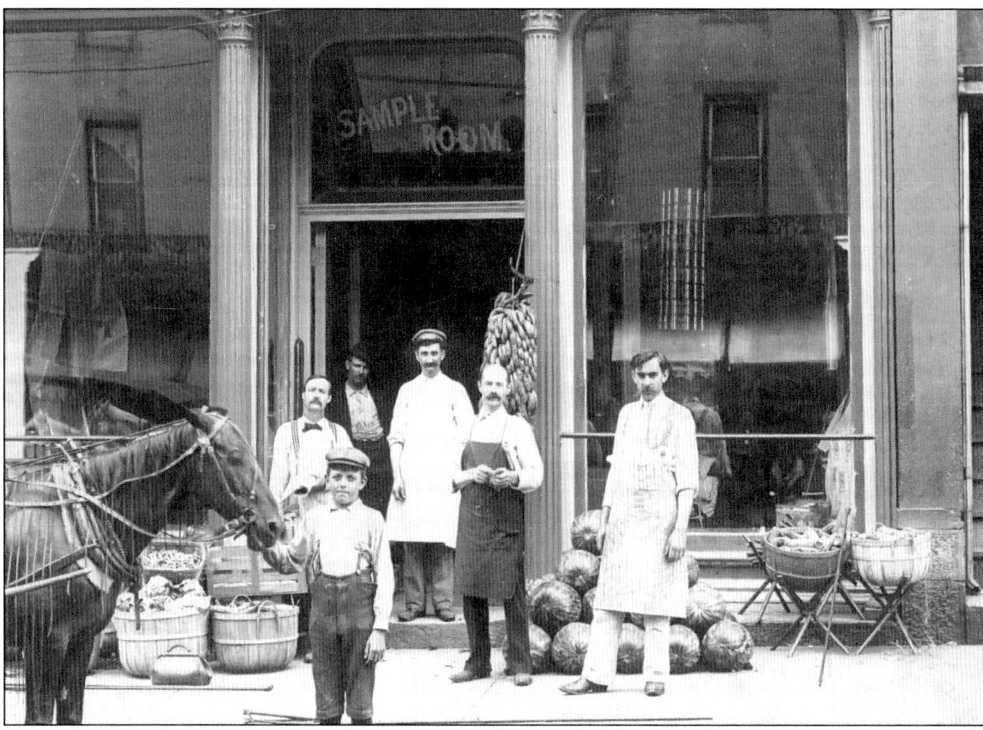

"C.W. Landis, your grocer, handles a full variety of quality goods at right prices." This quote from a 1917 advertisement was referring to Charles Wesley Landis, a man known for integrity, cheerfulness, and willingness to serve. Not bothered by the large grocery chains, Landis served the town as a grocer for nearly 67 years. This 1896 photograph shows Landis wearing a cap in the doorway during his early grocer years at 95 Main Street.

Three

Money Makers

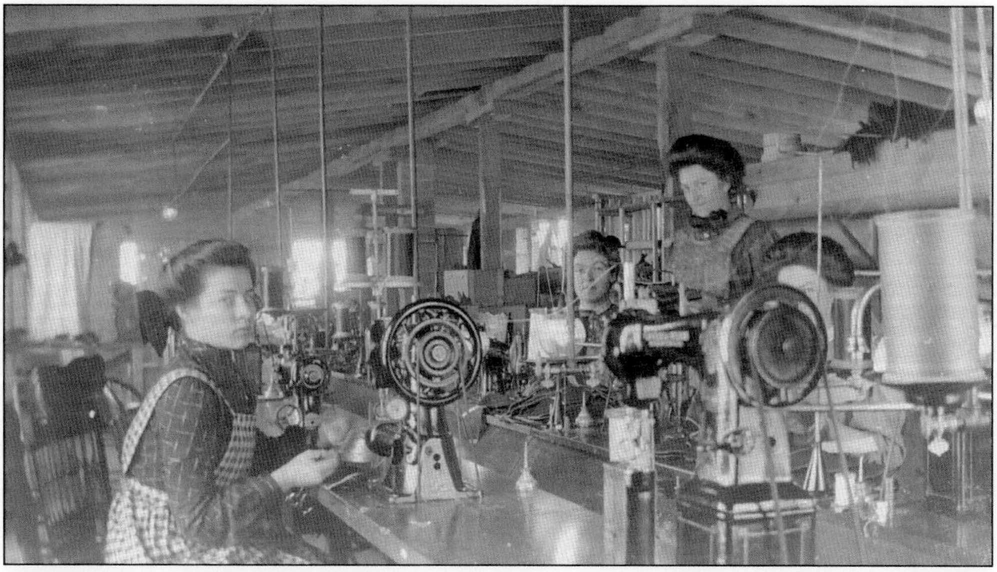

The Morr Shoe Manufacturing Company was founded in 1908 by G.M. and E.E. Morr. Located at 603 Miller Street, Morr Komfort Shoes sold directly to retail stores throughout Ohio, Michigan, and Indiana. The company flourished in 1918, employing 18 men and 10 women, but was later forced to lock its doors as leather became unavailable to those with no government contract to make military shoes during World War I.

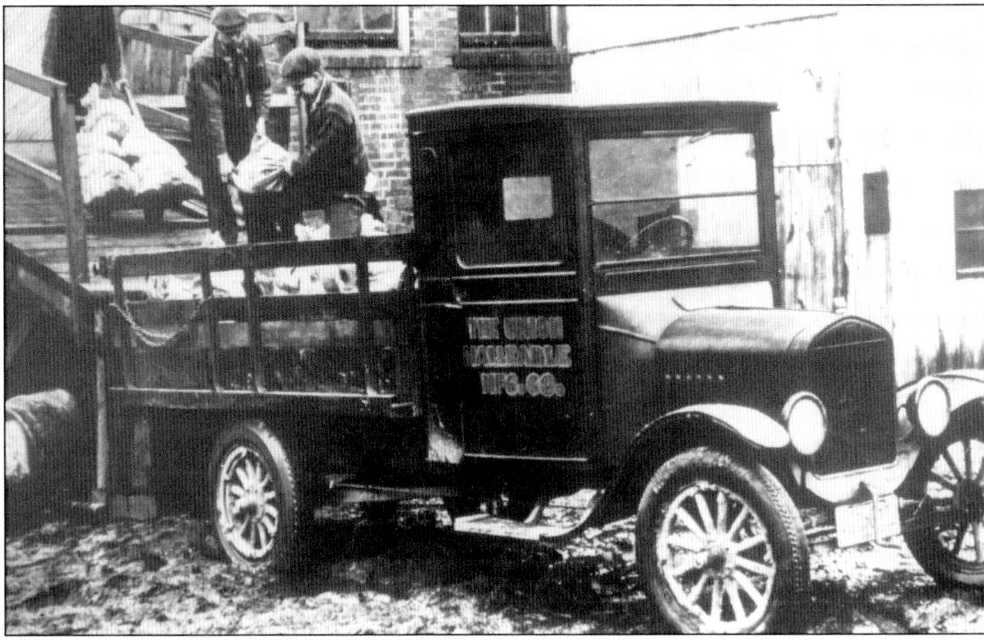

The Ashland Manufacturing Company, located at 701 Miller Street in 1910, manufactured a line of auto jacks and plumber's supplies and sold their goods across the country and beyond. Unable to receive iron in a timely manner, the company started producing its own malleable. To that end, in 1925, the Union Malleable Manufacturing Company, under the direction of Jack Jacobson, was formed. Also known as U-Brand for their production of "U" shaped fittings, the company, first located on East Eighth Street, became one of the largest mechanized fittings manufacturers in the world, covering 300,000 square feet and operating out of five plants at five locations. In a depressed market for iron fittings, the plant closed in 1992. The above photograph shows workers loading one of the Union Malleable Manufacturing Company's first delivery trucks, which replaced horse-drawn delivery wagons. Pictured below is a 1944 company catalog.

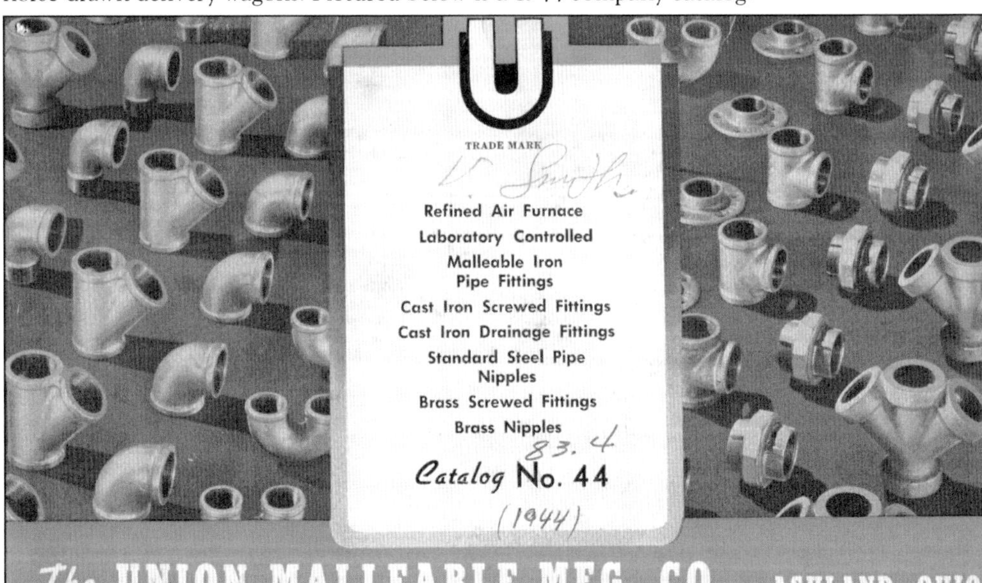

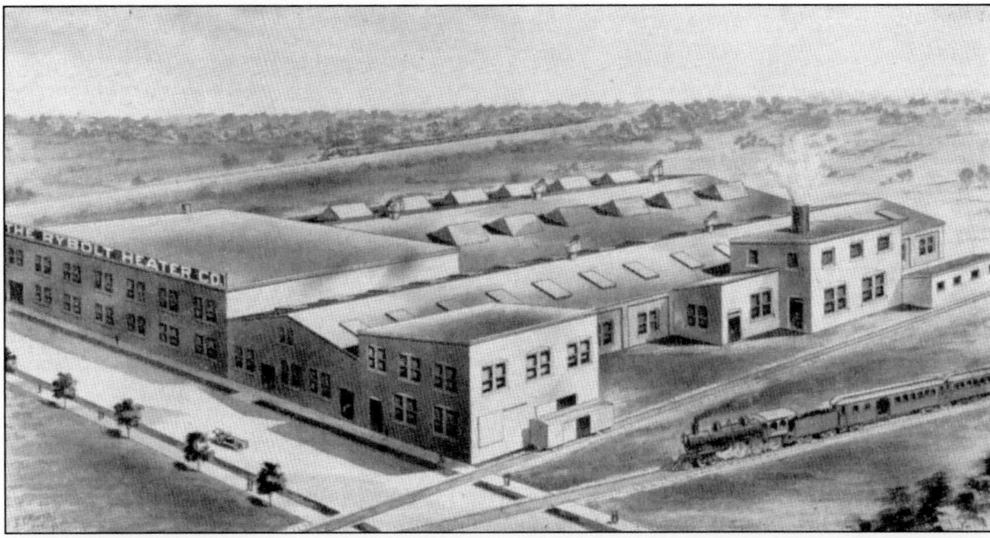

In 1915, Webster L. Rybolt started the Rybolt Heater Company. Located at 615 Miller Street, the maker of coal-fired warm air furnaces, Rybolt was considered one the most progressive businessmen in town. For nearly 50 years, Rybolt kept up with the times, adapting his operation to convert coal furnaces to oil, and later moved into the air-conditioning business, though ultimately closing his doors in 1966.

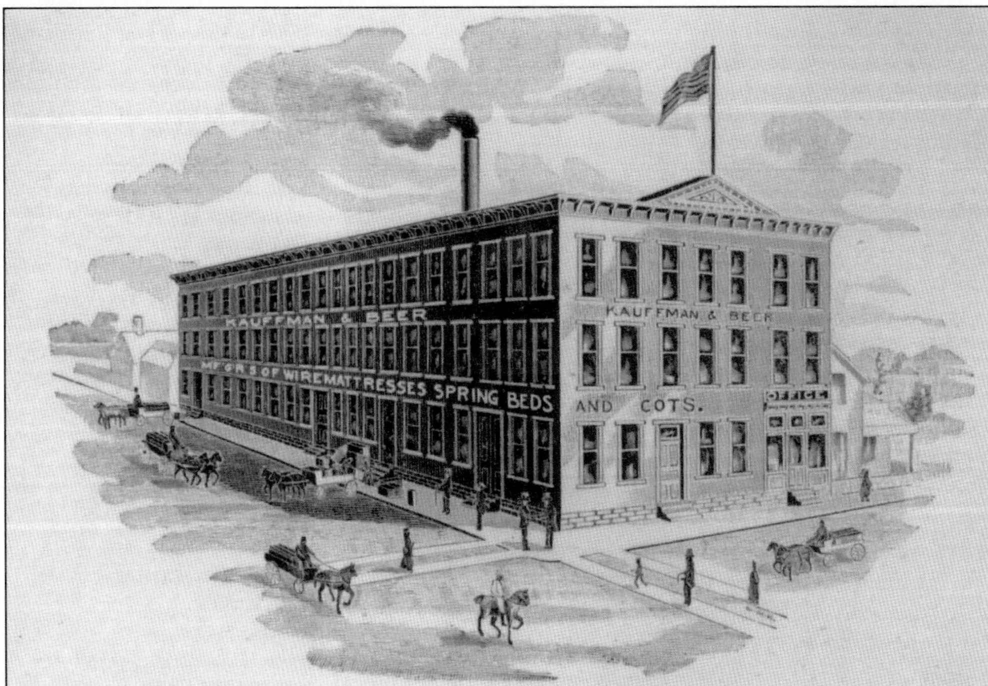

Making more than 80,000 bedsprings a year in 1895, the Kauffman and Beer Manufacturing Company opened its doors in 1875 under the ownership of J.J. Kauffman and S.W. Beer. With a wire-working machine, Kauffman wired its way to success, manufacturing bed springs, chairs, cots, and cribs, along with folding chairs for the Grand Army encampments. Located at 246 East Fourth Street, Kauffman closed its doors in the 1930s.

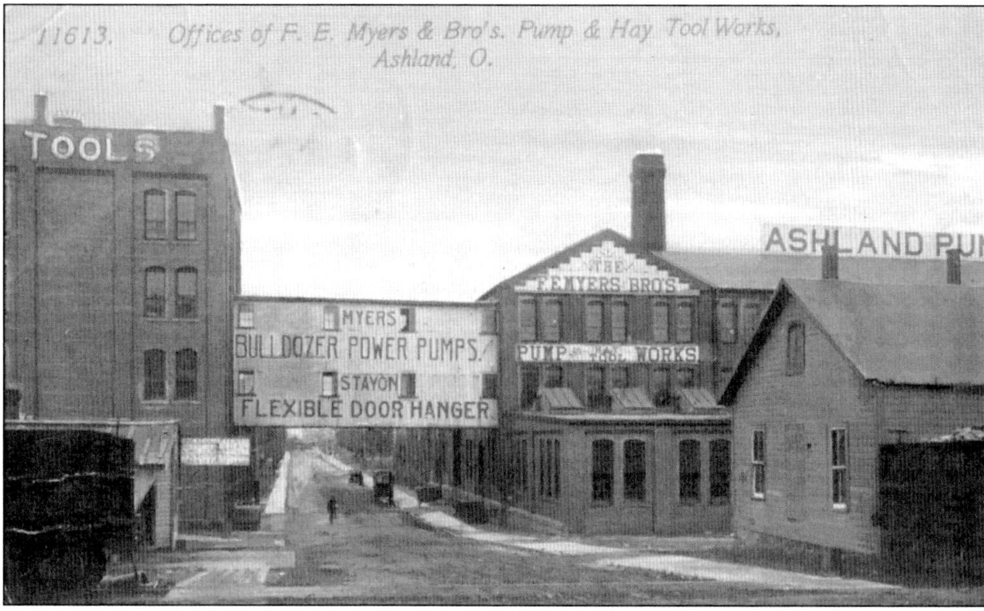

Francis E. Myers and brother Philip A. Myers started their venture in the business world in 1870 with a farm implement store on Center Street. They then moved to 29 East Main Street, adding more implements to their line. By 1879, Philip had secured a patent on the design of a double-acting pump that delivered water in a continuous stream. It was at this time that the F.E. Myers and Brothers Company was formed, growing to be the largest pump manufacturer of its kind in the world. With Francis at the sales helm and Philip as the inventor, the plant saw no end in site to its growing business on East Fourth Street, pictured above. In 1884, two more Myers brothers, Alvah N. and George D. Myers, joined the dynamic duo. Pictured below from left to right are Alvah, George, Philip, and Francis Myers. (Above, Cloyd McNaull collection.)

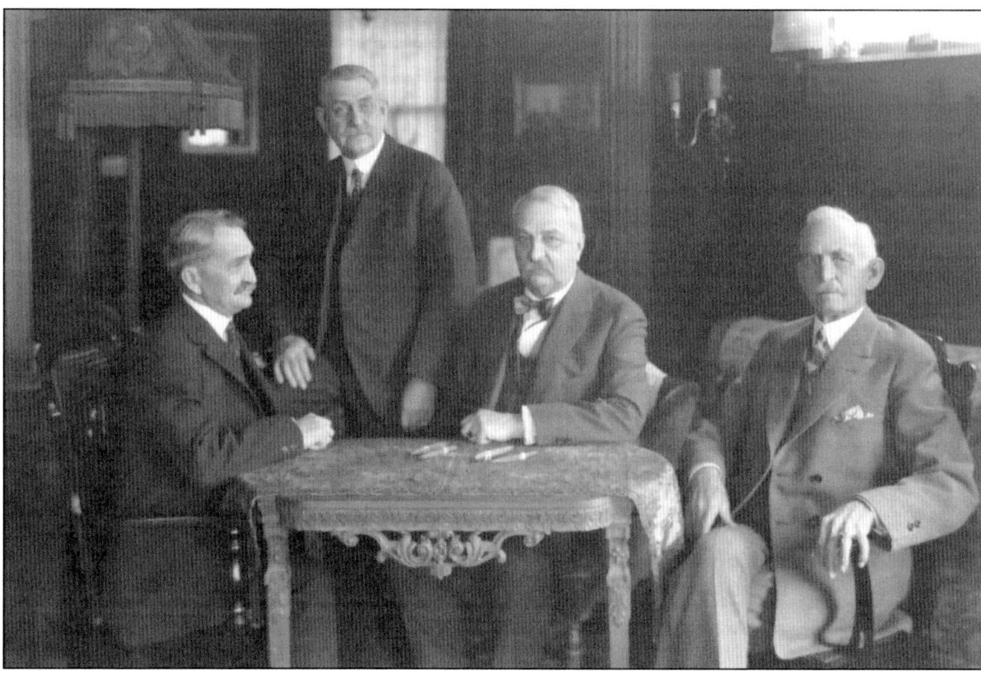

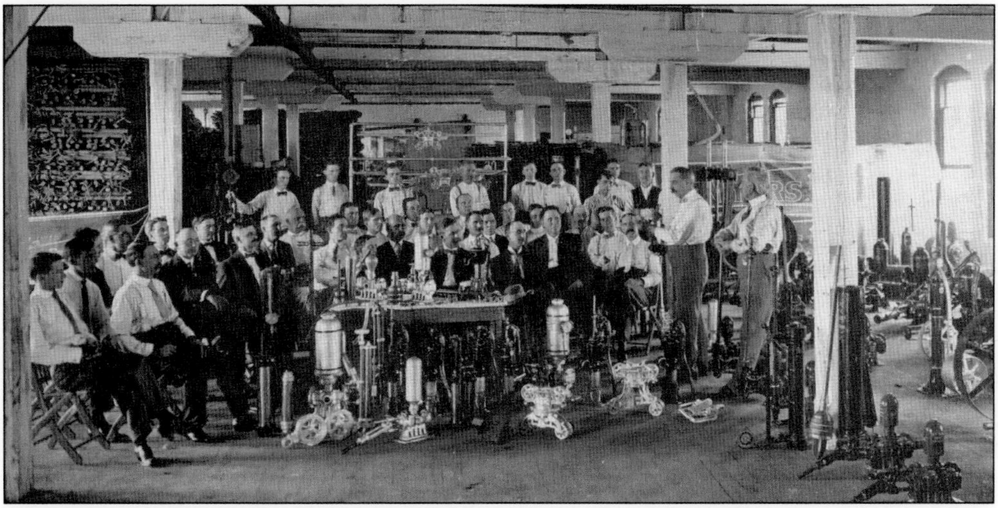

Through the years, the F.E. Myers and Brothers Company was controlled by three generations of family members before affiliation with the McNeil Corporation in 1960. By 1970, its 100th anniversary, the company was producing approximately 4,000 different items in five lines: water systems, industrial pumps, water conditioners, power sprayers, and hydraulic cleaners. With production of these products, the company enjoyed $22 million in sales. Branch offices were also maintained around the globe. In the early days, salesmen traveled the country either by train or locally by buggy. Annually, they gathered in town for sales talks and the introduction of new products, as pictured above. Below, salesmen tow the line in front of the Myers office building in 1920, ready to sell the new products of the Myers Company. Francis E. and Philip A. Myers are seen standing in shirtsleeves (with no jacket or hat) in the second row on the far right.

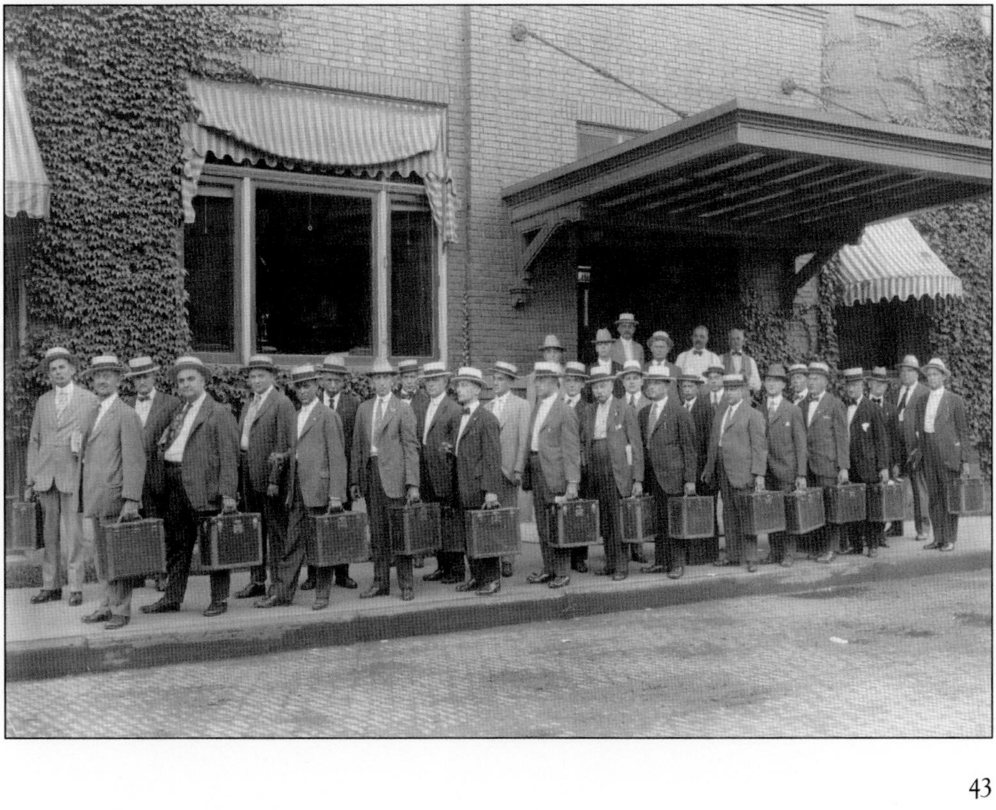

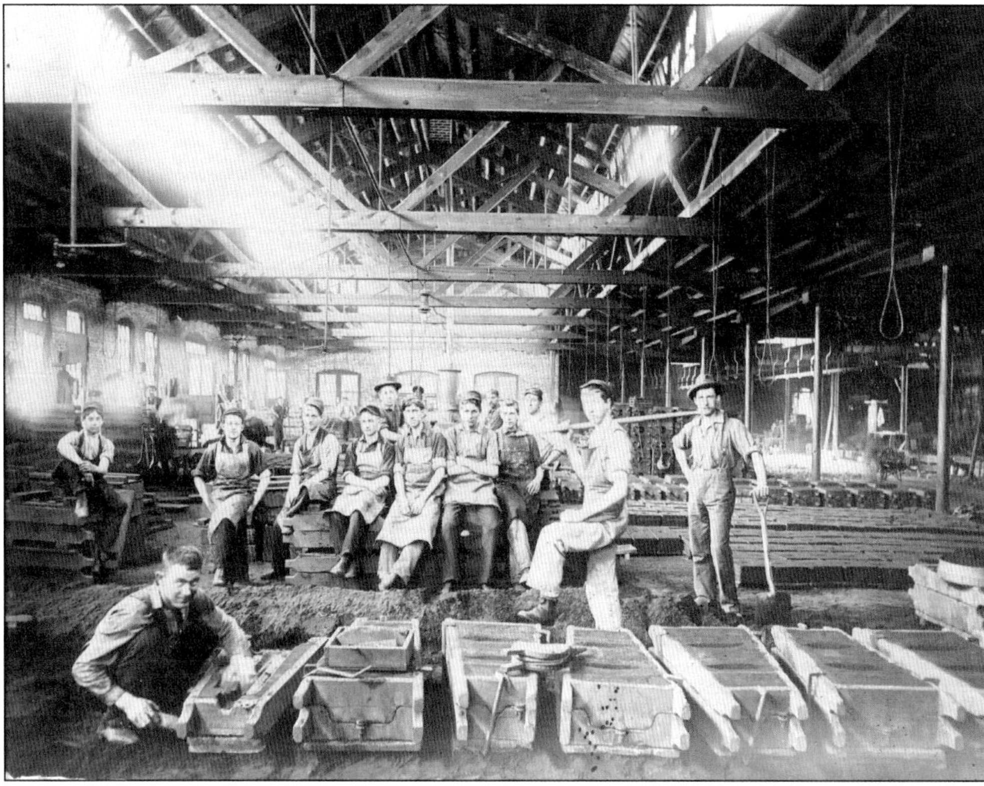

Although known for manufacturing pumps, the F.E. Myers and Brothers Company made ladders, lawn swings, bicycle stands, hay hooks, and other various items. In 1915, growing from a small building on East Main Street to more than nine-and-a-half acres of floor space and two acres of foundries, on East Fourth Street, production demands had factory workers logging 59 hours a week. The tinkering of Philip A. Myers paid off for the young inventor, through the years securing more than 100 patents; all the while, Francis, considered one of the leading captain's of industry, grew the company during this time, selling more than 175,000 pumps a year and employing 650 with 30,000 dealers around the world. Operating today as the Pentair Corporation, "Where Innovation Meets Tradition," the plant relocated to Myers Parkway in 1988.

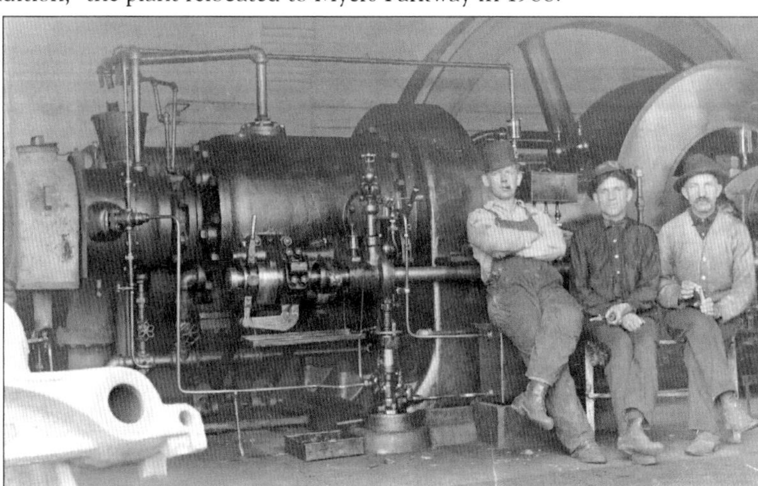

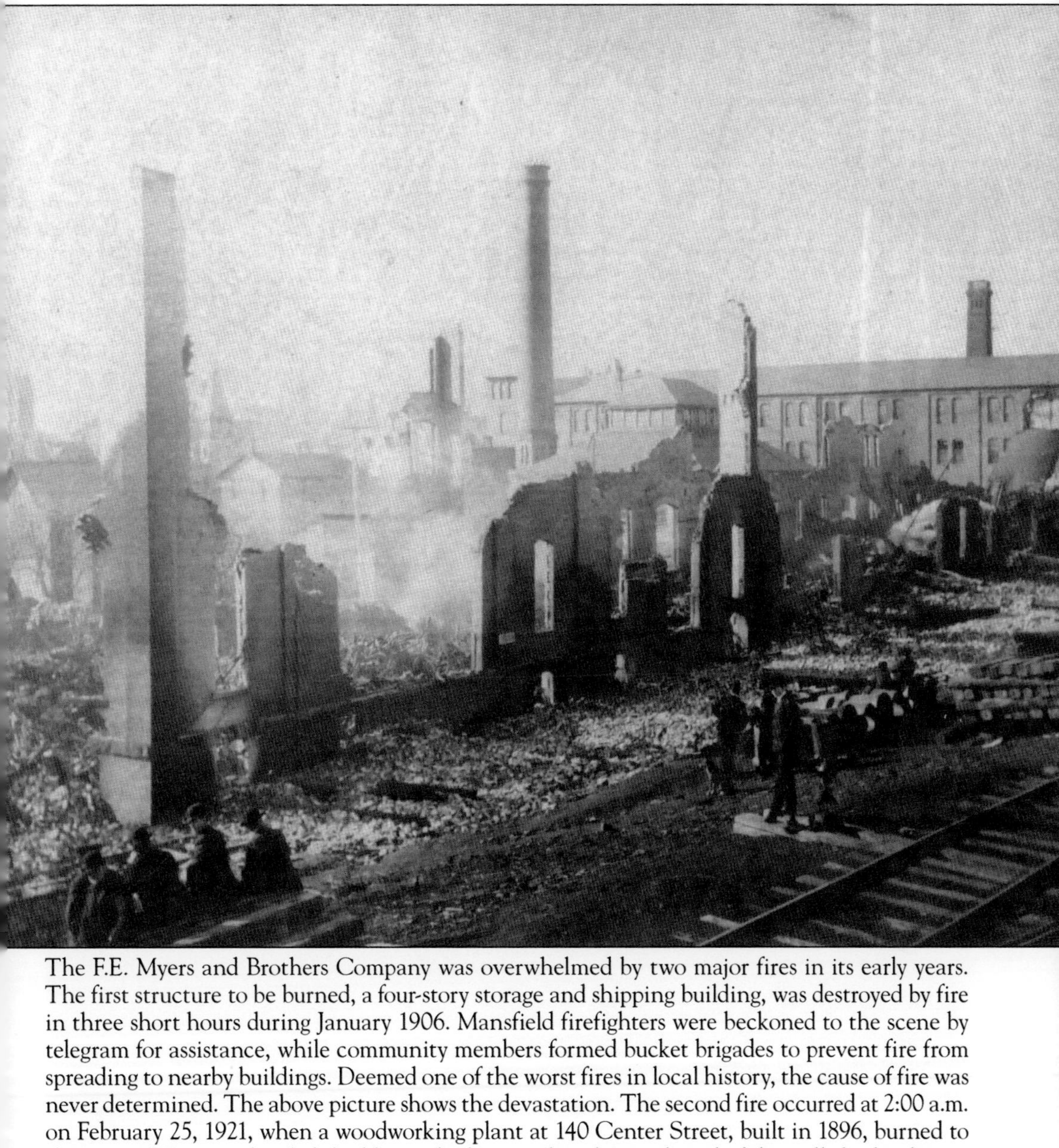

The F.E. Myers and Brothers Company was overwhelmed by two major fires in its early years. The first structure to be burned, a four-story storage and shipping building, was destroyed by fire in three short hours during January 1906. Mansfield firefighters were beckoned to the scene by telegram for assistance, while community members formed bucket brigades to prevent fire from spreading to nearby buildings. Deemed one of the worst fires in local history, the cause of fire was never determined. The above picture shows the devastation. The second fire occurred at 2:00 a.m. on February 25, 1921, when a woodworking plant at 140 Center Street, built in 1896, burned to the ground. Firemen battled the blaze, which started in the south end of the mill, for five hours. After the rubble was cleared away, the company did not rebuild the woodworking plant, but rather leased the property, eventually selling it in 1941. (Cloyd McNaull collection.)

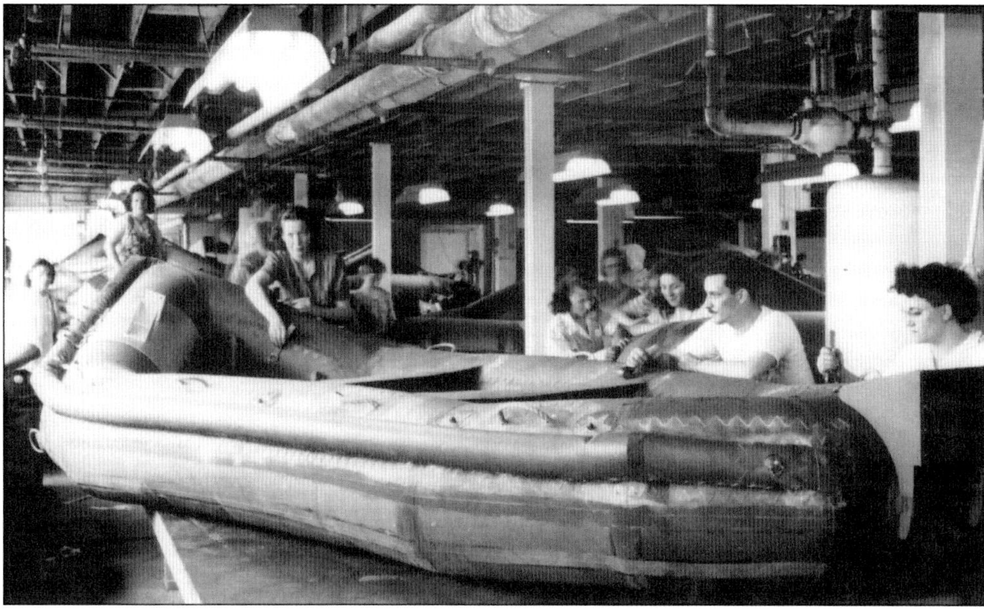

When Harry Gill Sr. incorporated the Eagle Rubber Company, located on the corner of Union and East Seventh Streets, he soared with success. Formed in 1913, the Eagle manufactured toy balloons and, during World War II, produced military equipment, as shown above. Having relocated to Orange Street along the Erie tracks, with the most modern dipping plant in the country, Gill sold products of the highest quality around the globe. In 1939, Gill left the firm, and under a new management team of Kenton Cravens and John Sweeney, the plant continued its success. In 1943, the main plant was completely gutted from fire caused by a train wreck on the Erie tracks. Upon reconstruction, the Eagle continued to grow and change ownership, becoming the Hedstrom Corporation. In this 1951 photograph below, a plant employee strips a balloon from its mold.

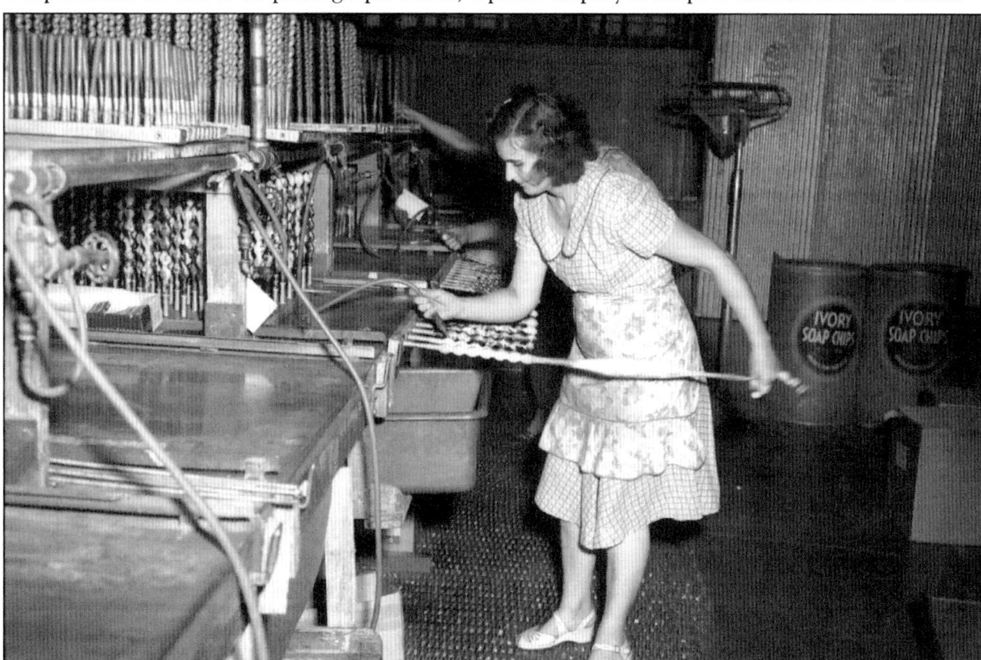

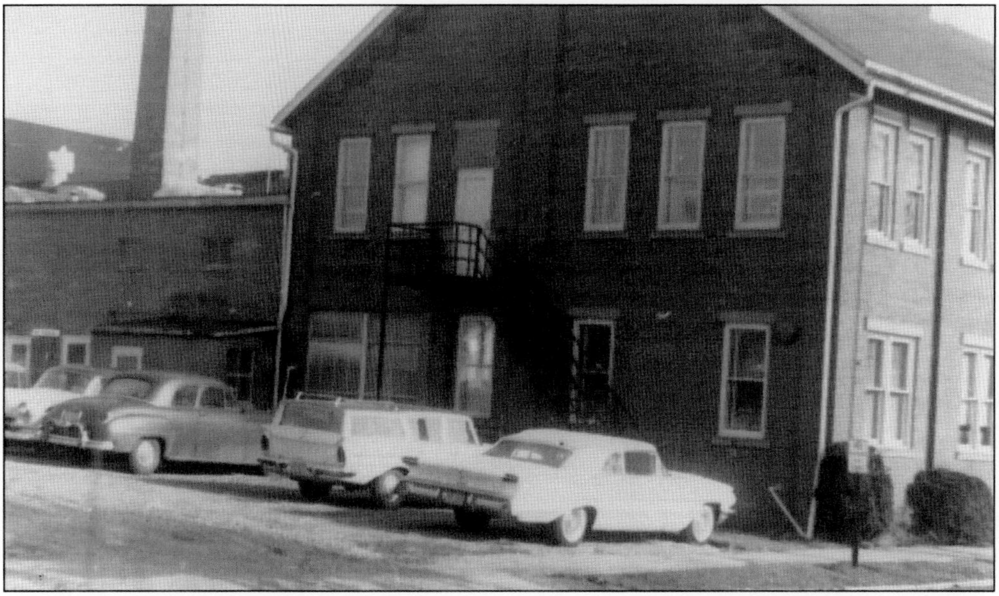

The founder of the Eagle Rubber Company, Harry Gill Sr., established the National Latex Products Company in 1939 on East Fourth Street, seen above. Selecting the bluebird, a symbol of happiness, for his new company trademark, Gill was very happy as the latex company prospered to the top in the industry with daily shipments to points around the globe. By 1953, the company was producing the vinyl play ball, a first in the business, which was a highly profitable conception. Joined in the 1940s by his two sons, David and Harry Jr., Gill continued to lead the firm into his later years. It is because of companies like the National Latex Products Company and the Eagle Rubber Company that Ashland was known as the balloon capital of the world, at one time producing 70 percent of the world's balloons. Pictured below are Latex employees dipping balloon molds.

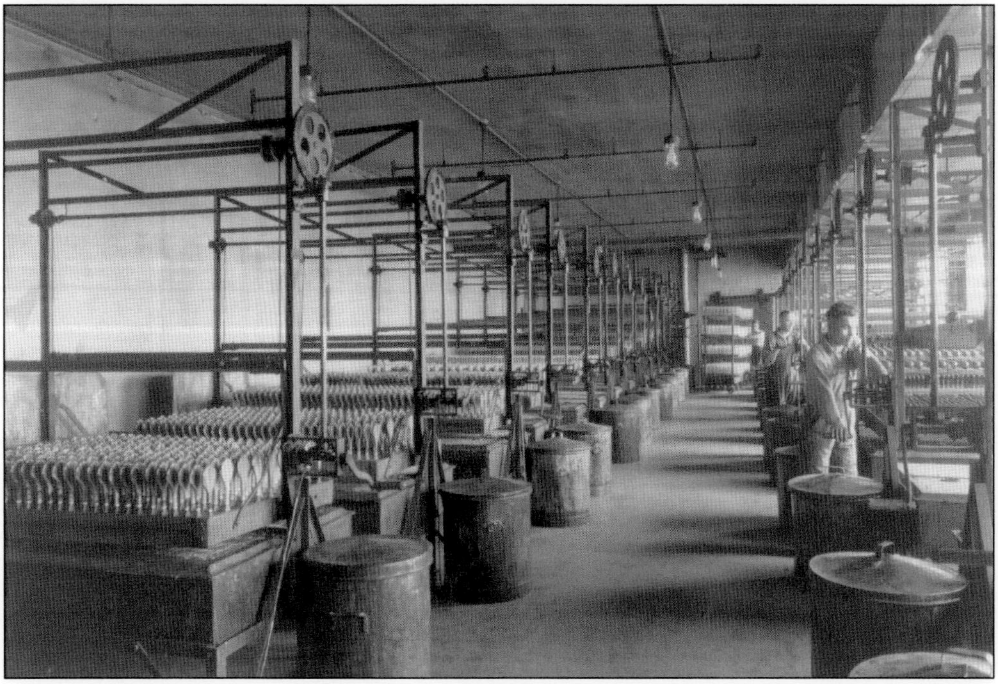

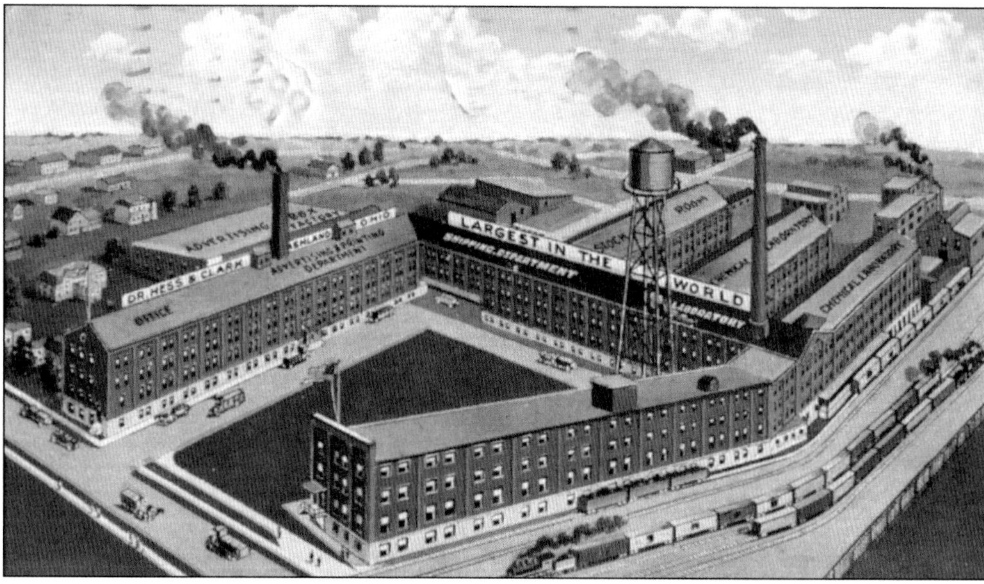

In 1893, Gilbert Hess, MD, DVS and Jesse Lewis Clark joined forces, converting an old stable into a veterinary hospital, forming the Dr. Hess and Clark Company. Previously a salesman for the F.E. Myers and Brothers Company, Clark made a $250 investment in Dr. Hess's product. He then traveled the surrounding counties in his buckboard, selling their first product, Dr. Hess Stock Tonic. In those early years, Nettie Hess, wife of Gilbert, and Mary Clark, wife of Jesse, assisted their husbands by filling orders at night to keep up with the demand in company sales. Eventually manufacturing feed medications and animal health products in 1900, a three-story factory was built on Orange Street, which through the years became a U-shaped complex, covering nearly three-and-a-half acres, becoming the largest manufacturer of its kind in the world. The photograph below shows a covered wagon used in the delivery of products. (Robert C. Ingmand collection.)

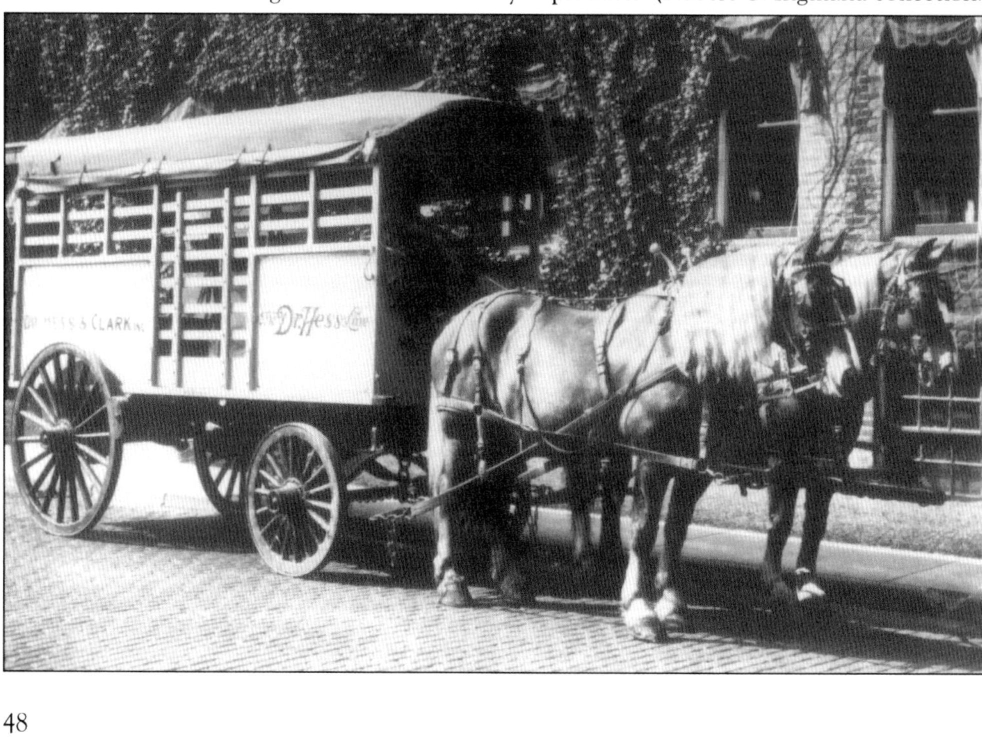

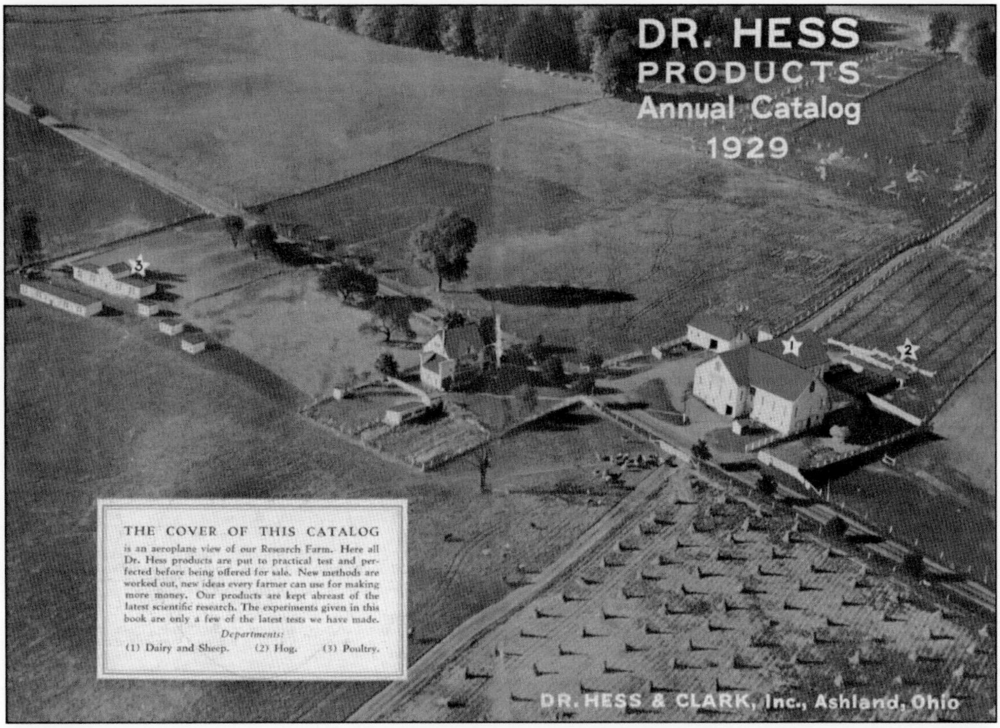

In 1924, a year after the death of Dr. Hess, Jesse Lewis Clark opened a 476-acre research farm, pictured above, on Route 250 East for the purpose of conducting experiments and tests under practical and on-the-farm conditions. Scientists studied all types of animal and poultry diseases. Knowing that healthy animals grow faster and are vital to more wholesome human food, the experimental station played a crucial role in the development of new products produced at the Orange Street plant. The Hess and Clark Company became associated with a division of Vick Chemical in 1955, carrying on its unending battle against sickness and disease in animals. In 1980, it was sold to WIL Research Laboratories, which specializes in animal toxicology, metabolism, and analytical chemistry studies. Pictured below is an undated aerial farm view in later years. (WIL Research collection.)

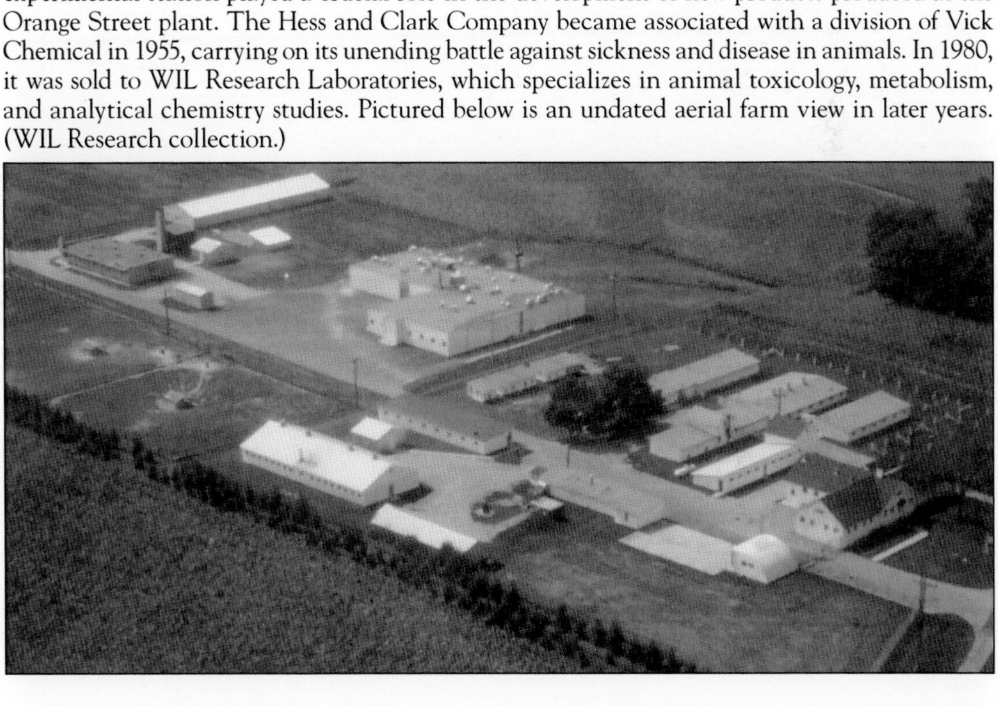

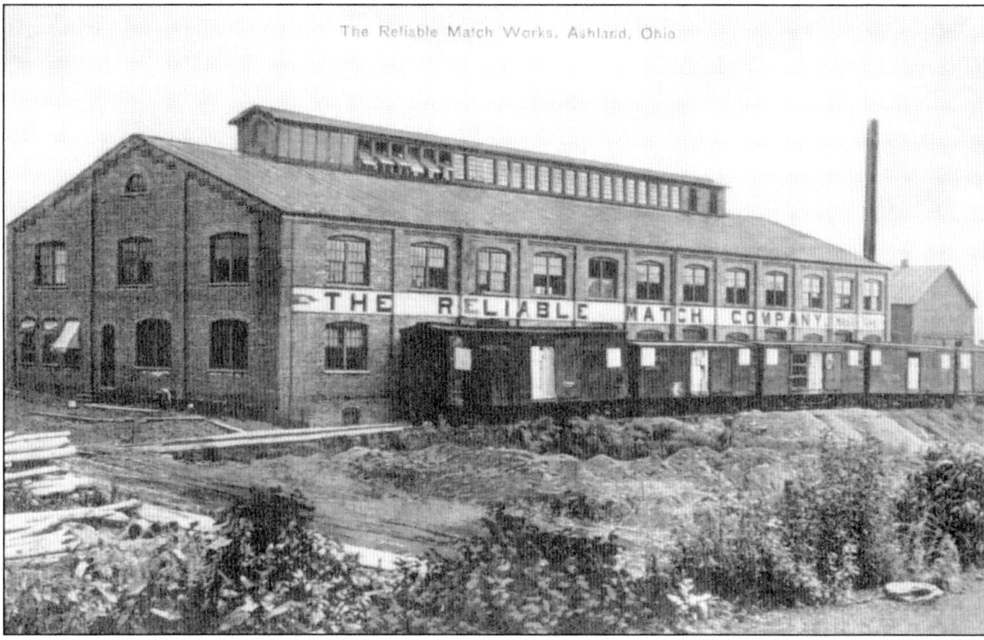

Magic Tips was the brand name, and they were sold across the country and beyond. Formed in 1903, the Reliable Match Company was burning up with the production of 400 gross boxes of matches per day. Located at 609 Union Street, the company eventually was purchased by the Federal Match Corporation. Covering 60,000 square feet of floor space, Reliable produced matchsticks of white pine shipped from Idaho.

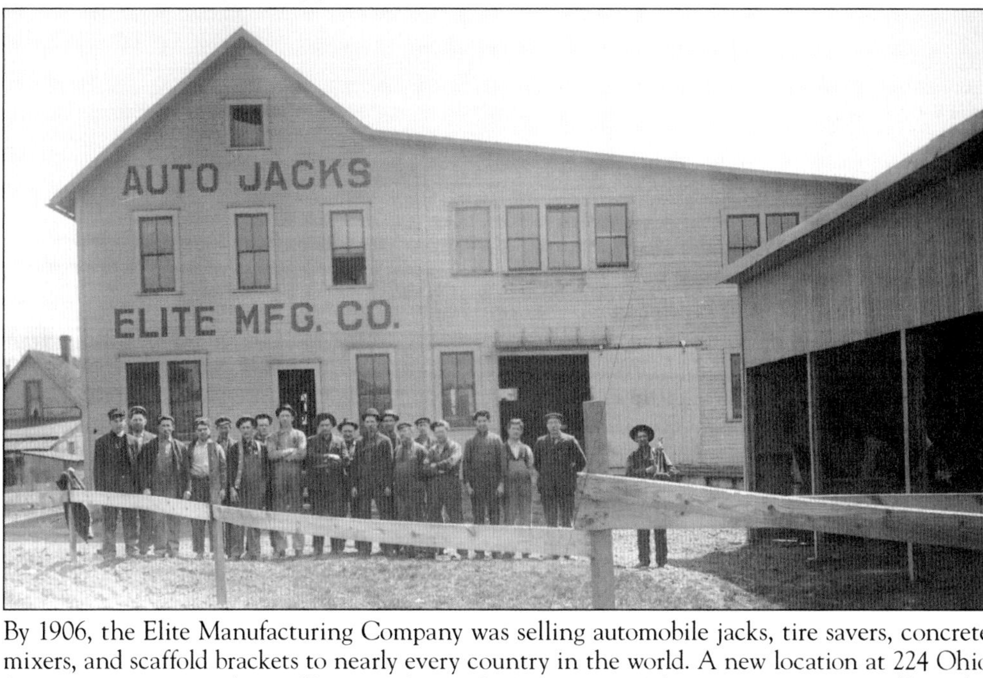

By 1906, the Elite Manufacturing Company was selling automobile jacks, tire savers, concrete mixers, and scaffold brackets to nearly every country in the world. A new location at 224 Ohio Street saw expansion from 450 square feet to 30,000 in 1914. The company grew rapidly under the direction of owners E.L. Kilhefner, J.H. Burkholder, and P.E. Countryman. In 1929, the plant was sold to J.H. Channon Company of Chicago.

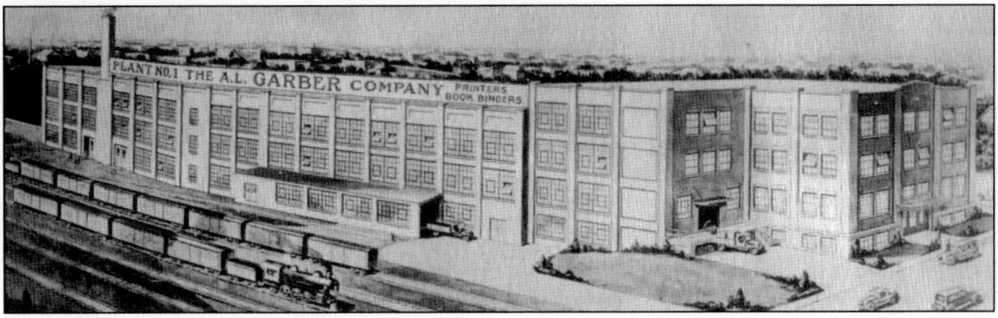

Similar to their winning 1935 Garber softball team, the A.L. Garber Company, located at 636 Orange Street at the Erie tracks, was also a winner. In 1879, founder Aaron L. Garber saw a vision for commercial printing with his first big job, a catalog for the F.E. Myers and Brothers Company. In 1929, changing its name to Garber Publishing Company, Garber was on the move, printing quality catalogs, booklets, and display materials. "We Serve to Serve Again" became the 1929 company motto. During World War II, as armed guards kept watch, they printed training materials, literature, manuals, and maps for the military, becoming one of five printing firms to receive the US Navy Commendation Award in 1945. The Garber family, with O.M. Garber pictured below, led their company to success and eventually sold the firm in 1969.

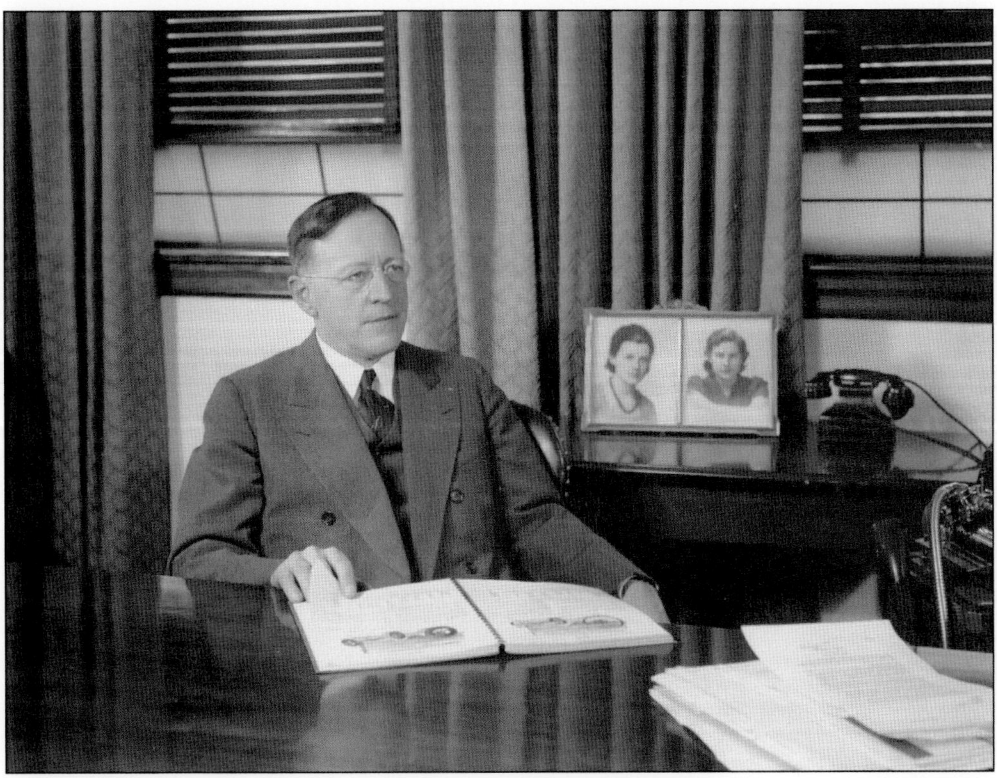

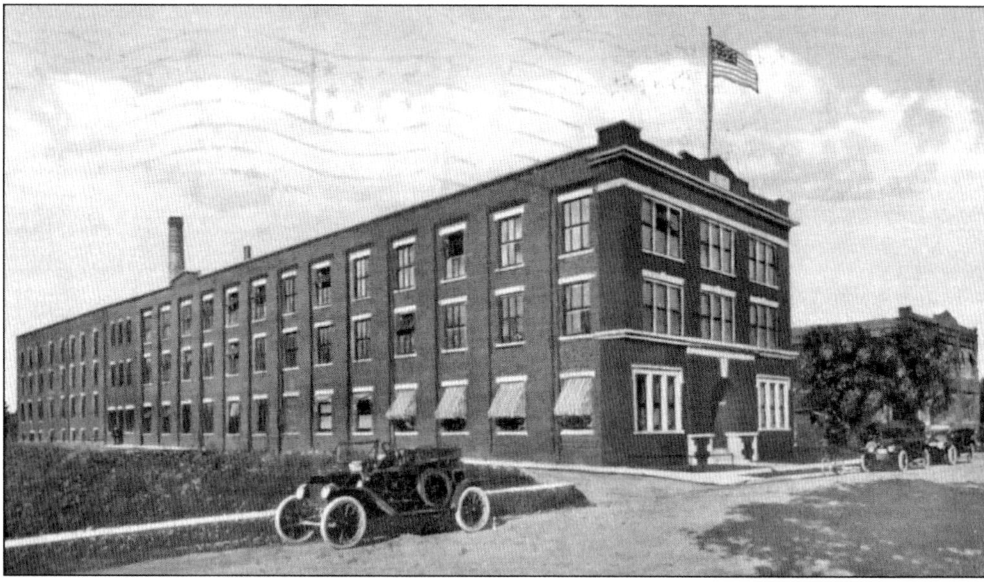

A high standard of quality gave the Faultless Rubber Company, shown above, an early reputation as one of the top special rubber goods manufacturer in the world. Owner T.W. Miller got his start in 1898 in Akron, Ohio, before moving operations to Ashland in 1907. The craftsmen in rubber were among the first to produce one-piece molded water bottles and chemically blown sponge rubber. The production of rubber sundries, rubber specialties, rubber surgical goods, and balloons were amongst the 600 items the plant manufactured. Pictured below, operators work with extruding machines. Situated at 268 East Fourth Street and covering nearly nine acres in 1965, Faultless was a leader in its field. In 1966, a merger with Abbott Laboratories took place. By 2004, a merger with the Hospira Corporation occurred, though it was short lived, as Hospira doors closed in 2008.

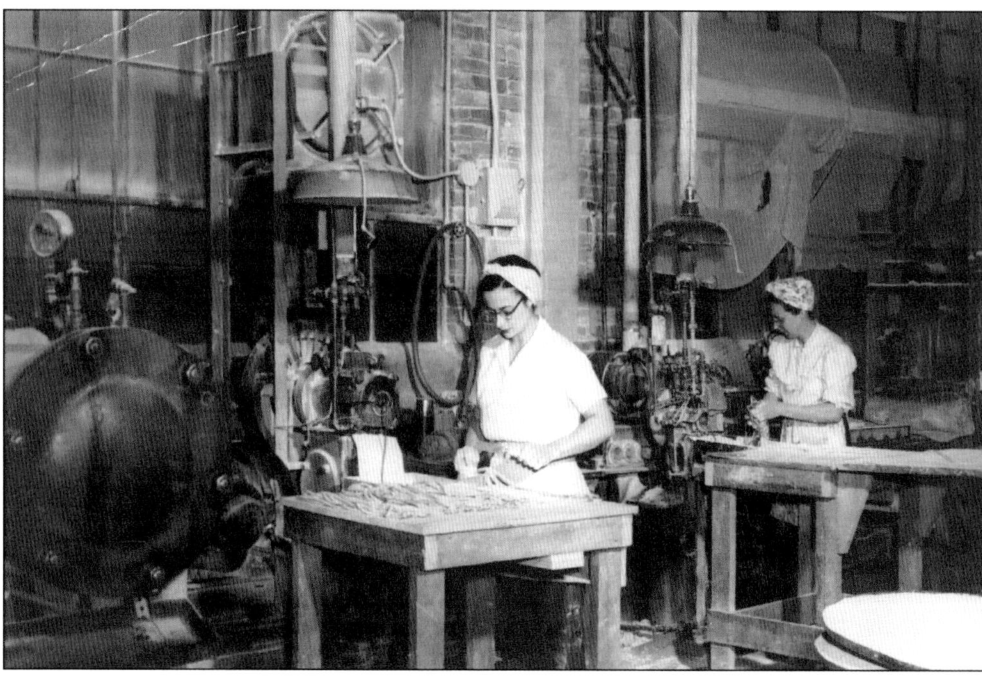

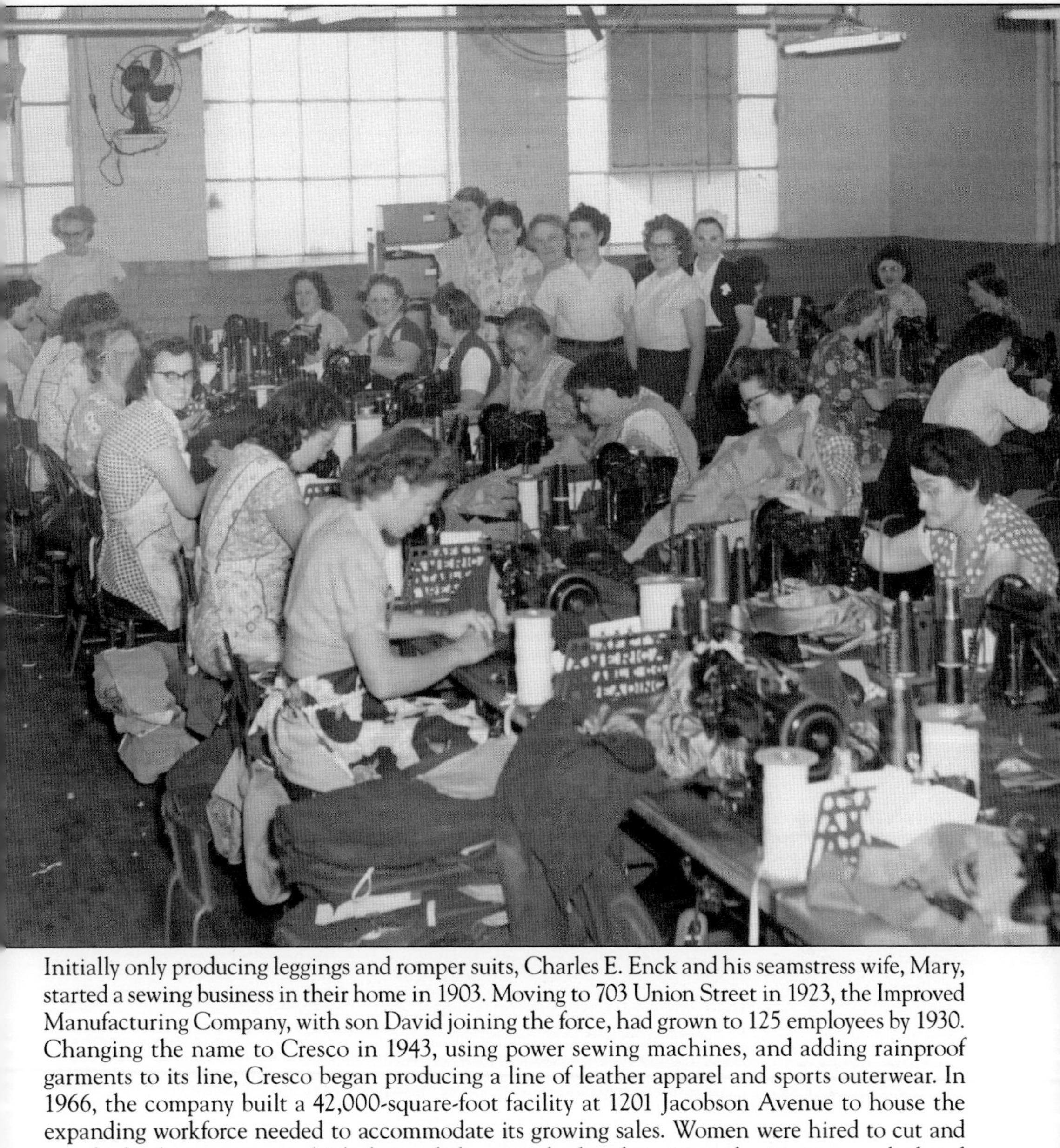

Initially only producing leggings and romper suits, Charles E. Enck and his seamstress wife, Mary, started a sewing business in their home in 1903. Moving to 703 Union Street in 1923, the Improved Manufacturing Company, with son David joining the force, had grown to 125 employees by 1930. Changing the name to Cresco in 1943, using power sewing machines, and adding rainproof garments to its line, Cresco began producing a line of leather apparel and sports outerwear. In 1966, the company built a 42,000-square-foot facility at 1201 Jacobson Avenue to house the expanding workforce needed to accommodate its growing sales. Women were hired to cut and sew the leather garments, which demanded a special talent because each piece was cut by hand and sewn to perfection, shown above, with "Integrity in Every Stitch." Advertising nationally, the Cresco Company was marketed in men's and ladies' magazines, from *Sports Illustrated* to Sears and Roebuck, realizing $12 million in total sales at one time. Cresco was ultimately sold, with the doors closing in the 1980s.

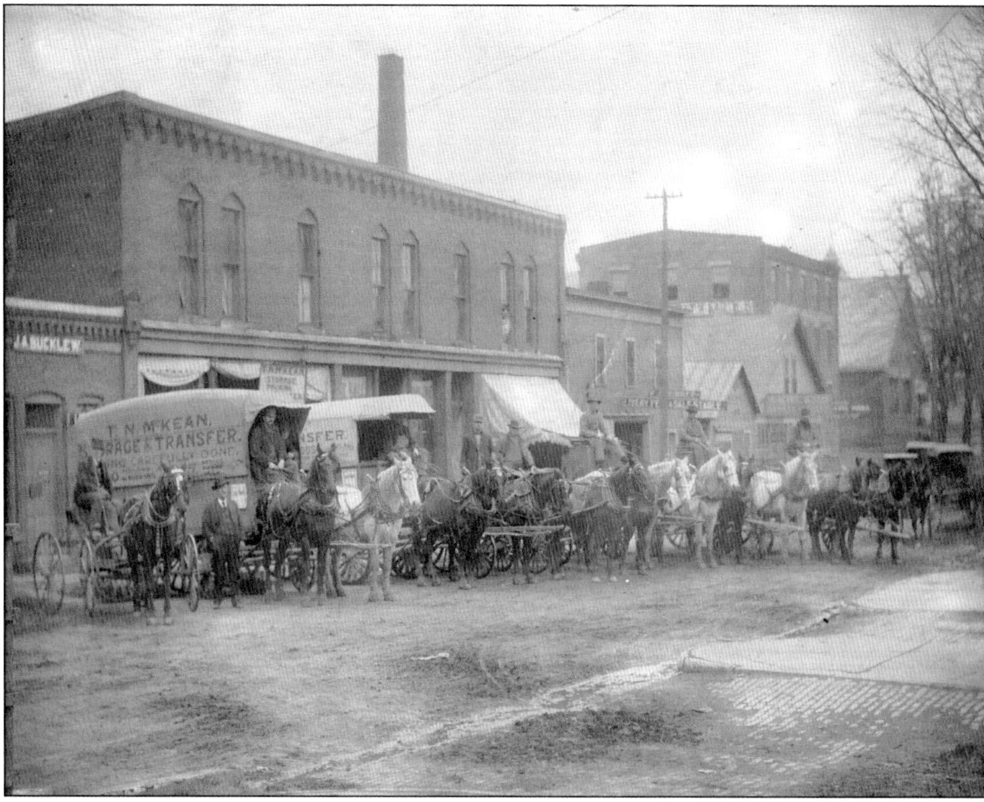

The McKean Storage and Transfer Company, pictured above in 1911, was located at Nine Center Street, situated between the Home Company and the Ashland City Mills and owned by Thomas Newton McKean. McKean's business was known for transferring and moving, using reliable, experienced men, one-horse wagons, and heavy drays. They advertised piano moving as their specialty. (Samuel G. Markel collection.)

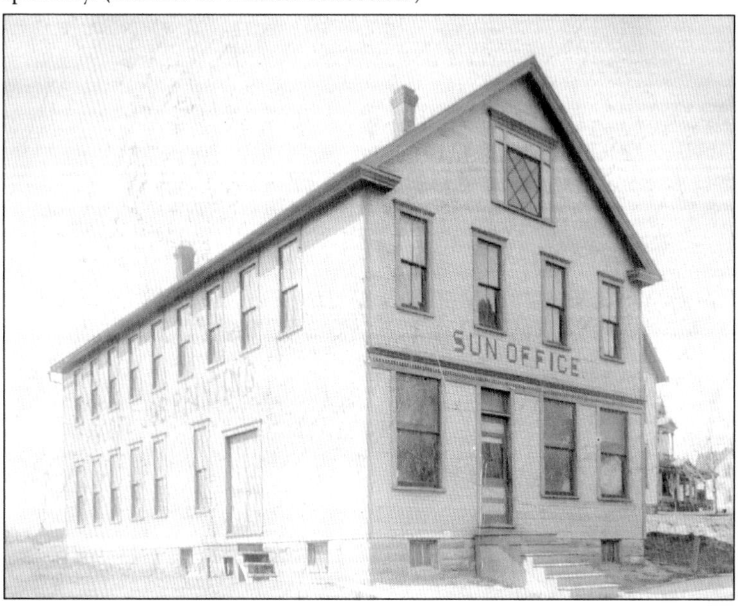

The *Ashland Sun*, a weekly newspaper published by Aaron L. Garber, was established in 1879. Garber came to town when the Brethren Church organized Ashland College in 1878 and first printed church and school publications before starting the *Ashland Sun*. The *Sun*, located at 67 Orange Street, was the official beginning of the A.L. Garber Company.

Four

Faces on the Street

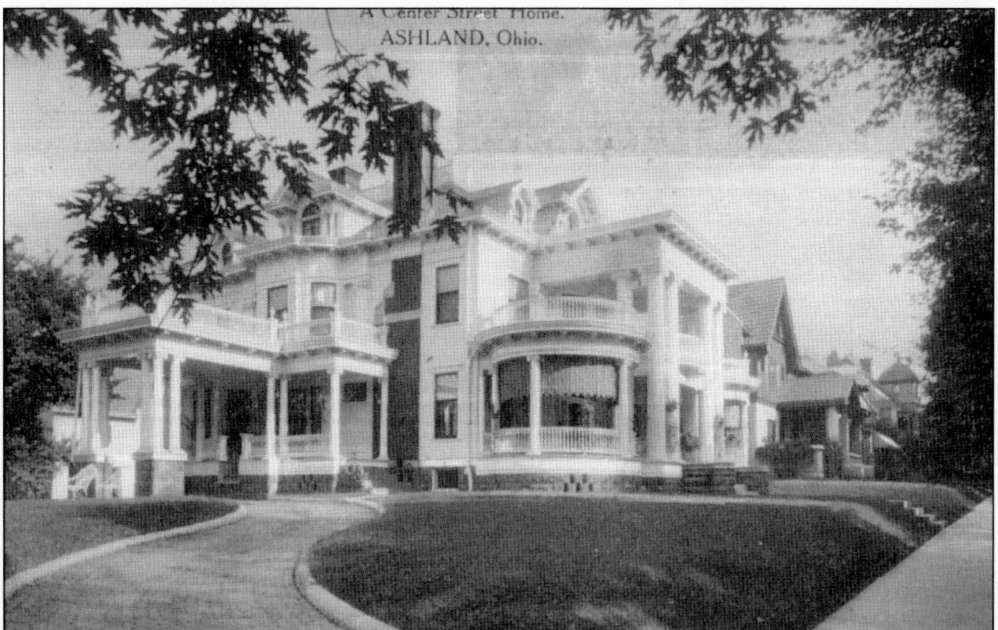

In 1903, this Georgian Revival home at 413 Center Street was built by Samuel H. Grabill, founder of the Ashland Gas and Electric Company and cofounder of the Star Telephone Company in 1899. The three-story home, with its impressive two story columns, two rounded verandas on either side of the entrance, and the extended carriage entrance on its north side, makes an extraordinary presence on the street.

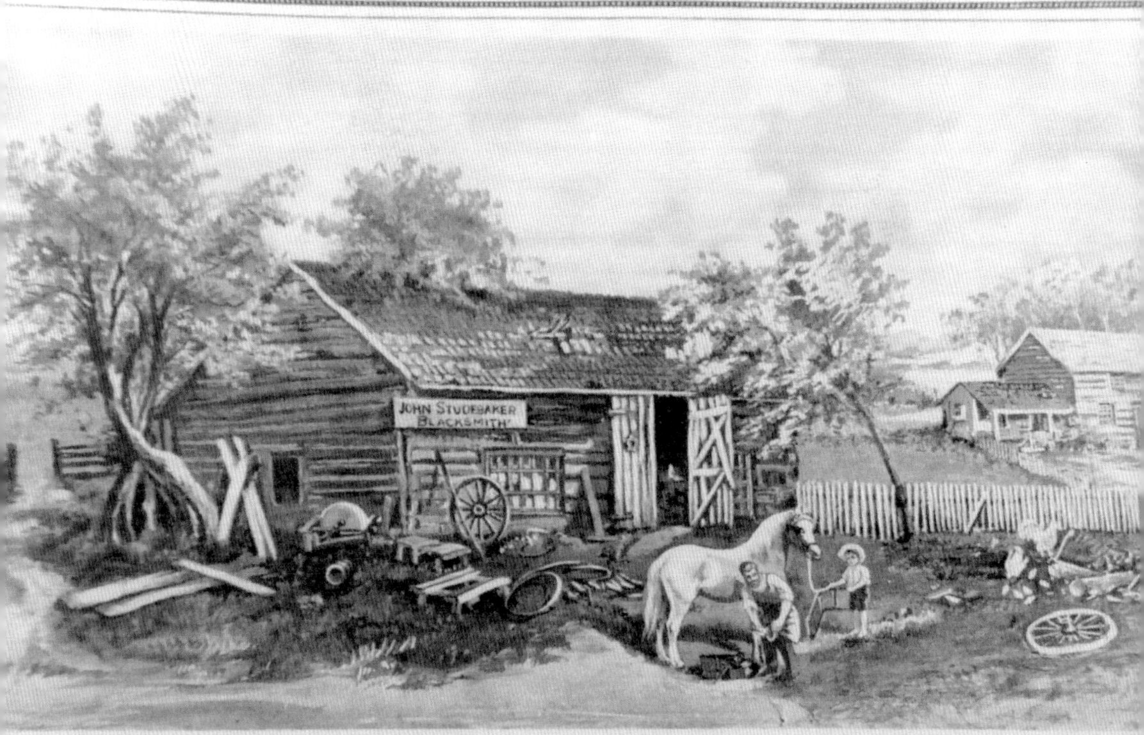

STUDEBAKER SHOP AND HOME, ASHLAND, OHIO, 1835

Standing strong along Route 250 East, a granite monument proudly rests where one of the town's most noteworthy families once called home. Minutes east of the Ashland community atop Studebaker Hill, a memorial with a bronze tablet honors John Studebaker and his family, symbolizing the site of the Studebaker home and blacksmith shop. In 1835, astride a bulky wagon pulled by four horses, Studebaker and his wife, Rebecca, arrived in a carriage that carried their then six of 10 children. They relocated to Ashland from Pennsylvania and purchased a 160-acre farm they called Pleasant Ridge, pictured above in 1845. Family struggles reduced the farm to a small tract of land, where Studebaker turned out iron parts for wagons with neighbor George Myers, father to Francis E. Myers, doing the woodwork. Three of Studebaker's sons learned the blacksmithing trade, and amongst the hard times of the 1850s, they moved west, settling in South Bend, Indiana. It was here that Clem, John M., and Peter Studebaker started their own blacksmith shop, eventually becoming the world's largest producer of horse-drawn vehicles, ultimately manufacturing the Studebaker gas-powered automobile.

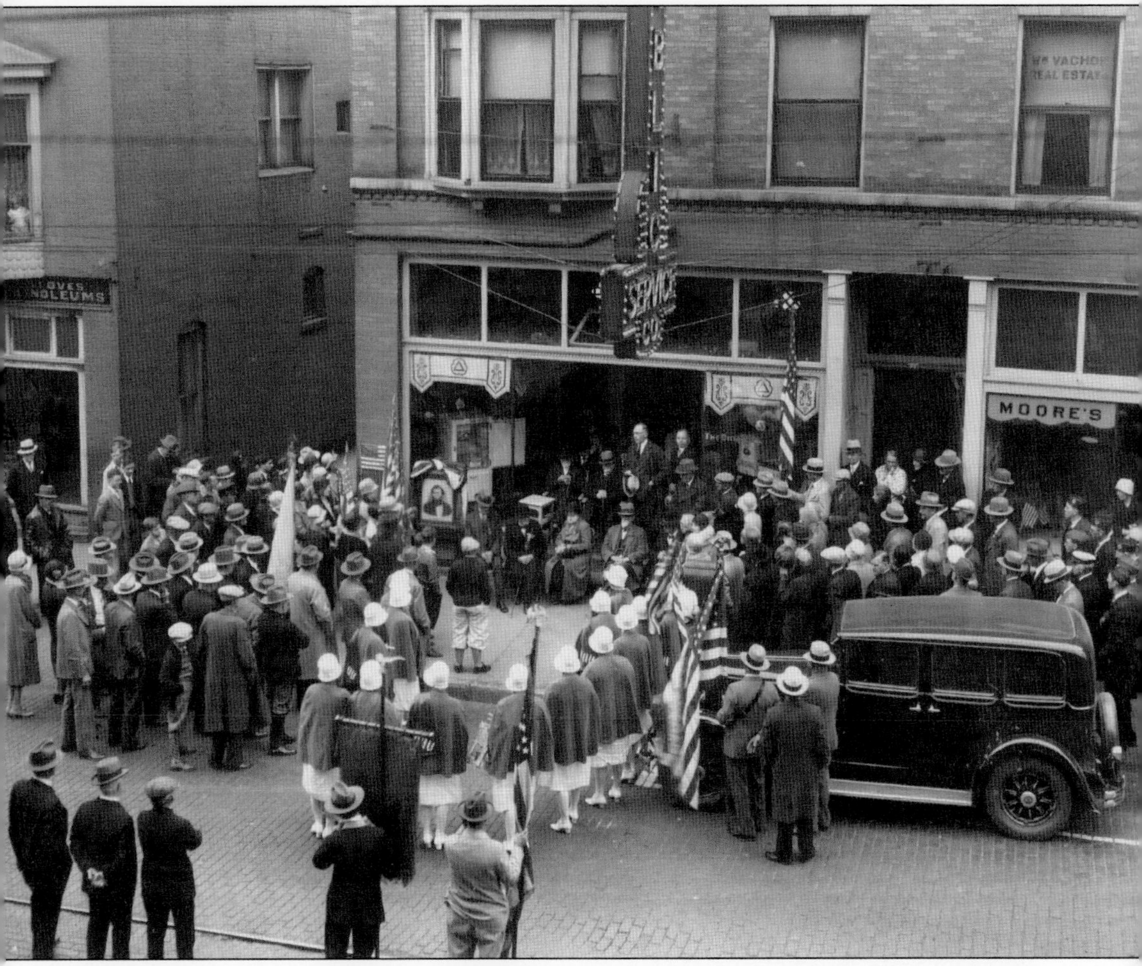

In 1819, Lorin Andrews was the second child to be born in Uniontown, now known as Ashland, in a log cabin on Main Street. A man of great success, he became the sixth president of Kenyon College in 1854. In 1861, he was granted a leave of absence from his position with Kenyon to become the first man from Ohio to volunteer in the Civil War. Made captain by Gov. William Dennison, he mustered into the Union army. As a member of the 4th Ohio Volunteer Infantry Regiment, Andrews was then promoted to colonel for his discipline and command of his men. Before his regiment saw action, Andrews contacted typhoid fever and died at the age of 42. The untimely death of Andrews stunned Ohio. Looking closely at this photograph, one can locate a picture of Andrews in the store window as Judge Charles Chapman unveils and dedicates a bronze tablet on May 30, 1930, at 29 East Main Street, commemorating Andrews and marking the site of the log cabin where he was born.

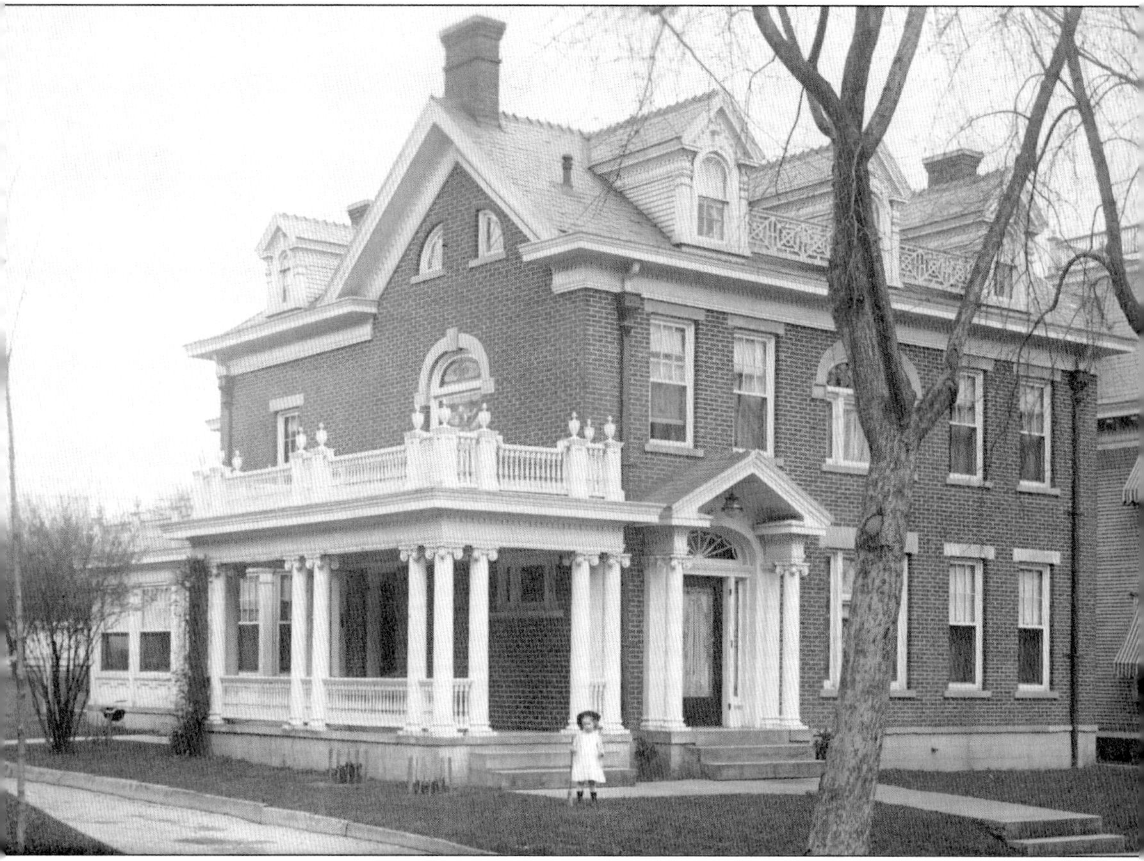

Situated at 414 Center Street, this Georgian-style home is one of the oldest on the street. It was built in 1859 by Dr. Jacob P. Cowan on a lot purchased for $200. In addition to being a doctor, Cowan also served in the legislature and the Ohio House of Representatives for many years. In 1905, Philip A. Myers purchased the home as a wedding gift for his son Guy C. Myers. It was then that central heating and gas lighting brought the home a much-needed update. In 1920, additions to the south and west created its current appearance. Additionally, a unique feature added to the third floor was a holding tank for water, which provided gravity-fed water throughout the house. The Cowan home stayed in the Myers family until 1952 when it was given to Ashland College to be used as the residence of the college president. It then became the Ashland College Historical Center in 1969. In 1981, the property was sold to the Ashland County Historical Society to accommodate its extensive collection.

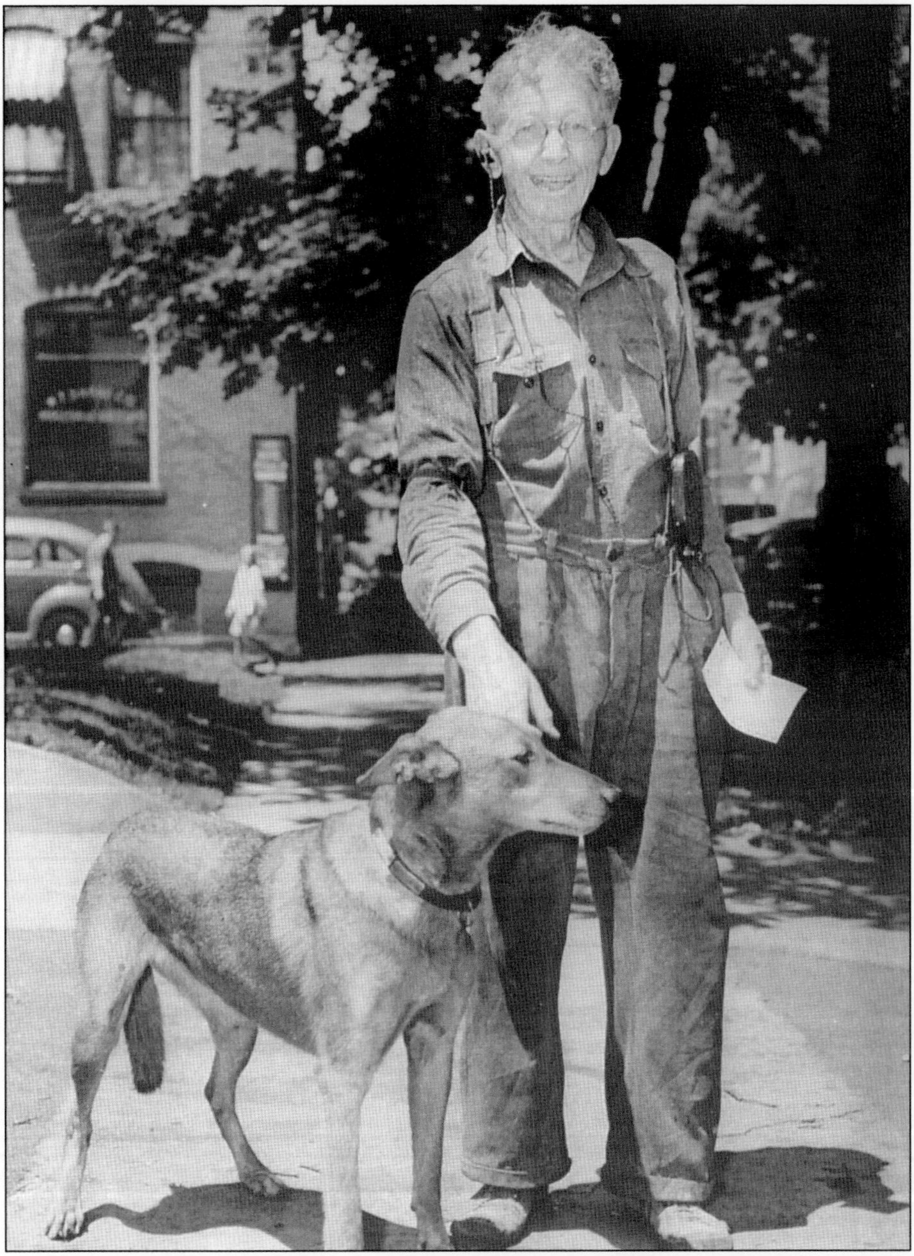

Often seen walking the town with his companion dogs and teaching Sunday school, coal dealer and cement contractor Ard Blackford, pictured above, imprinted the hundreds of sidewalks he made with the words "Keep Sweet," the words he chose to live by. "Keep Sweet" was not only stamped into sidewalks, but in 1917, Blackford began publishing a pamphlet titled with the popular slogan, distributing 3,500 copies each year free of charge, believing, "It was more blessed to give than to get." Additionally, in 1911, the first Boy Scout troop was organized under Blackford's command. Three years before his 90th birthday in 1949, Blackford was named the Golden Rule Honor Citizen of the town. Living a good life, Blackford died at the age of 90. The Savannah Cemetery boasts a monument with his philosophy: "I have always been a great giver. I enjoyed life and enjoyed giving more than any property I might possess."

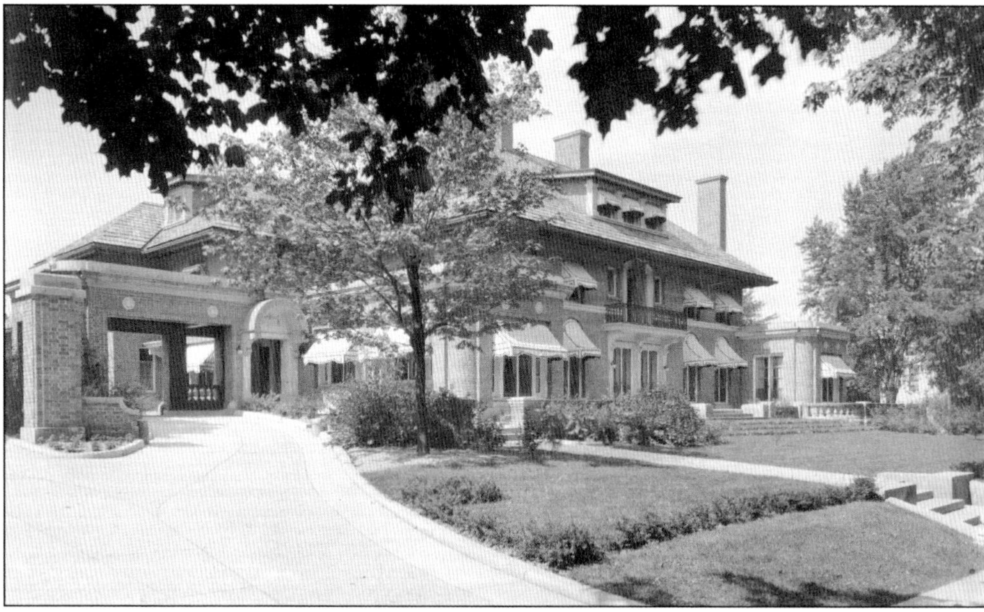

An inventive genius, with nearly 100 patents in his name, Philip A. Myers, cofounder of the F.E. Myers and Brothers Company, married Samantha Alice Chase in 1879. In 1915, they built this Italianate-style home at 508 Center Street that proudly features an interior of oak and walnut, vaulted ceilings, several fireplaces, an enclosed porch, and an exterior of Greendale rug brick, Indiana buffed limestone, and a roof of slate. Myers, shown below with daughter Phyllis, was a millionaire industrialist that was proud of his Ashland heritage. Favoring a bow tie, the inventor was happy designing and manufacturing pumps, staying close to home, involving himself in civic affairs, and holding the position as second chief in the Citizens Relief Fire Company for 30 years. The beautiful Center Street home was gifted to Trinity Lutheran Church and incorporated into the house of worship in 1963.

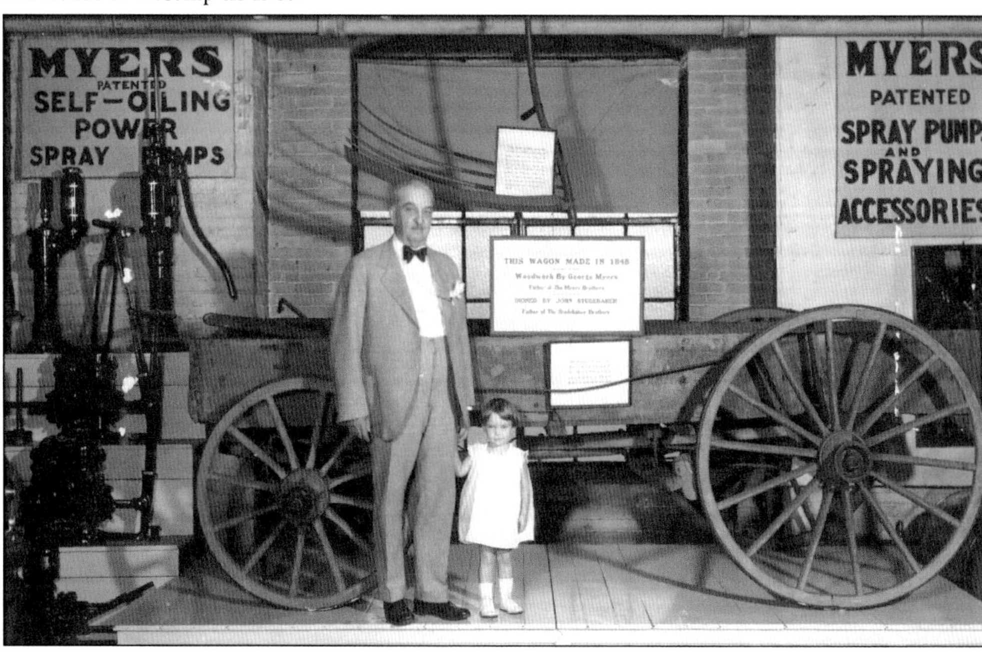

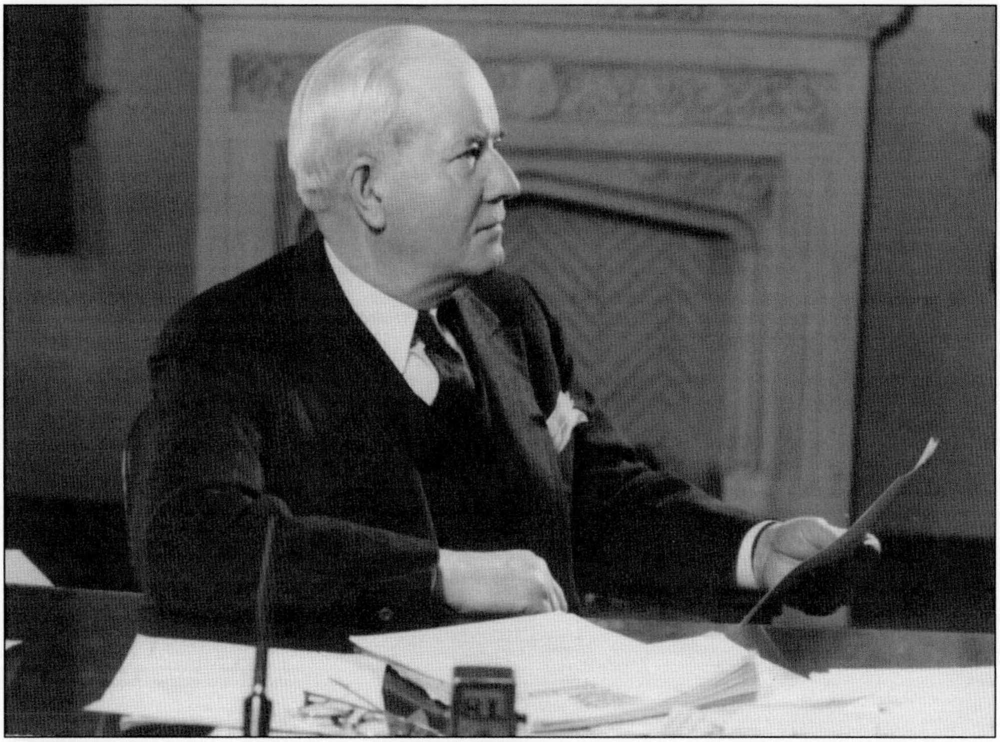

Jesse Lewis Clark, pictured above, was determined to succeed, and succeed he did. In 1893, Clark, along with partner Dr. Gilbert Hess, formed the Hess and Clark Company in 1893. By 1920, the livestock and animal care company became the largest of its kind in the world. In 1912, with the heart of a true Samaritan, Clark donated $100,000 for the town's first hospital, aptly named Samaritan Hospital. With the encouragement of his wife, Mary, Clark had numerous interests, serving his community in countless ways. Clark built this Jacobean-style home in 1918, pictured below at 622 Center Street, setting itself apart with triangular gables rising above the roofline, bay windows enhanced by stone mullions, leaded glass windows boasting distinctive medallions, and a third floor that included a ballroom. Clark's family gifted the house to the Good Shepherd Nursing Home in 1957. (Robert C. Ingmand collection.)

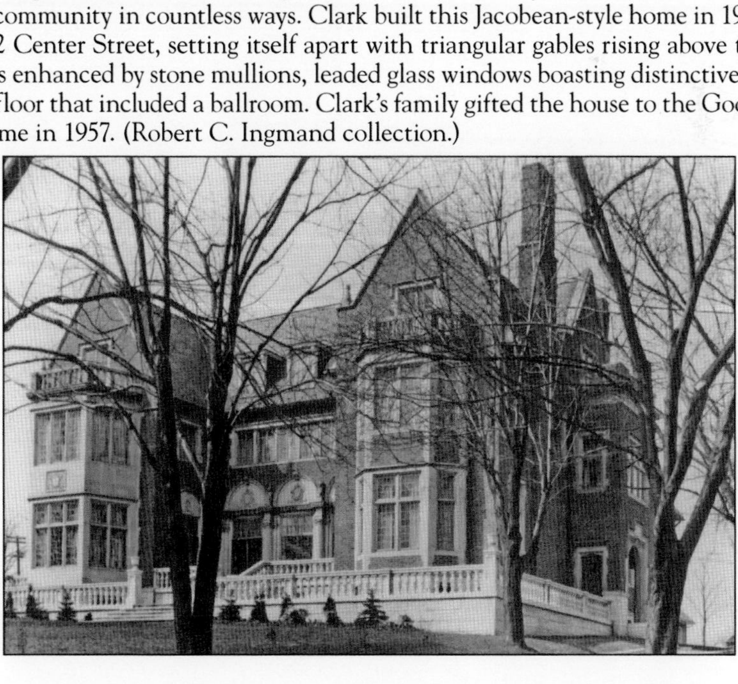

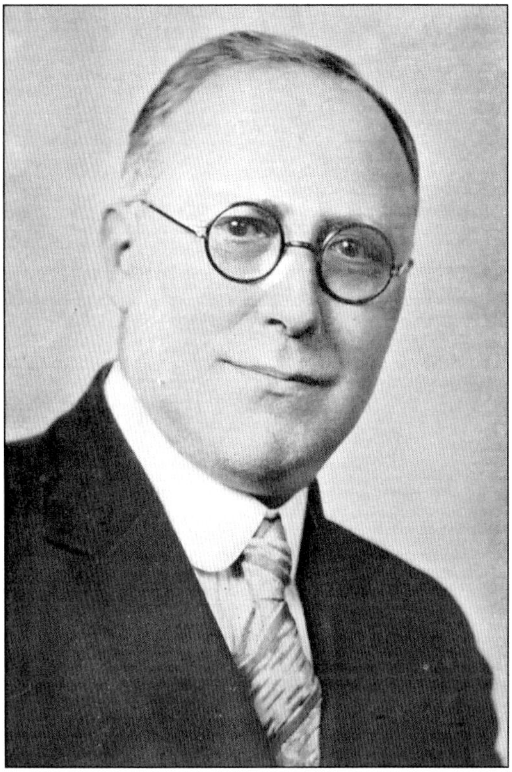

Remembering Ashland's past for future generations, Will Duff, at left, wrote the news column "Today's Observations" during his retirement years for the *Times-Gazette*. On Sundays at 3:00 p.m., he was at the microphone of the town's radio station WATG, sharing his *Reflections*. In 1915, he composed the centennial book for the city's 100th-year anniversary, and in 1931, he published a three-volume book entitled *History of North Central Ohio*. It was a good bet that Duff knew the answer to any question about Ashland County. Always to be remembered through Duff's efforts is Johnny "Appleseed" Chapman. In 1915, the children of the county raised money to build a monument in Chapman's honor, below, which stands in Brookside Park today. Duff Drive and Duff Field, the farmland where he lived with his wife, Carrie, was named after this much-loved historian.

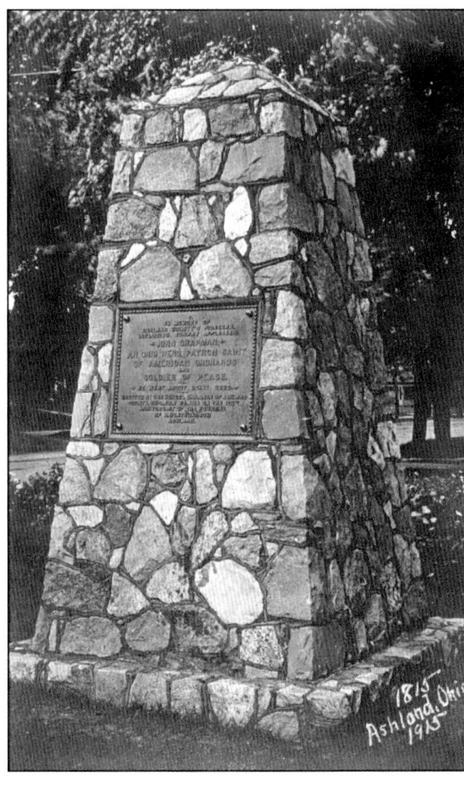

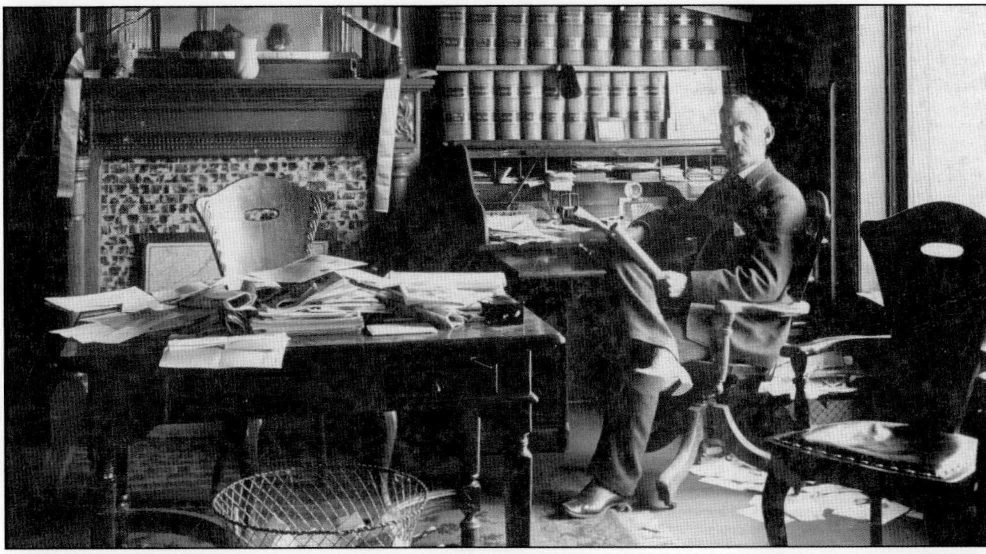

A partner in the town's largest industry, Francis E. Myers, pictured above, built this stone palace at 726 Center Street in 1896. Resembling a castle of heavy brown limestone with red and white striped awnings, a candle-snuffer roof, and a three-story turret, the home, shown below with company salesmen in 1906, was similar to that of William Vanderbilt's in New York City. Myers made many contacts around the globe, forging a closer link to the industrial world. This put the town on the map, leading Myers on a quest to improve rail connections with a line to Wooster that opened in 1899 and connected with the Pennsylvania railroad. As president of the Cleveland and Southwestern Railway, Myers brought the electric interurban to town. He also owned a private interurban car, named "Alvesta" after his wife, treating family and friends to numerous excursions.

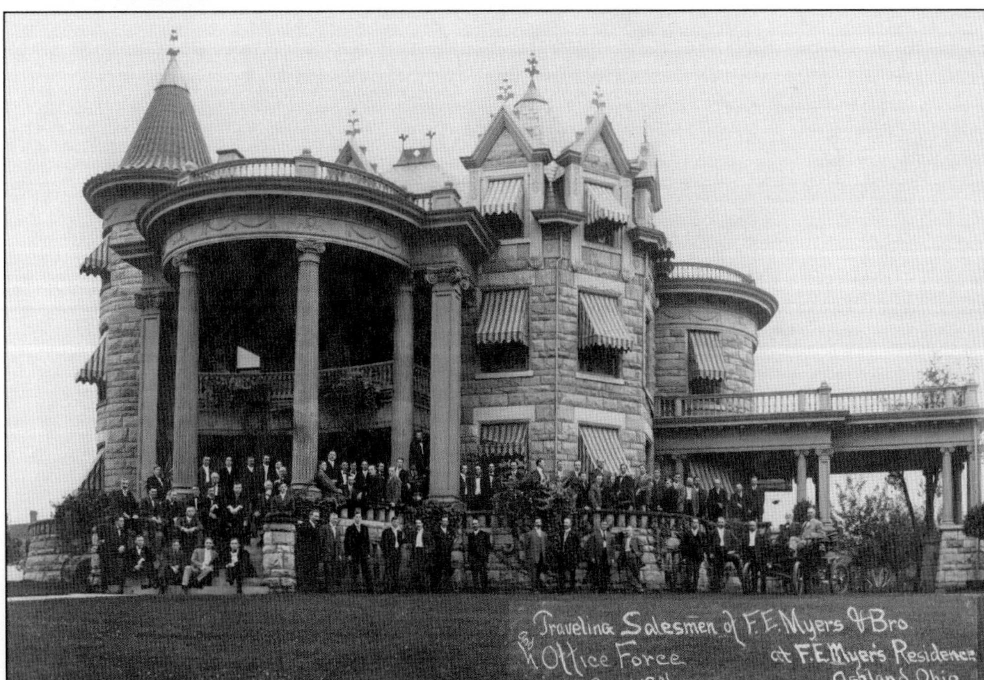

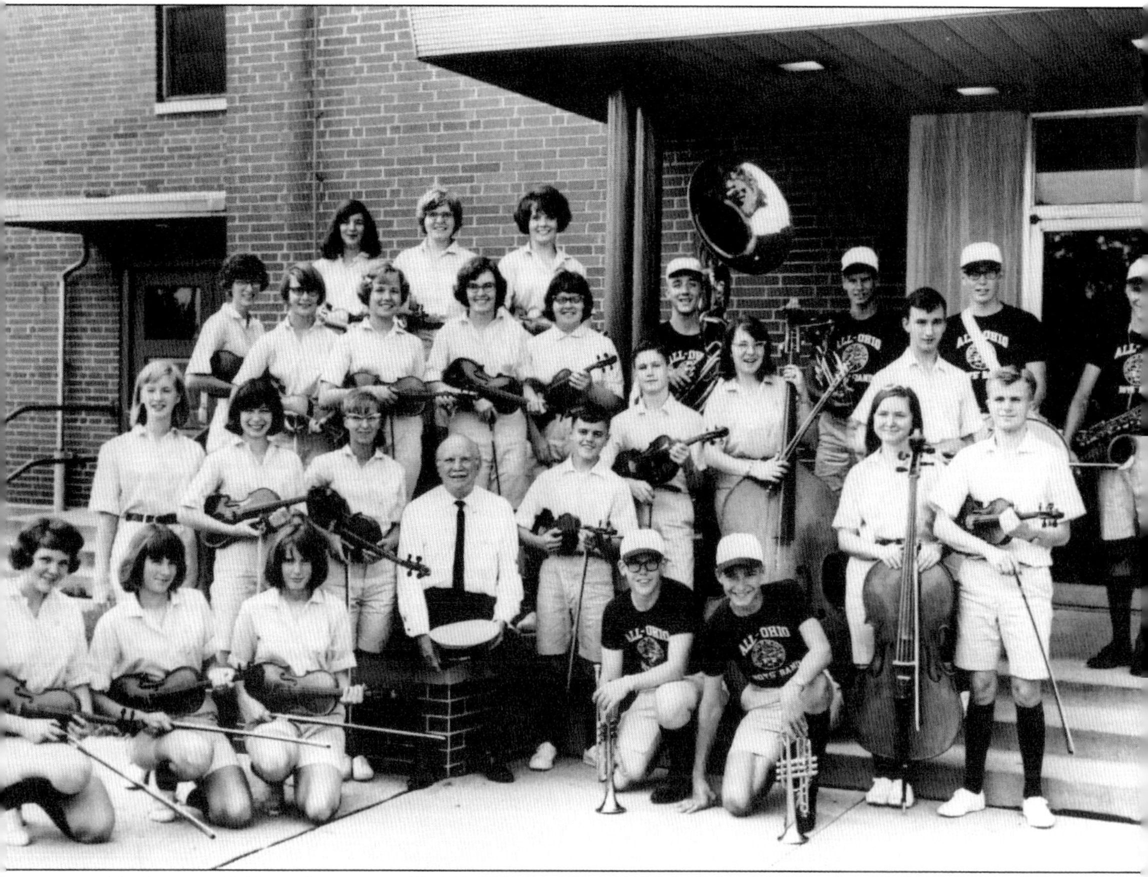

Dr. Louise E. Pete, known as "Ashland's Music Man," was the organizer and director of the 300-piece All-Ohio State Fair Boys Band for 35 years. Additionally, in 1956, Pete was coordinator and conductor of the first of many school musicals, *Brigadoon*, and the founder of the Ashland Symphony Orchestra. At the 1964 Balloon Festival, he was honored with a "Doc Pete Day" for his achievements in the world of music. Many times, Pete received statewide recognition for his musical talents, including honors from governors O'Neil and Rhoades. Those with a passion for playing music were inspired to perform their best for him, and those with a passion for listening to music were inclined to provide financial music support for him. One such financial request by Pete was granted in 1949 with a donation from Kate Moore Myers for the Guy C. Myers Memorial Band Shell. Pete is pictured above center with several members from the Ohio State Fair Orchestra members and the All-Ohio Boys Band in 1965.

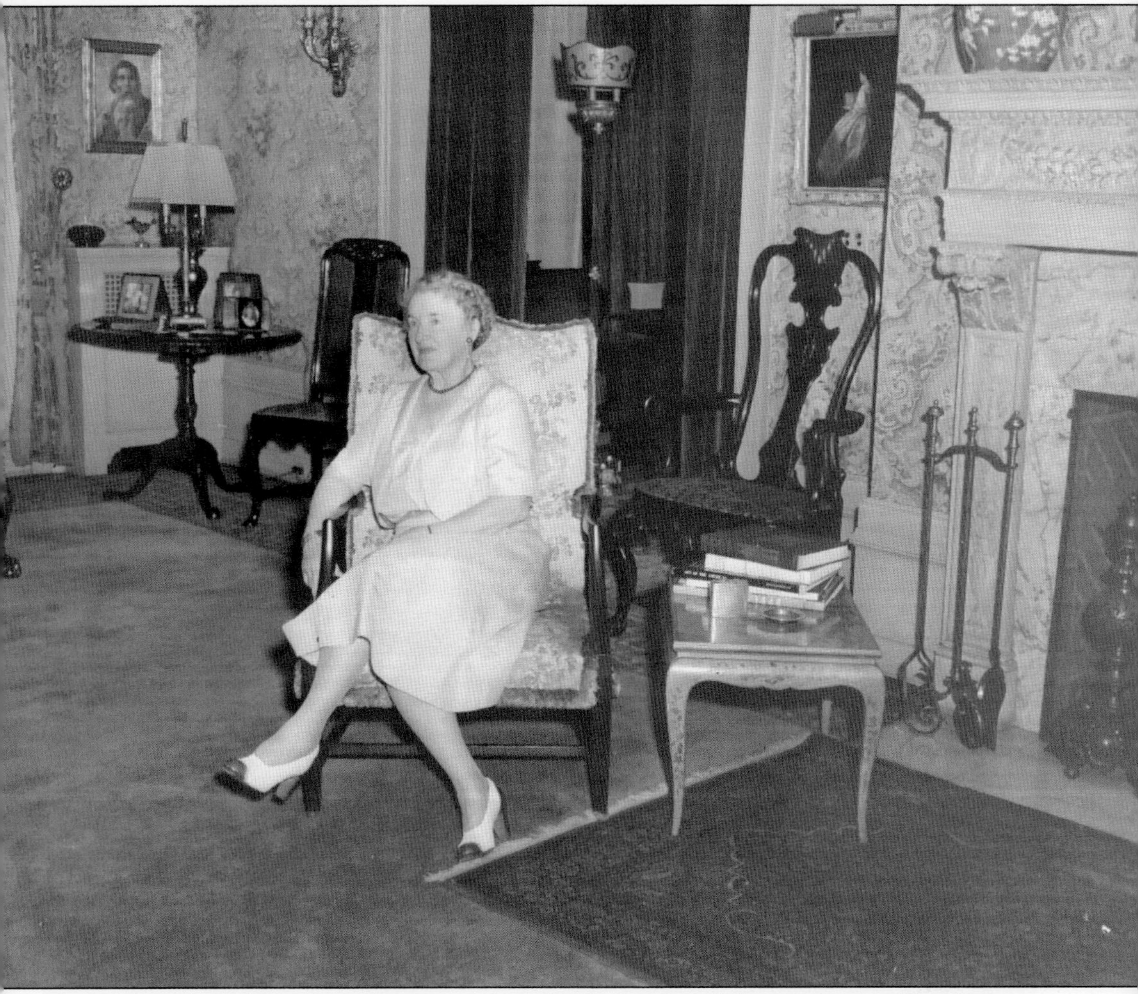

The town has been honored with many great philanthropists, including Katherine "Kate" Moore Myers amongst the leaders. In 1906, the daughter to W.C. Moore became the wife of Guy Chase Myers, son of Philip A. Myers. Always a supporter of the arts, Myers blessed the city with one of her greatest gifts: the Guy C. Myers Memorial Band Shell, donated to Brookside Park in 1949. Additionally, she touched a wide circle of friends, including the YMCA, Trinity Lutheran Church, Samaritan Hospital, and Ashland College, sponsoring the Kate Moore Myers Woman's Dormitory and the gift of her first home, located at 414 Center Street, for the use of the college president's home. Myers, along with her chauffeur, was tragically killed in an automobile accident in 1957 while returning home from a meeting in Columbus. The gifts Kate Myers showered the community with, as well as her kindness and thoughtfulness, will long be remembered.

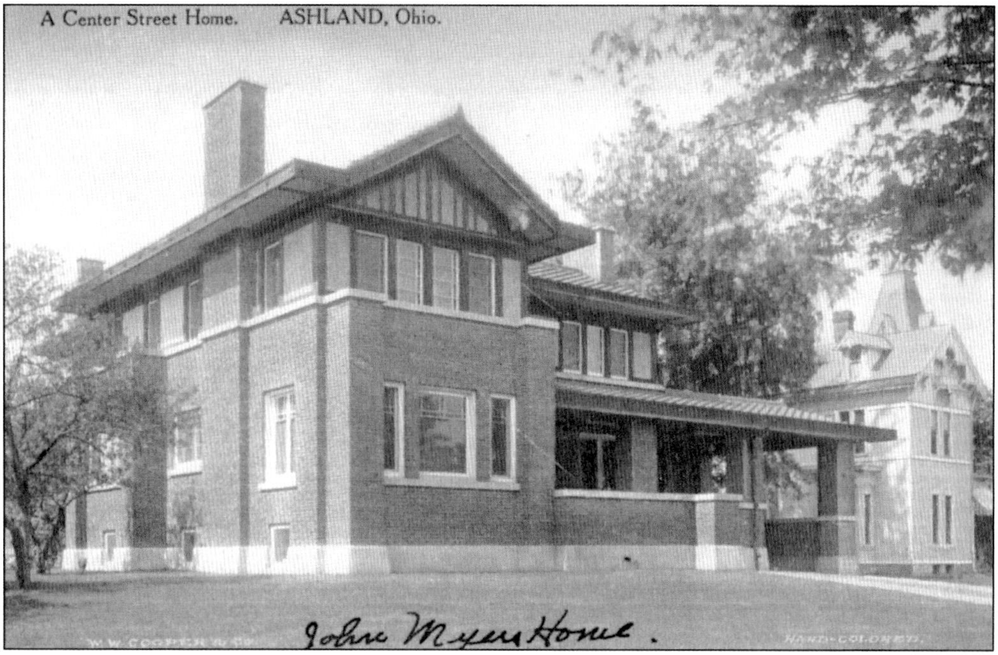

John C. Myers also comes to mind with his generosity to the community, with Ashland College boasting the John C. Myers Convocation Center. Ashland Theological Seminary cherishes the gift of his Frank Lloyd Wright–style home at 910 Center Street with its brick and stucco exterior and low-pitched roof and broad overhang, as pictured above. A graduate of Harvard and the son of Francis E. Myers, John C. Myers married Alice Mould of Cheboygan, Michigan, in 1908. Becoming a collector of fine art, he owned one of the largest private collections in the United States. Much like Kate Moore Myers, he was very generous to the musical wishes of Dr. Louise Pete. Myers is captured below anticipating an Ashland High School music performance conducted by "Doc" Pete. This was an annual event held in the Myers' home garden on Center Street.

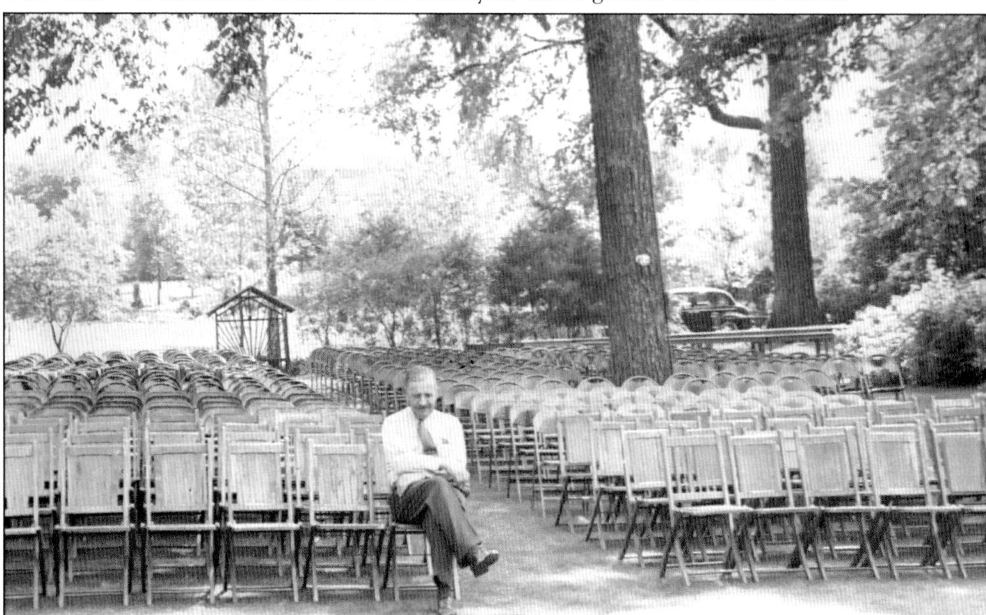

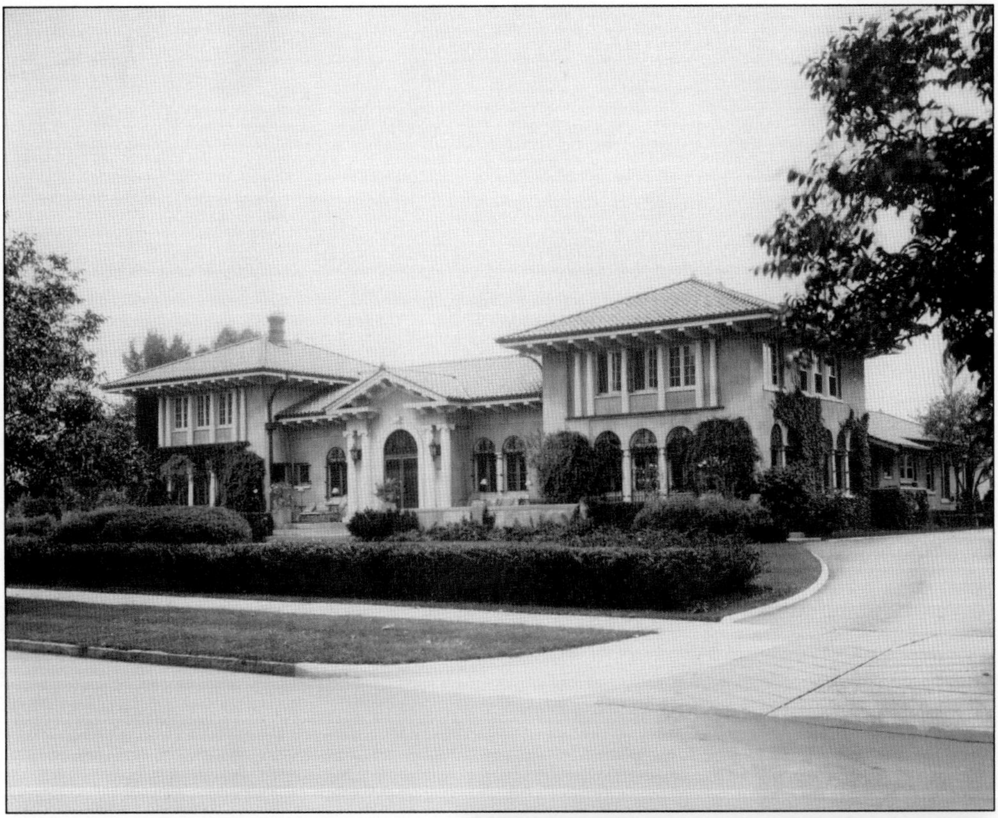

Thomas W. Miller built this home at 934 Center Street in 1914, just doors south of the home of his father-in-law, Francis E. Myers. The Faultless Rubber Company owner, who secured his first patent in 1901, married Helen Myers, forming a bond between the Faultless and Myers companies. Similar to Myers, Miller used his new residence to entertain company executives and salesmen at annual meetings. The Spanish-style architecture of this home, with a central entrance flanked by two-story wings, a drawing room boasting a vaulted ceiling with gold inlaid filament, and a large fireplace with symbols depicting the voyage of Christopher Columbus, was quite impressive to guests that entered under the Miller coat of arms above the arched front doorway. Miller is shown at right in an undated photograph.

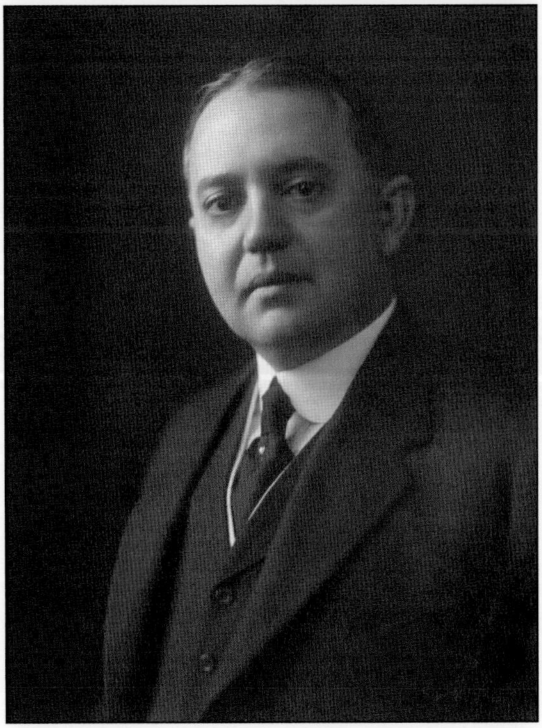

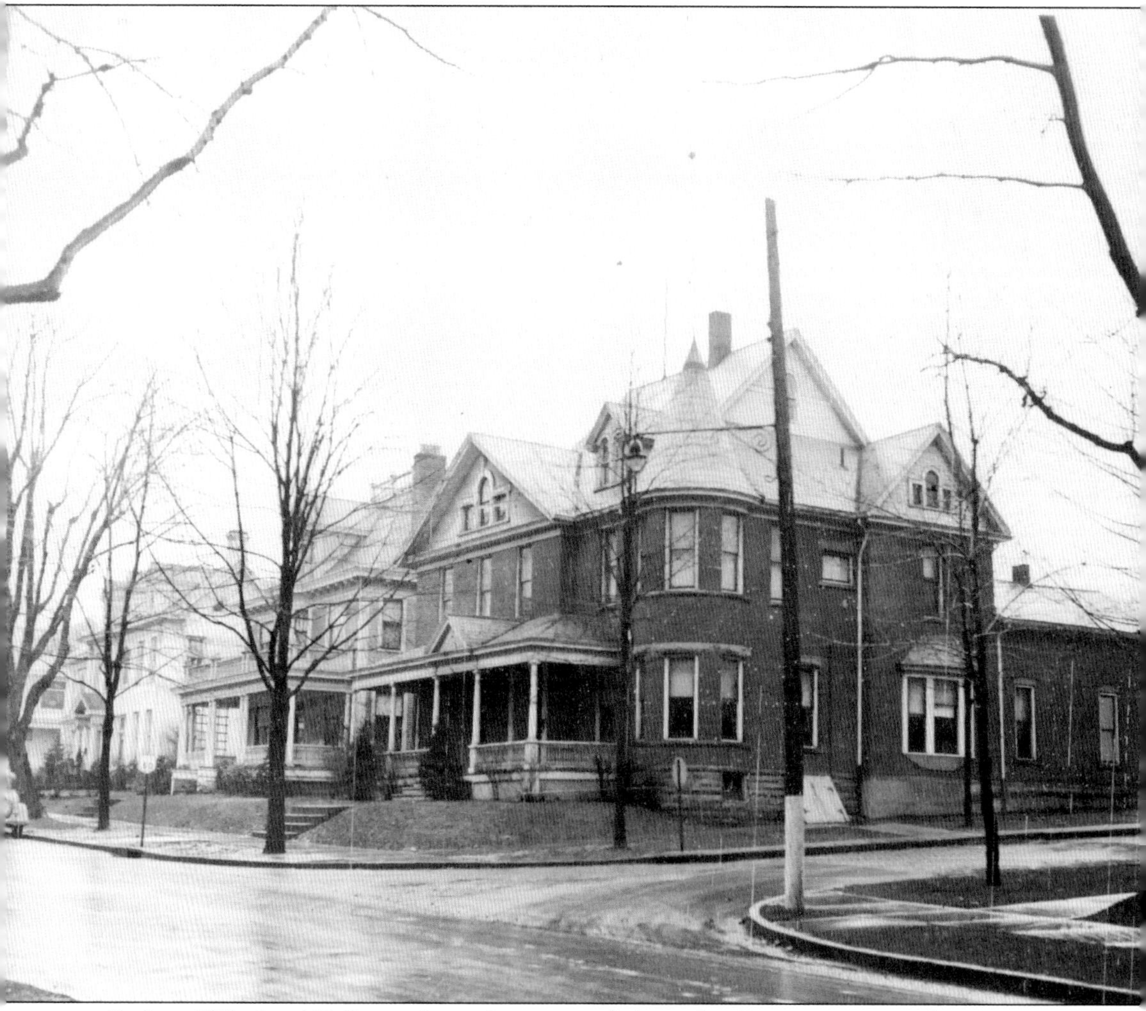

Built in 1851, this 402 Center Street home once belonged to Dr. George W. Hill. Hill moved to Ashland in 1845 and accomplished a list of many occupations in his short 61 years of life. Topping that list would be working as a lawyer, physician, politician, principal, orator, and a newspaper publisher, though he is most remembered for writing *History of Ashland County* in 1880, as well as writing histories for Marion, Wyandot, and Allen Counties. One of his greatest honors came when he was chosen to deliver the address at Ashland's Centennial celebration in 1876. Married to Rebecca Draper in 1850, the couple had three children. Daughter Rena became an artist and enjoyed brief success before dying in a fire in New York City. In 1910, the Elks Lodge became owner of the Hill home, razing it for a new club at the same location in 1966.

Five

The Rails to Success

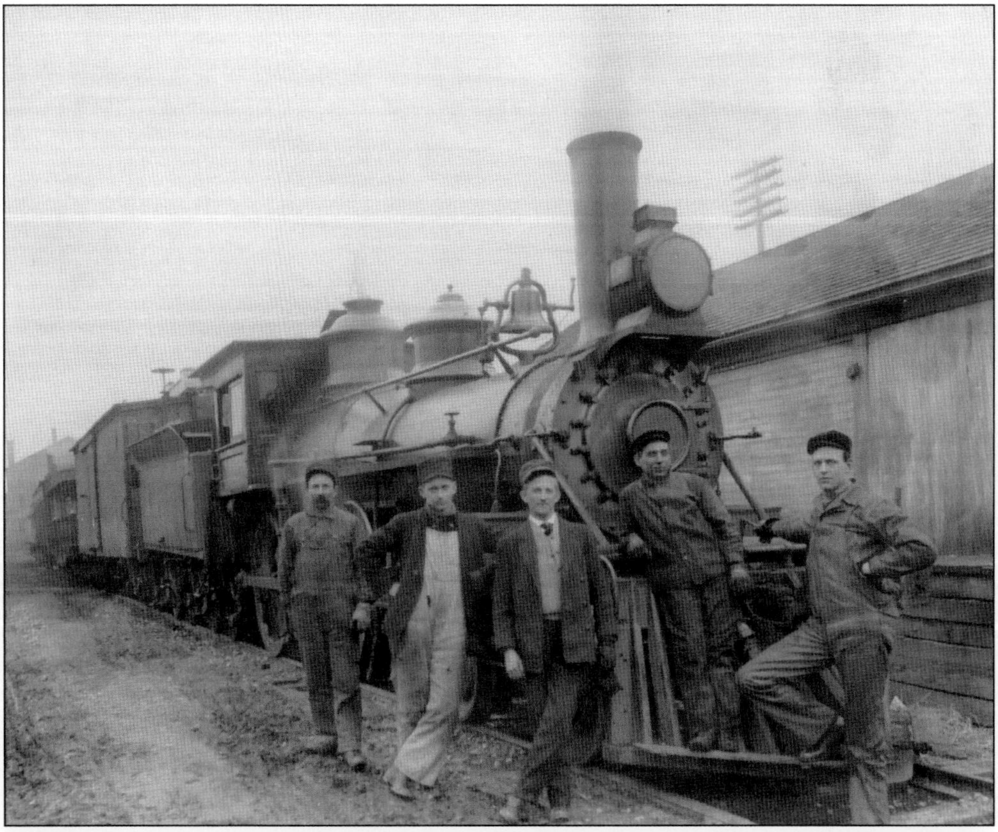

Pictured above during a city stop in the early 1900s is locomotive No. 6 of the Ashland and Western Railway with conductor Jay B. Jackson in the center. The Faultless Rubber Company is seen in the background on the left. The Ashland and Western Railway provided freight and passenger trains between Ashland and Custaloga (a station at the junction of the Lorain, Ashland, and Southern Railroad) and the Pennsylvania Railroad in Wayne County. (William S. Snyder collection.)

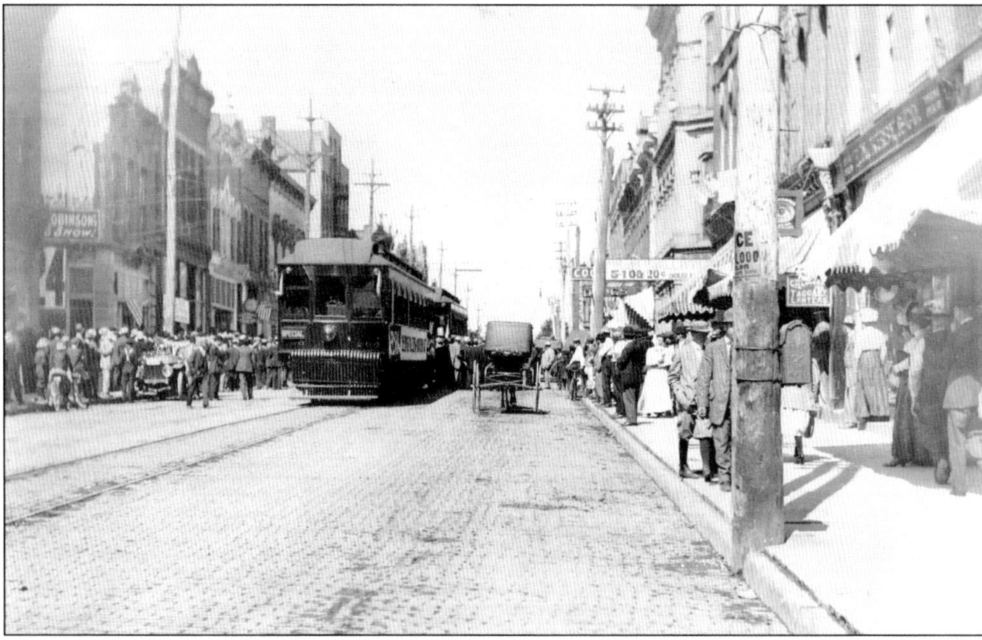

Travel by bicycle, car, trolley, or buggy became the question of the day on January 14, 1909, when the electric interurban line arrived in town. The Green Line ran from Cleveland through Ashland and ended in Mansfield and Seville. It was at these points that riders would catch other lines to their final destinations. The electric line provided direct freight and passenger service to Berea, Medina, Elyria, Oberlin, Wellington, Shelby, and Bucyrus. The town had three interurban depots, and one is pictured below, situated near Cleveland Avenue. Interurban travel was at its peak in 1921 when the paving of roads and the refinement of the automobile drew business from them. Ashland service ended on January 31, 1931, when the last car of the Cleveland, Southwestern, and Columbus Railway passed through town. (Below, William S. Snyder collection.)

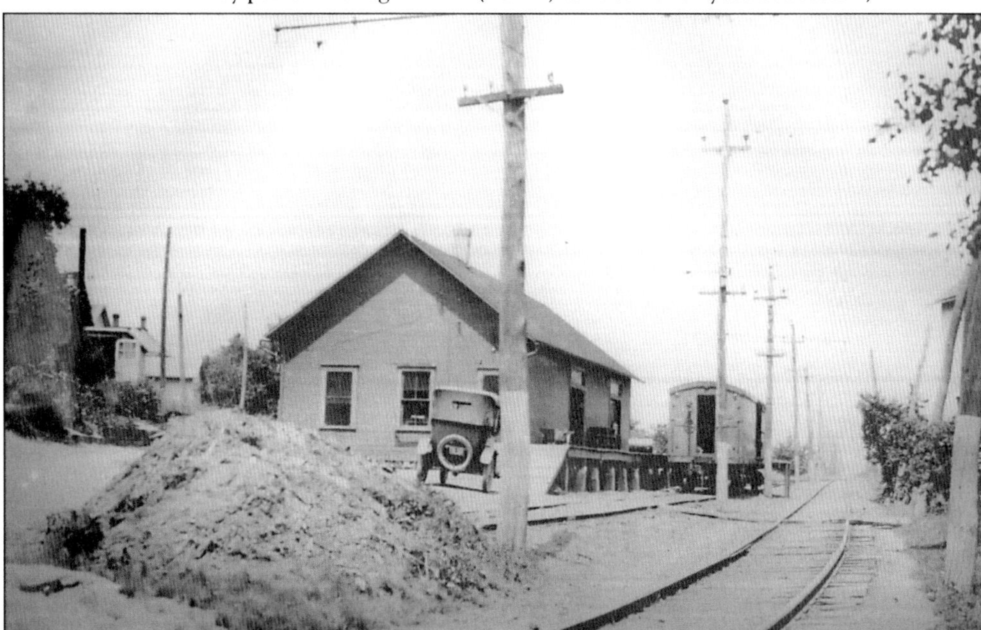

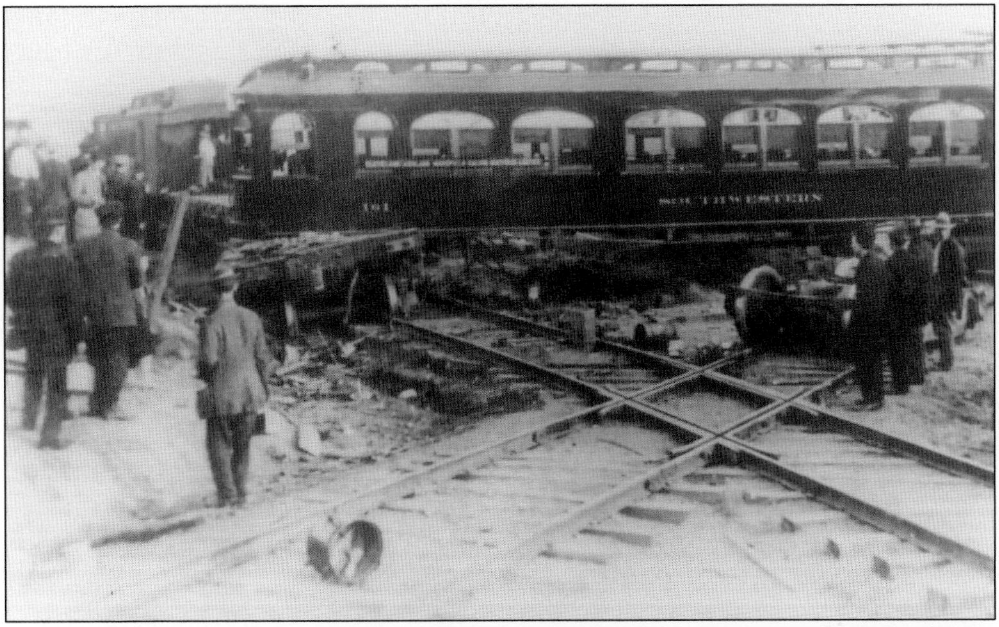

Just outside of town, on May 15, 1914, a Cleveland Southwestern interurban coach heading to Cleveland, and a Lorain, Ashland, and Southwestern train carrying railroad laborers heading to Ashland collided. The work train engineer crossed over the diamond of the interurban line without checking the crossing while passing, not noticing the interurban coach. The coach struck the last car of the work train, causing a derailment. (William S. Snyder collection.)

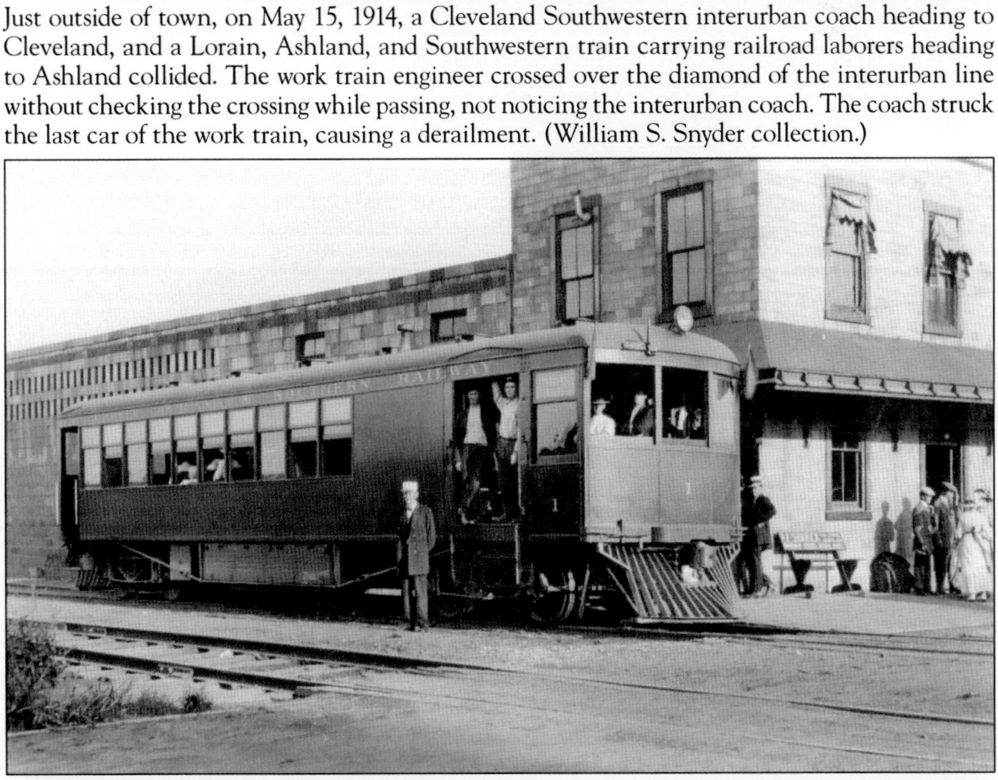

In 1915, conductor Theodore George stands in charge of battery car No. 1 at the Lorain, Ashland, and Southern Railroad station at the Union Street depot. Seeking to provide a similar service as the interurban, this railway car, which ran on batteries located in the center section underneath the car, was used strictly for passengers traveling between Ashland and the Custaloga station in Wayne County. (William S. Snyder collection.)

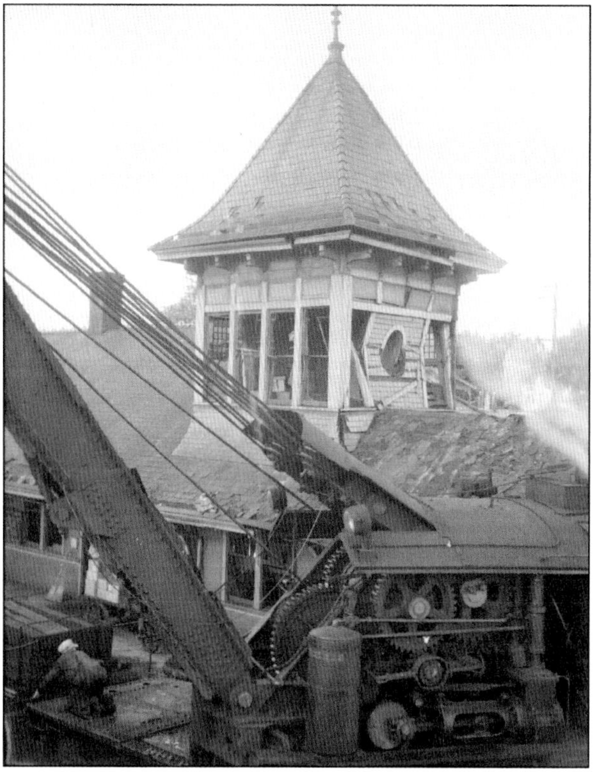

On June 23, 1943, an explosion of paint cans in a boxcar at the Erie Railway depot shook the city. Shattering windows in a five-block area, it damaged a portion of the depot cupola, shown at left, as well as caused $15,000 worth of damage to railway property and destroyed railway cars, as pictured below. When the explosion occurred, two railroad workers were loading fireworks from the Spencer Fireworks Company of Polk. As a result of the explosion, the fireworks erupted and exploded through the air, killing the two workers and seriously injuring three others. People were thrown from their beds, and workers in war-related industries rushed home to their families, while thousands of onlookers packed the area, forcing crowd control by the police and sheriff.

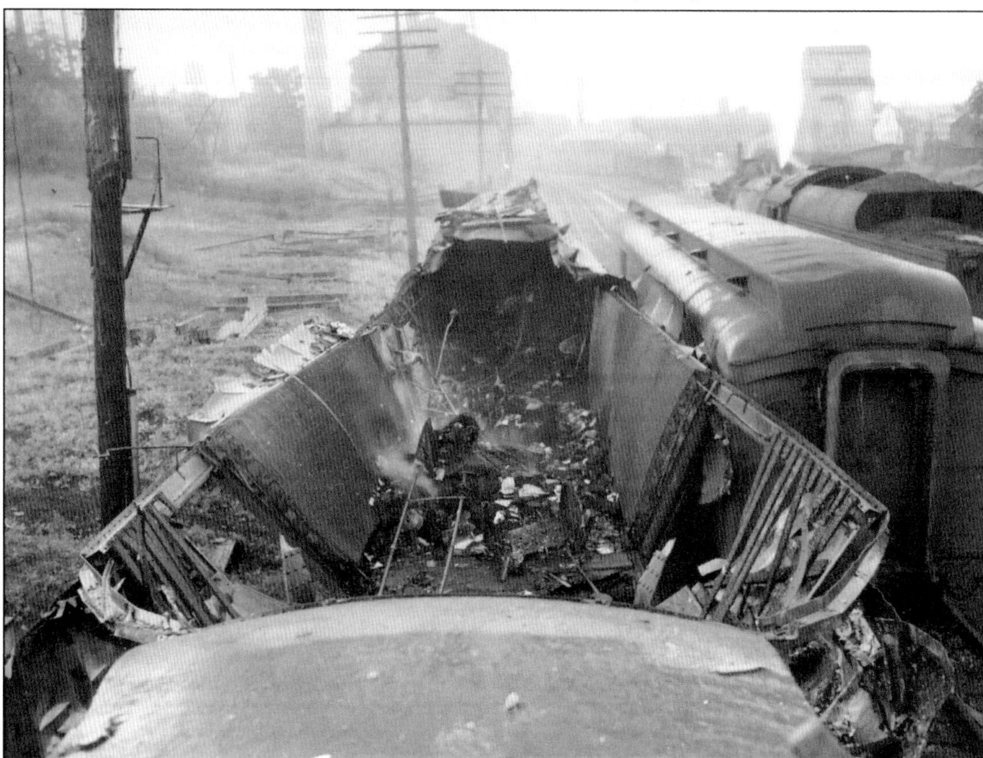

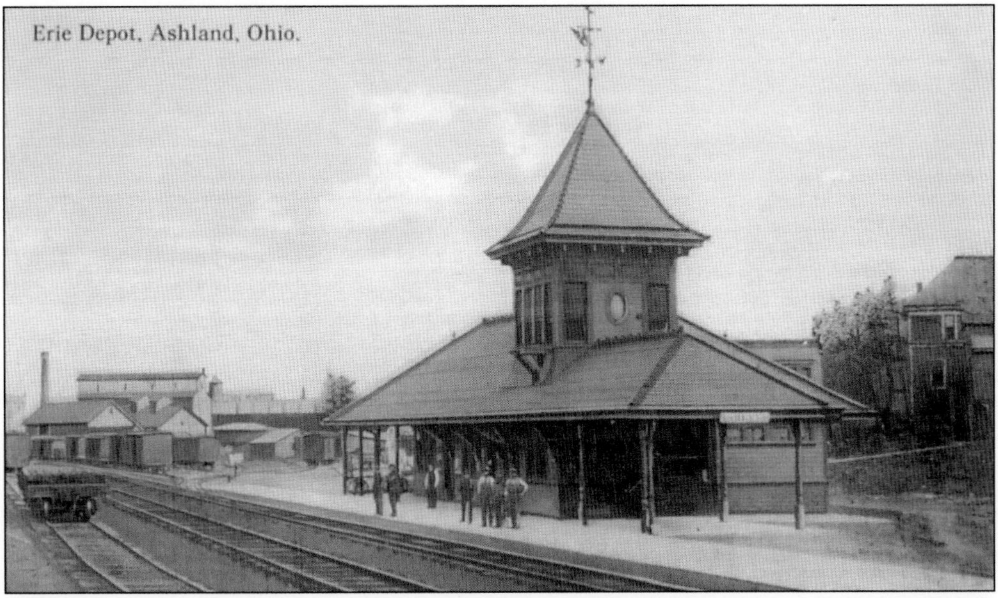

Being one of the main lines on the Erie Railway between New York and Chicago, the community felt that the first train depot, located near the Cottage Street crossing, was an eyesore for the popular and growing town. Virtually one-and-a-half years after a fire destroyed the original depot on October 17, 1891, a new depot, pictured above, was dedicated on February 9, 1893, at nearly the same location, just east of the Cottage Street crossing. Switch operators of the early 1900 depot, shown below, would either push or pull the large levers to divert trains from one track to another. Upon using the levers, a portion of the track would switch locations, forcing the train to a different section of the track. (Above, William S. Snyder collection.)

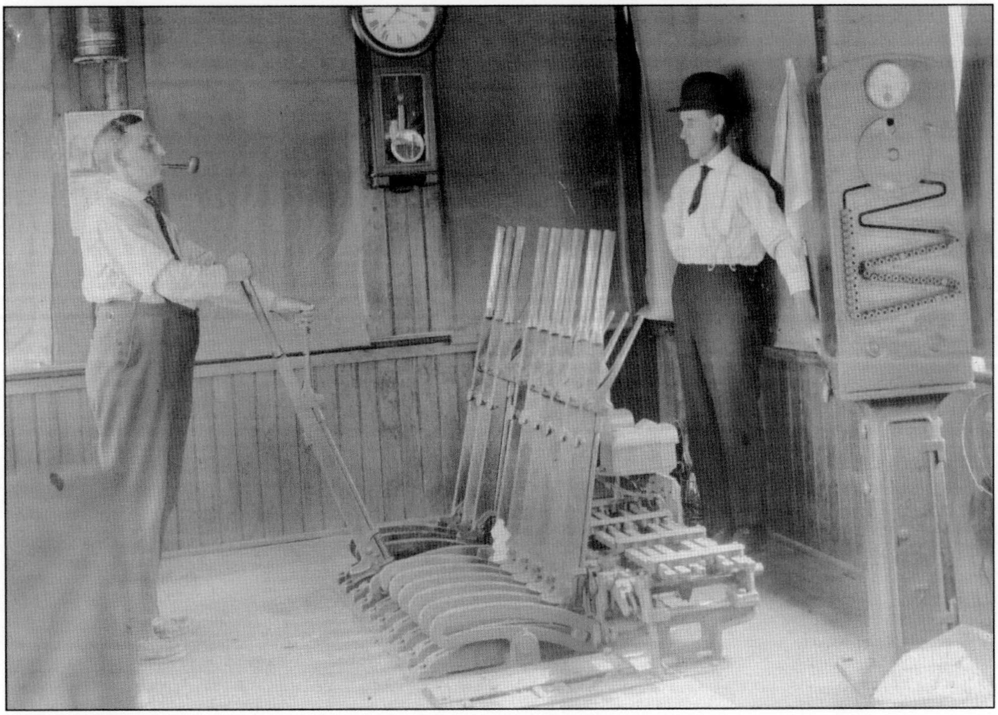

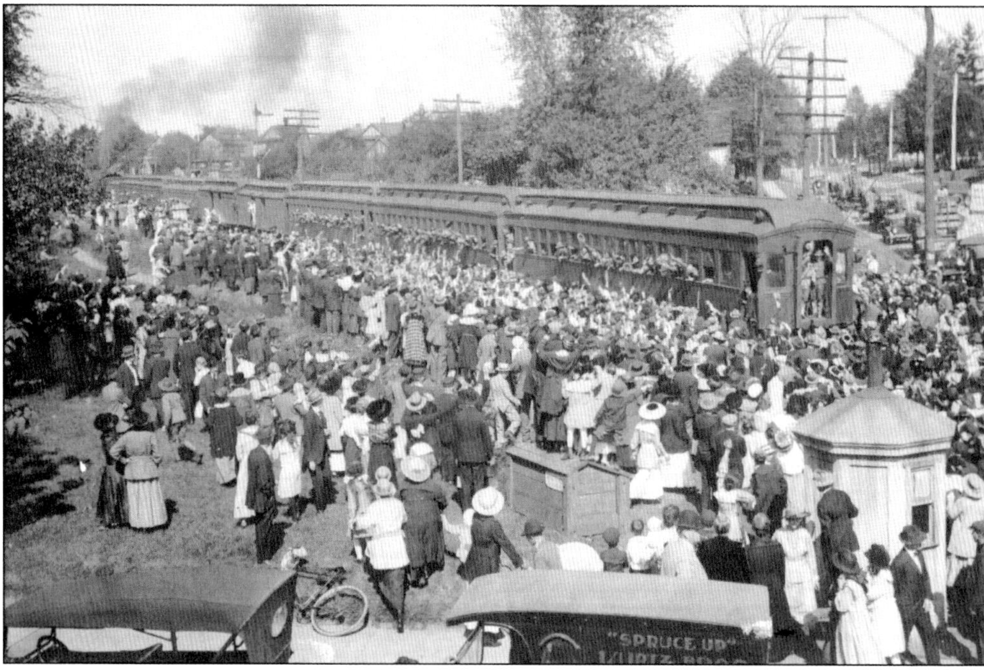

Leaving town by way of rail to serve in the Spanish-American War, 24 men traveled to Polk to join Company C of the 8th Regiment, Ohio Volunteer Infantry on April 24, 1898. With nearly 1,000 people at the Erie depot, pictured above, their send off was a memorable event. The men first traveled to Polk, then to Akron, followed by Camp Bushnell in Columbus and later to Cuba. In the image below, World War I soldiers, 175 men strong, receive a warm send off by family members and friends at the Cottage Street railroad crossing near the Erie depot. On September 29, 1917, the men departed for training at Camp Sheridan in Montgomery, Alabama. This group of Company E soldiers of the Ohio National Guard served in the 146 Infantry of the 37th Division in France.

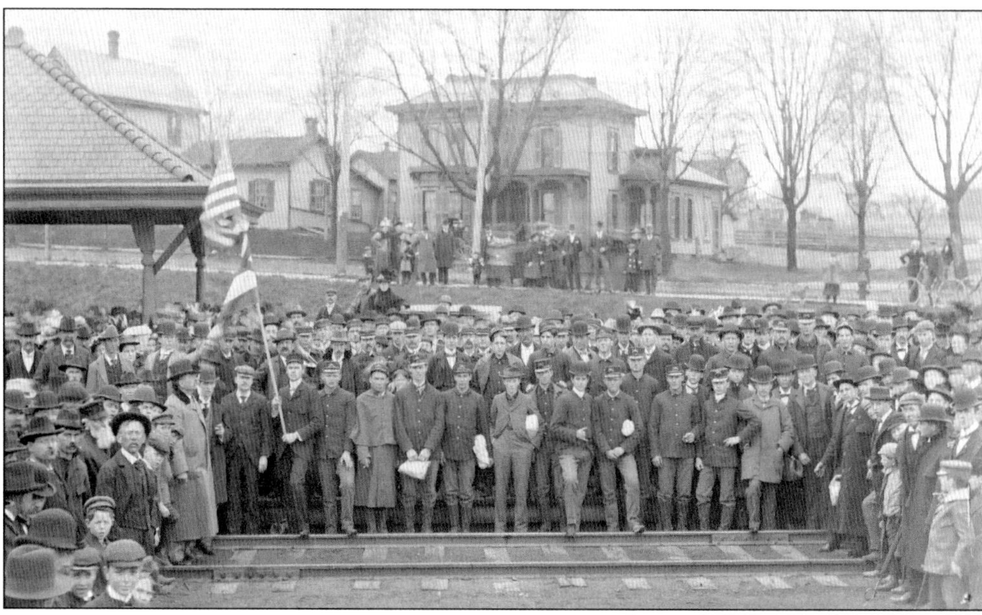

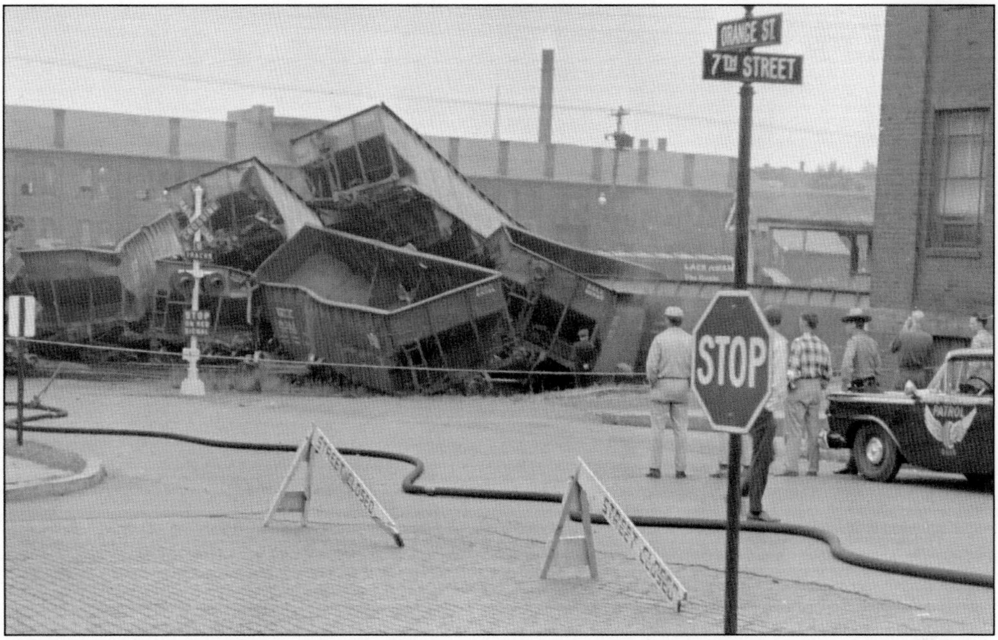

The September 25, 1943, train derailment and gasoline explosion at the Erie Railway depot brought alarm to the city. Most feared that the explosion they had just heard or witnessed was an enemy attack as a consequence of World War II. As it was, the wheels of a railway car tore loose, causing the derailment of 23 tanks and cars with 230,000 gallons of gasoline going up in flames. Creating chaos throughout the town, fire and explosions caused a total of $250,000 in damages. Amongst the destruction, the depot and the Eagle Rubber Company were destroyed and thousands of windows were broken at the Hess and Clark, A.L. Garber, and F.E. Myers plants. Flaming oil shot through the sewer system, which generated gas that popped manhole covers into the air. Miraculously, there were no serious injuries.

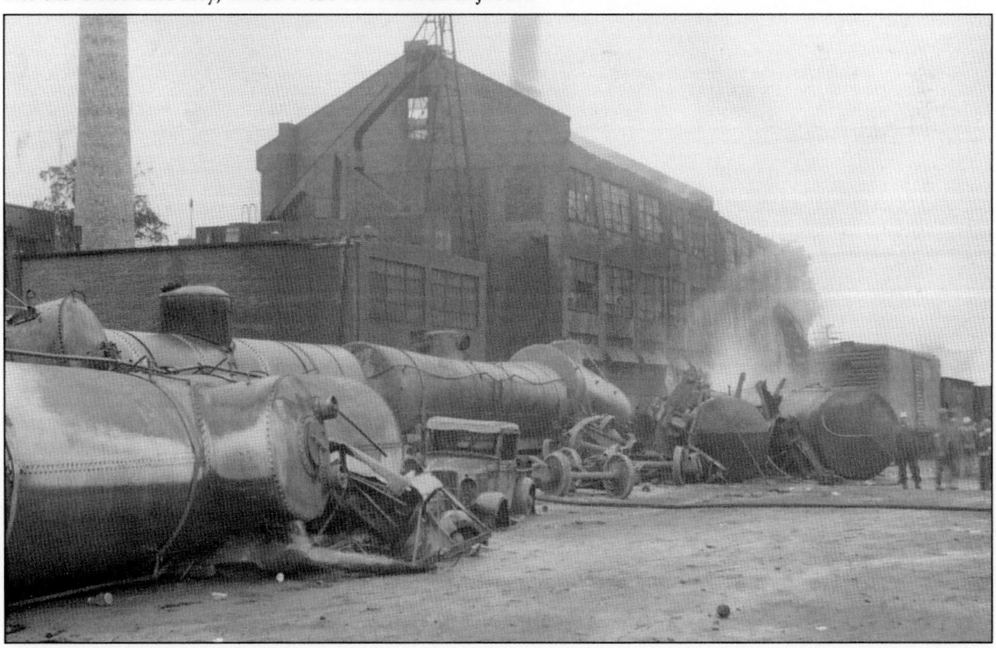

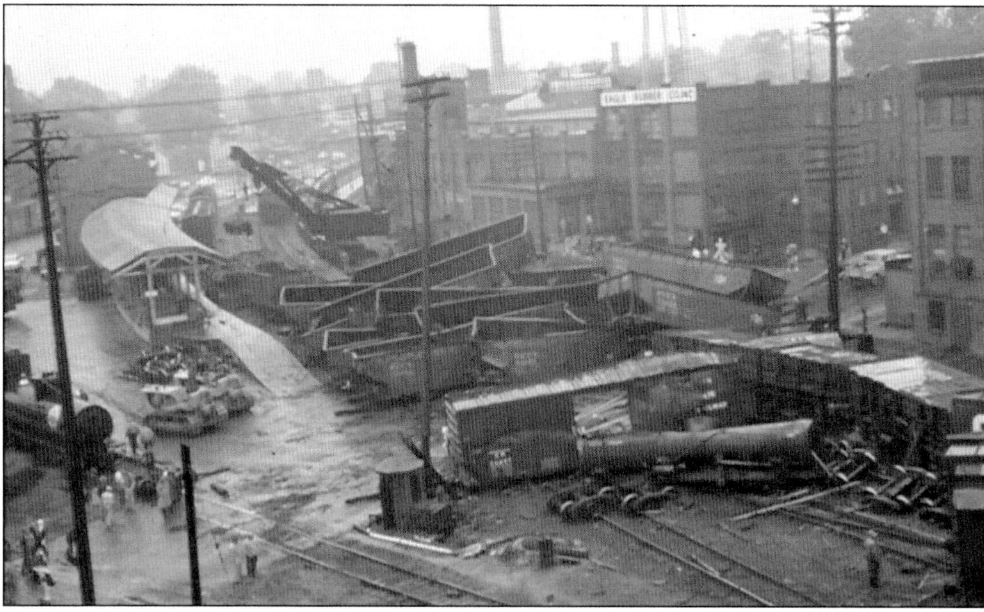

Picking through the derailment of 36 freight cars is a delicate task, especially when one car is full of butane and situated near the bottom of the pile. On July 5, 1961, a train running from Marion to Kent jumped the track, narrowly missing the Hess and Clark factory at the Orange Street crossing. Wrecker cranes were brought in from Marion and Kent for aid in lifting the derailed cars from the scene, cautiously working their way to a butane car that escaped rupture in the wreckage, as firemen kept continuous watch and water on the car. It was not until a day and a half later that the butane car was freed with nearly 10,490 gallons of gas unloaded into a tank truck from Galion at the Orange Street crossing. (William S. Snyder collection.)

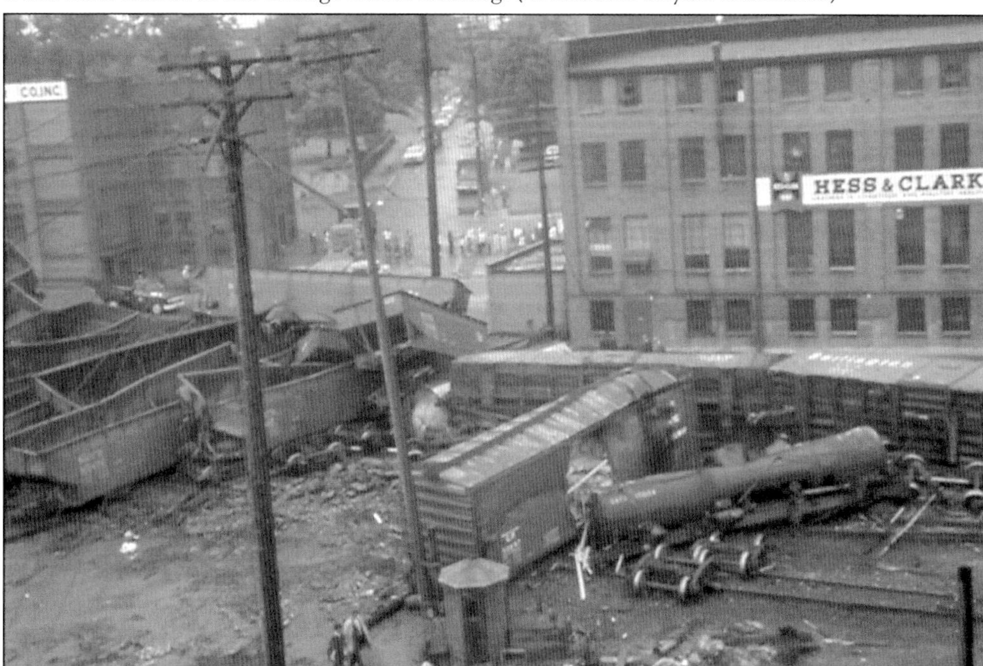

Six

Teaching and Preaching

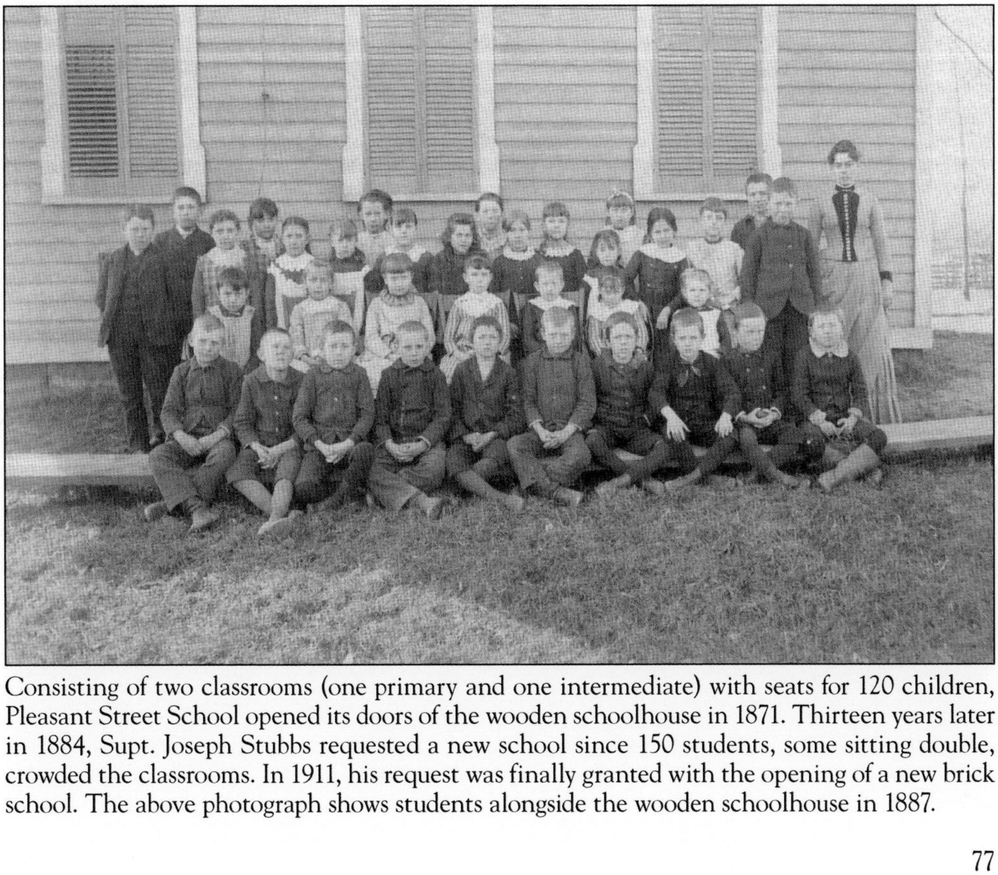

Consisting of two classrooms (one primary and one intermediate) with seats for 120 children, Pleasant Street School opened its doors of the wooden schoolhouse in 1871. Thirteen years later in 1884, Supt. Joseph Stubbs requested a new school since 150 students, some sitting double, crowded the classrooms. In 1911, his request was finally granted with the opening of a new brick school. The above photograph shows students alongside the wooden schoolhouse in 1887.

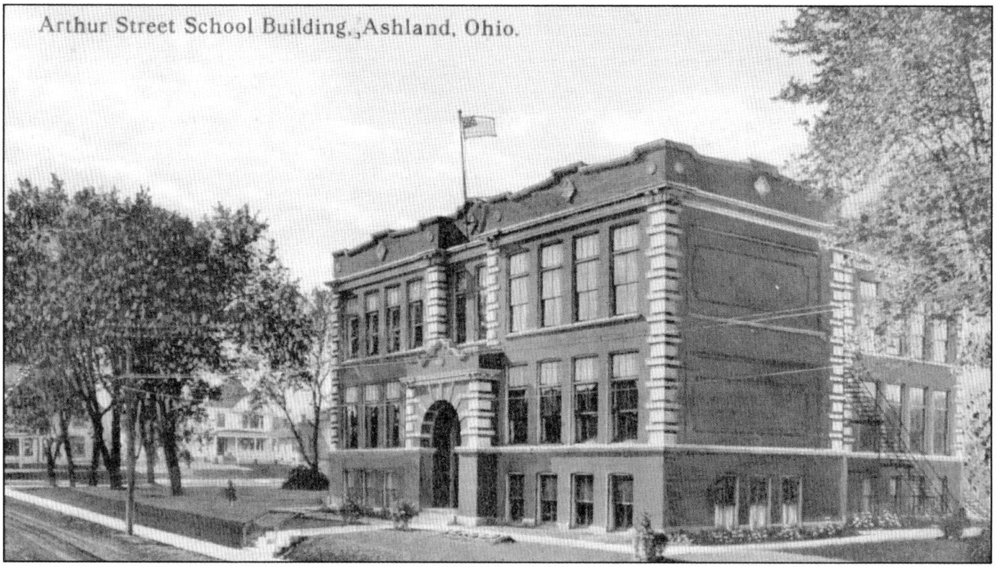

Steady growth of the town in the early 1900s led to the construction of Arthur Street School, pictured above, which opened during September 1908. Situated on the corner of Arthur and Walnut Streets, the brick schoolhouse replaced an earlier wooden structure known at this location as the Walnut Street School. During a time when schools were overcrowded, a bond levy was passed for two more schools: Lincoln and Pleasant Street. In 1911, three years before the start of World War I, Lincoln School opened its doors. Situated on West Eleventh Street, construction cost was $54,000. In 1912, with an elaborate program and the unveiling of a portrait of President Lincoln, students celebrated the birthday of the school's namesake. Pictured below is a fifth grade class of students from the Lincoln School in 1921.

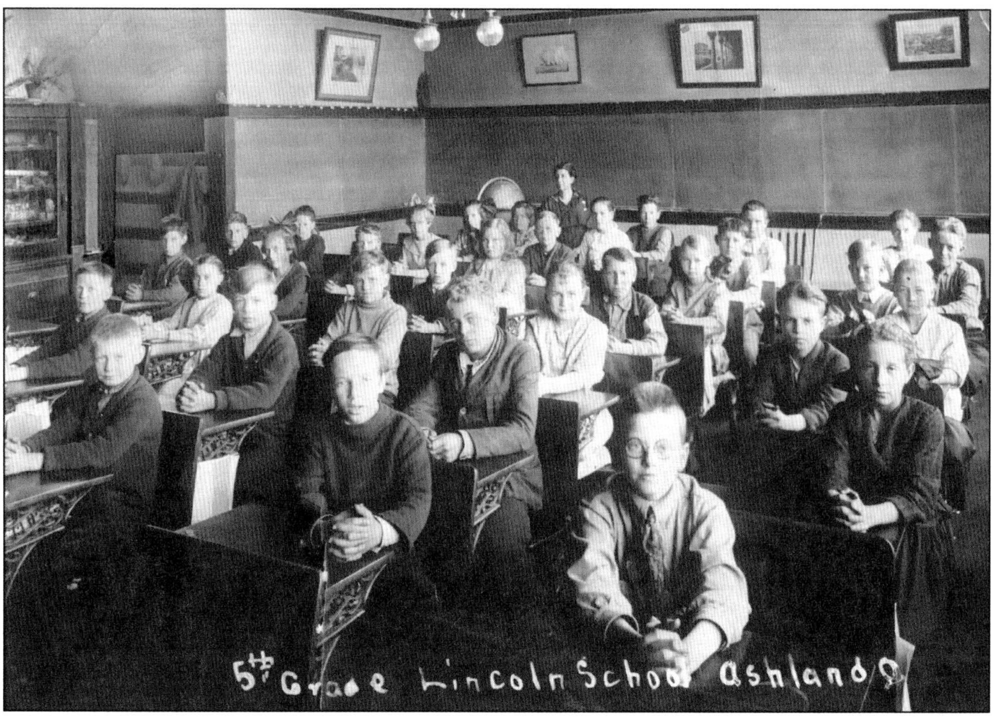

Three times the Presbyterians fulfilled their worship needs by building and rebuilding their house of worship on the corner of Church and Third Streets. Built in 1842, the Reverend Dr. John D. Robinson ministered to the church from 1844 to 1884. Robinson is seen here at the church gate with his horse and buggy in the background. Parishioners are barely visible around the steeple. The church was torn down in 1879, and a new place of devotion was built and dedicated in 1883. In 1933, this second church, pictured below, was damaged by fire while parishioners, on their way to attend Sunday services, witnessed the devastation. In 1935, the cornerstone was placed for the third Presbyterian church, which still stands today.

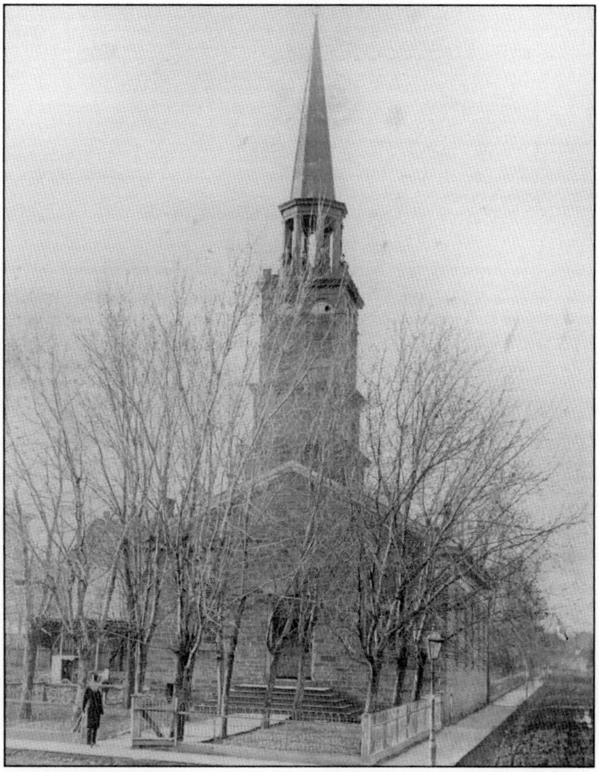

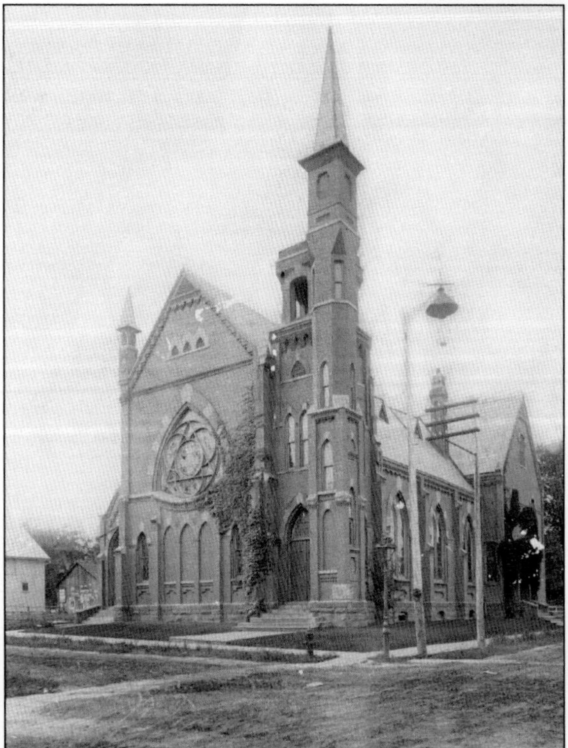

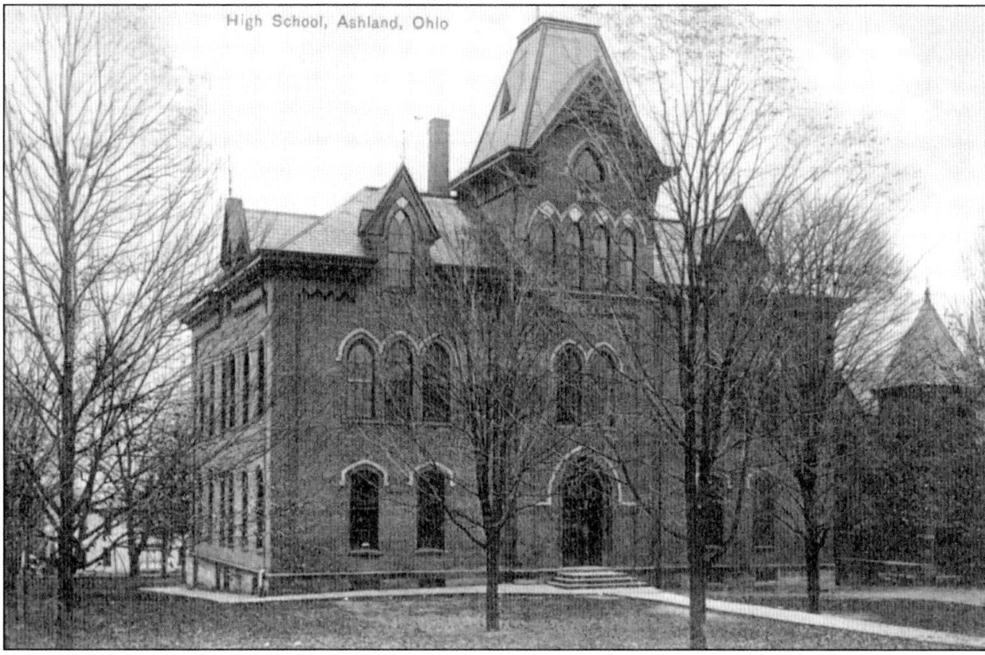

Boasting a price tag of $32,000 in 1874, the first high school, pictured above, was built facing Cottage Street near the corner of Fourth Street. In 1915, this school was replaced by another school, shown below, that boasted a $100,000 price tag. Built to house 360 students, this school was situated on the large front lawn of the first school. Through the years, three wings were added to accommodate students in 7th through 12th grade. In 1926, the first school was razed, making room for a gymnasium and auditorium. By 1961, the crowded school with the packed halls and cramped front lawn on Cottage Street saw the construction of another high school, this time on Katherine Avenue. This school, which carried a $2.39-million price tag, housed 10th through 12th grade, while the 7th through 9th grades remained in the former school.

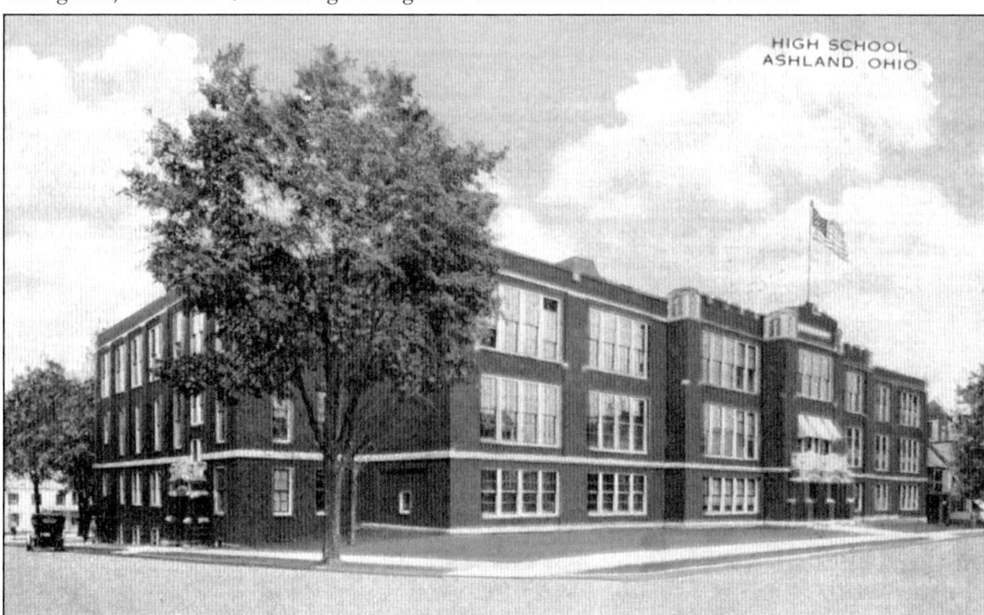

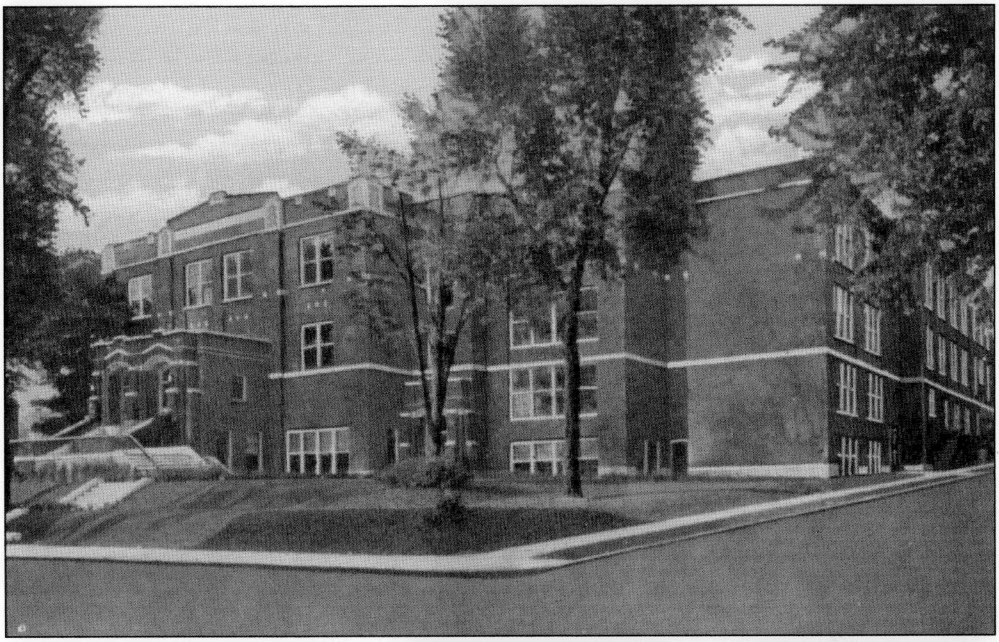

By the time the 1926 auditorium addition, pictured above, was made to the high school, John A. McDowell, a former US congressman, had been school superintendent for 19 years, the longest tenure in school history. Since McDowell was well respected in the academia community, naming the auditorium in his honor was quite appropriate. Through the years, the much-esteemed McDowell, right, served as a Kent State University trustee, additionally serving on the board that established the teachers' retirement system. He lived long enough to collect his first retirement check. With a seating capacity of 1,500 people, McDowell Auditorium has seen graduation ceremonies, musical productions, assemblies, concerts, orchestra performances, school proms, and dances. The auditorium also served a dual purpose of being a gymnasium, with daily physical education classes occasionally being held amongst the props of an upcoming school theater production or prom.

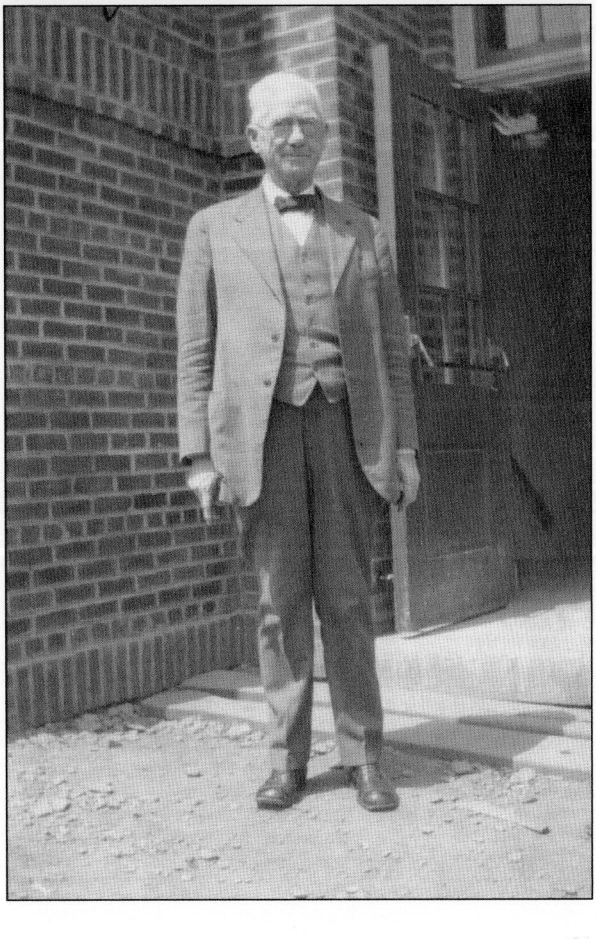

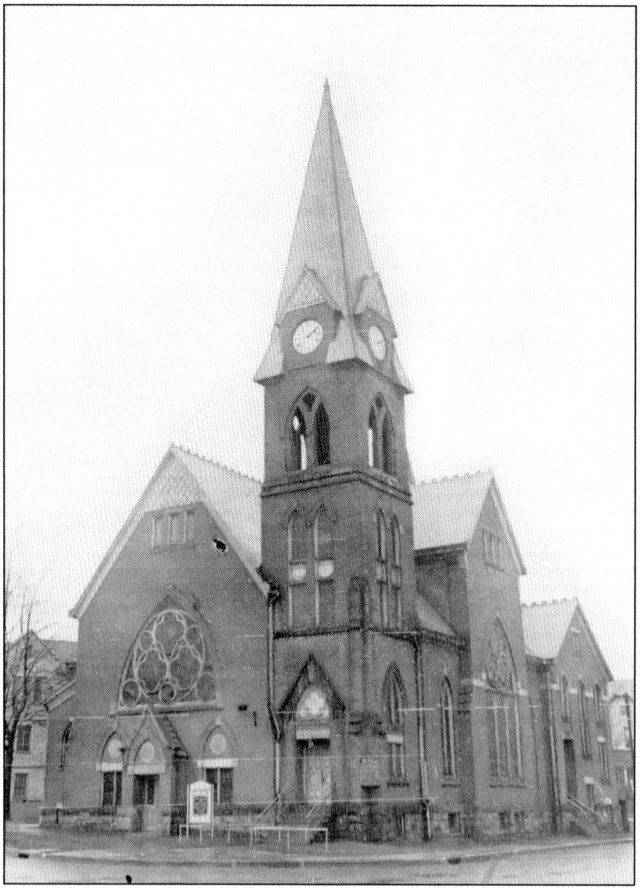

Once called the Methodist Episcopal, the Methodist Church first met in the home of John Smith on Cottage Street. In 1828, the church was the first to build a house of worship within the town. In 1846, the Methodists sold their church to the county commissioners, who established it as the first courthouse. Relocating to Church and Fourth Streets, they built their second church, which was later destroyed by fire. The church shown here, located at the corner of Sandusky and Cottage Streets, replaced the destroyed church in 1888. The clock tower in the steeple was a gift from Mary Freer, wife of merchant and banker Jonas Freer. In 1957, the need for a larger fourth church took place, razing the third church and rebuilding it under the name of the First United Methodist Church. The card below invites boys to Sunday school in 1917.

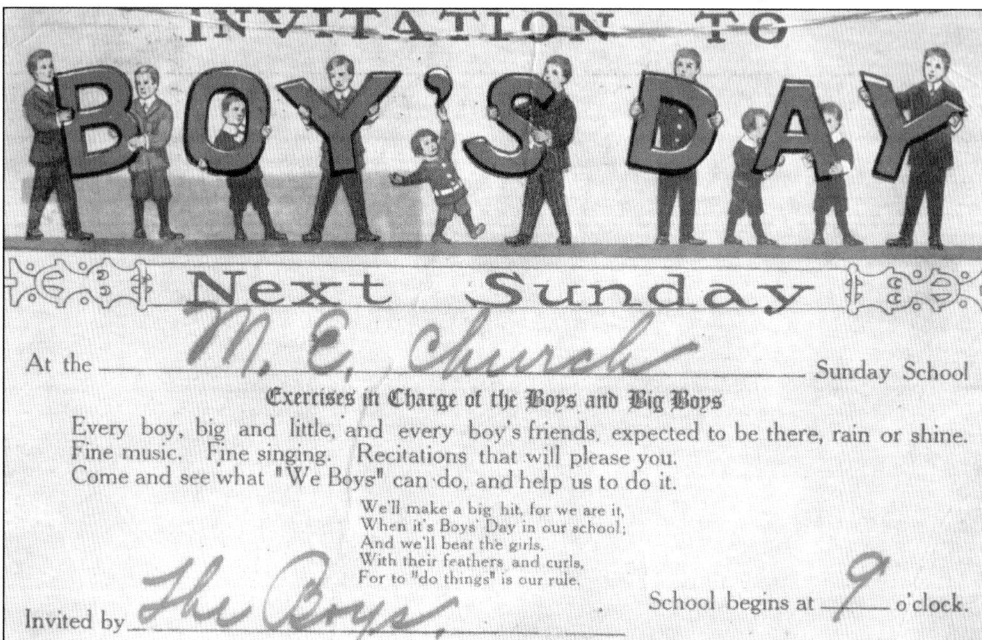

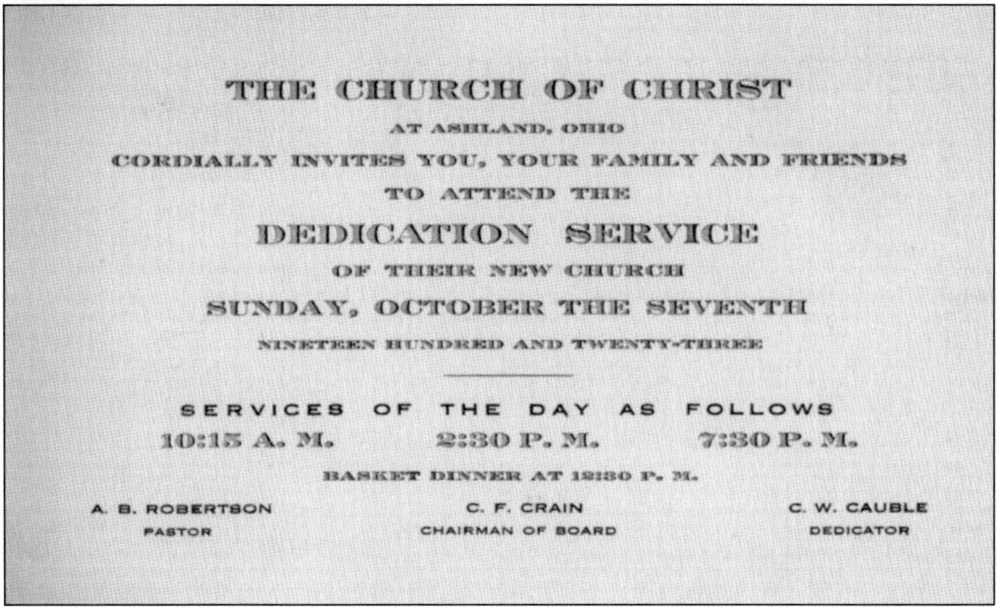

THE CHURCH OF CHRIST

AT ASHLAND, OHIO

CORDIALLY INVITES YOU, YOUR FAMILY AND FRIENDS

TO ATTEND THE

DEDICATION SERVICE

OF THEIR NEW CHURCH

SUNDAY, OCTOBER THE SEVENTH

NINETEEN HUNDRED AND TWENTY-THREE

SERVICES OF THE DAY AS FOLLOWS

10:15 A. M. 2:30 P. M. 7:30 P. M.

BASKET DINNER AT 12:30 P. M.

A. B. ROBERTSON
PASTOR

C. F. CRAIN
CHAIRMAN OF BOARD

C. W. CAUBLE
DEDICATOR

"The Church of Christ cordially invites you, your family, and friends to attend the dedication service of their new church, Sunday, October 7, 1923," as quoted from the dedication invitation shown above for the new home of the Church of Christ, located at the corner of Cottage and Fourth Streets, under the leadership of A.B. Robertson, pastor. First meeting in the homes of its members in 1824, the growing congregation continued to flourish, changing names from the Christian Church to the First Christian Church (Disciples of Christ). The congregation outgrew and relocated its house of worship several times over the years before settling on Cottage Street, only to grow again and change locations to King Road near Katherine Avenue in 2010. Pictured below is the front cover of the above dedication notice, which shows the Church of Christ on the Cottage Street corner in 1923.

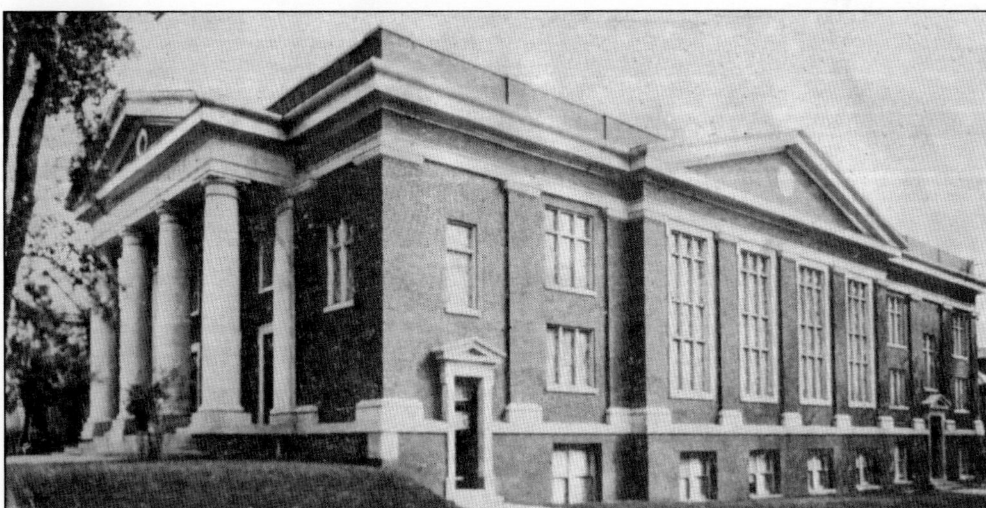

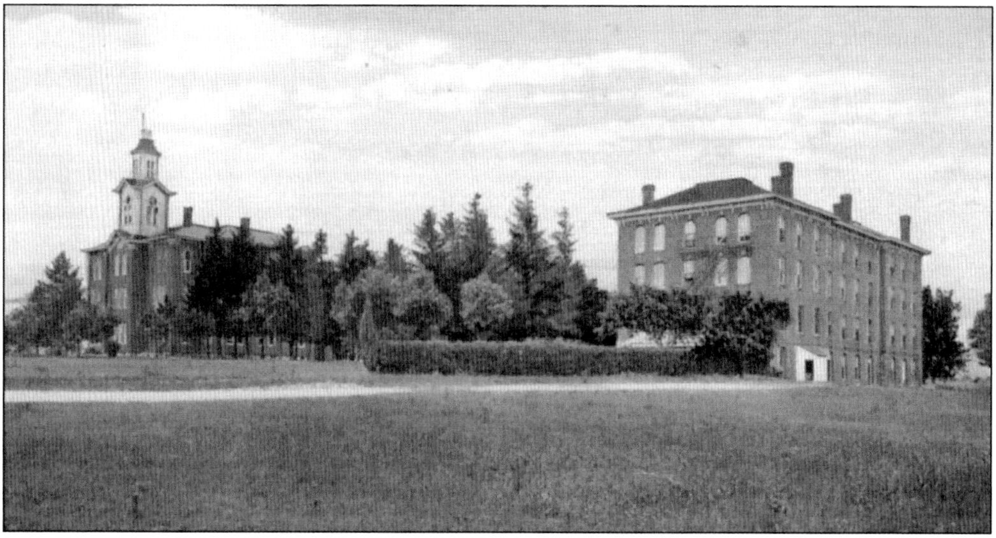

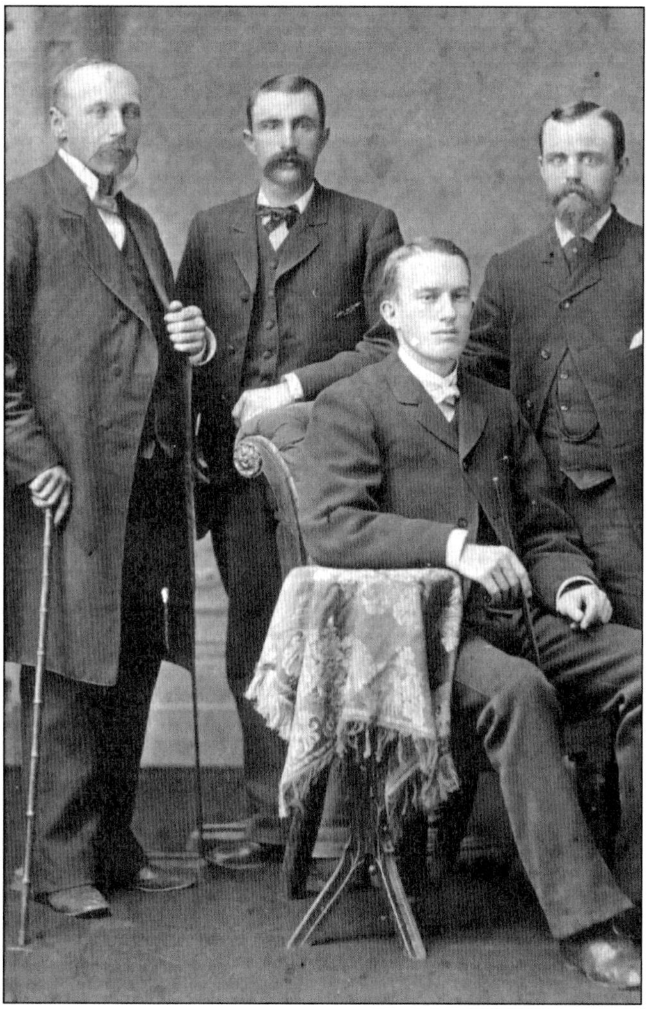

With community members contributing over $19,000 and additional funds donated by wealthy Church of the Brethren members, the Brethren Church chose Ashland as the home for their college in 1877. Construction began for the first building, Founders Hall, pictured above left, on the Ashland College campus in 1879. Experiencing growing pains during its first few years, the school graduated only four students in 1881, as seen at left. By 1888, fearing bankruptcy with a $44,000 debt, the college was rescued by several church members. Founders Hall proudly served its students for nearly 70 years before an October 1952 fire destroyed the building. A major fund drive pursued, and in 1954, a new Founders Hall was dedicated. The first boarding hall on campus, Allen Hall, above right, was named after Dr. J. Allen Miller, who served as college president from 1899 to 1906. (Left, Ashland University archives collection.)

The Reverend J.A. Schulze delivered sermons in German at the Die Evangelische Lutheriache Fredens Gemeinde Church on the corner of Main and Broad Streets in 1868, pictured at right. With the start of World War I, sermons were no longer spoken in German, and appropriately, the name was changed to Peace Lutheran. Growth forced relocation to the corner of Center and Maple Streets in 1944, then again to 1360 Smith Road in 1983.

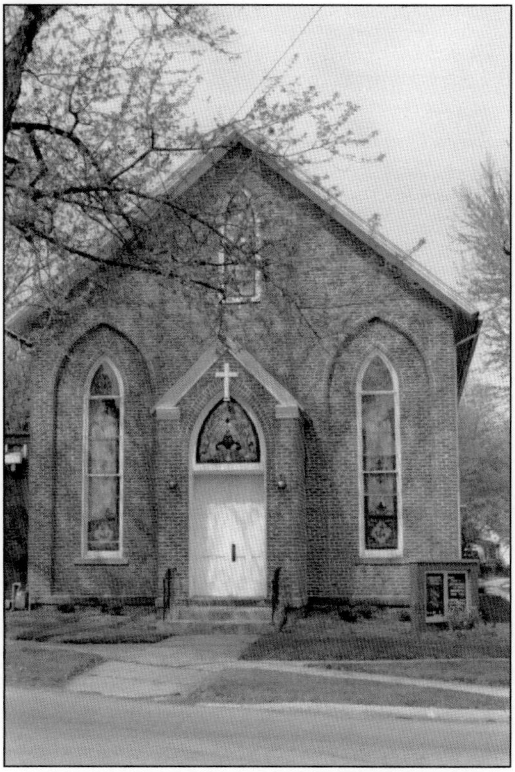

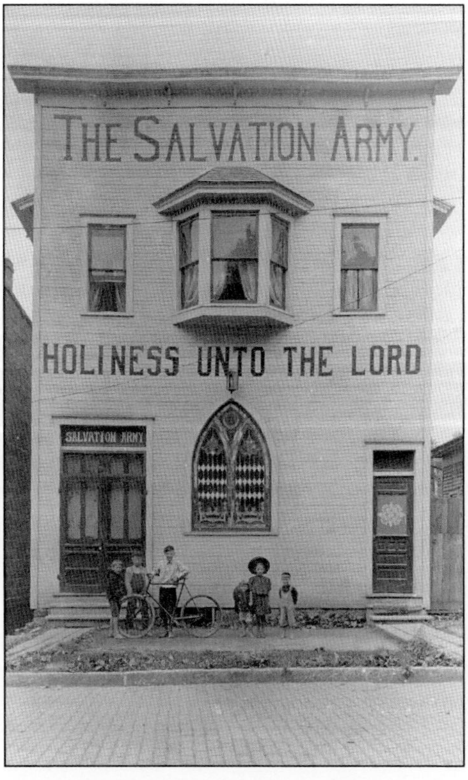

In 1885, the Salvation Army Corps began work in the town under the leadership of Captain Garner. Without a place to call home, church meetings were held at various locations. The corps had a vision for its own congregational hall, and under the direction of Capt. Fredrich Holzgrefe, a place of worship was built. Pictured here at 219 East Main Street, the church was dedicated on September 4, 1904.

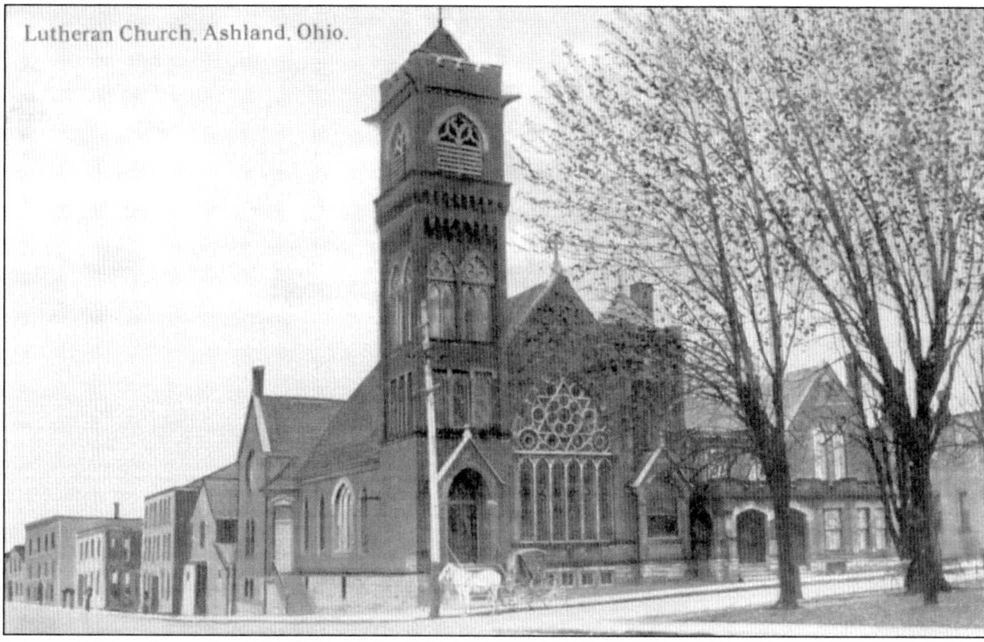

Prior to 1889, the Trinity Lutheran Church was referred to by different names such as the English, German, or Evangelical Lutheran. The Lutherans, like the Methodists, were not strangers to relocating, rebuilding, and fire. Initially under the leadership of Rev. F.J. Ruth, who preached in homes in 1821, the growing church established their first house in a converted brewery on the southwest corner of Orange and Third Streets in 1845. The Lutherans continued growing, and in 1859, a place of worship was built on Third Street between Orange and Church Streets. Falling under fire in 1883, the Lutherans rebuilt in 1884, pictured above with sanctuary below, on the corner of Church and Third Streets. Still growing, they built again in 1963, settling at 508 Center Street, and incorporated the donated home of longtime parishioner P.A. Myers, located at the intersection of Center and Walnut Streets, into the church.

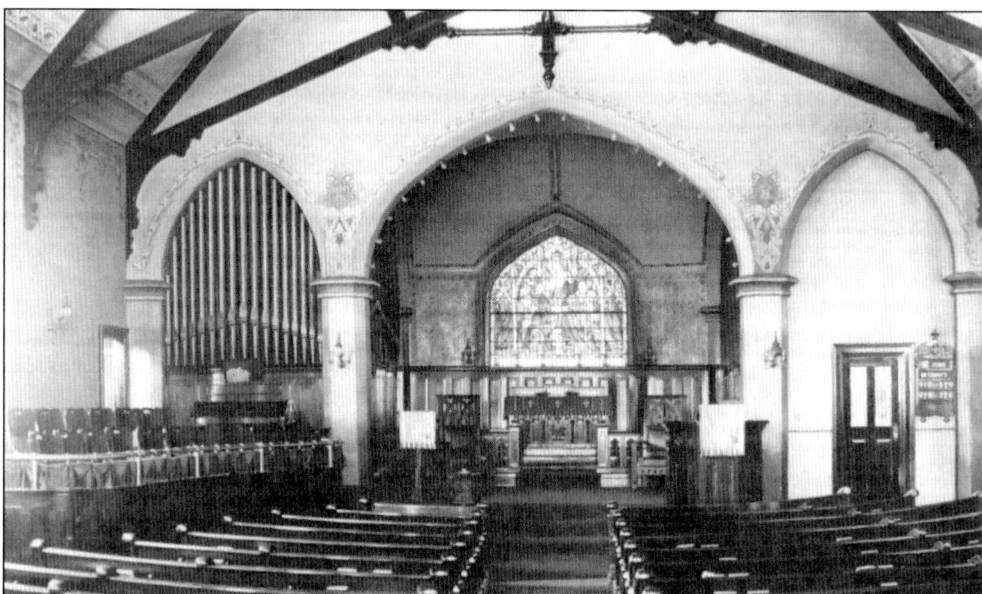

Seven

Entertaining the Town

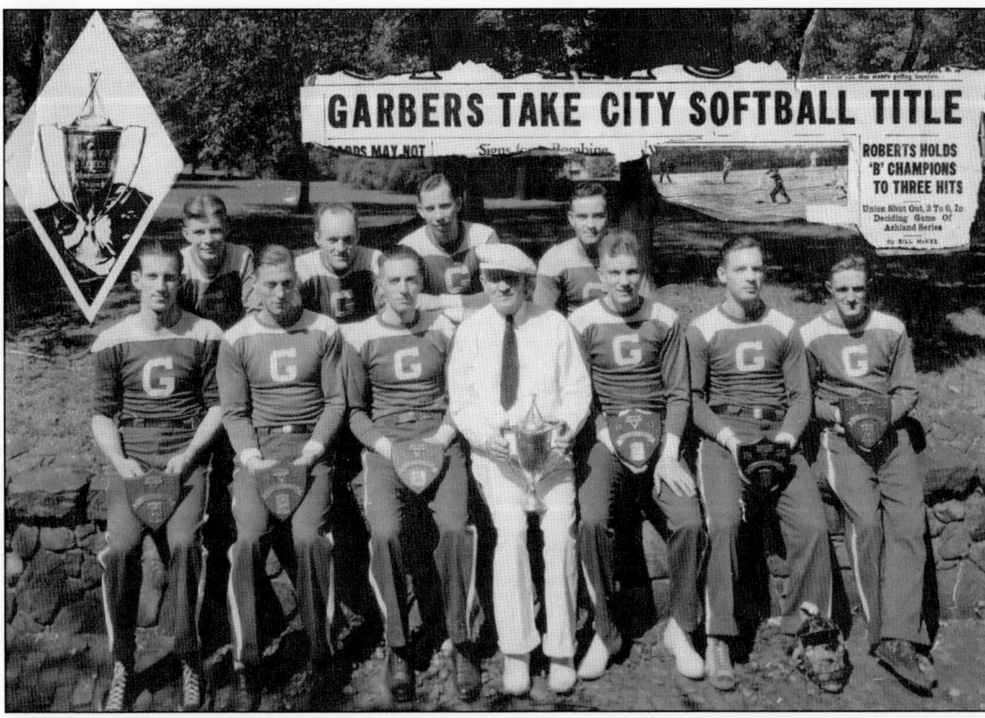

This 1935 Garber Publishing softball team (then referred to as kitten ball) took the winning YMCA City Kitten Ball Championship title, and it appears that it was not their first title. By closer examination of the photograph, one will see that city titles were won four years in a row, beginning in 1930. The team is pictured with manager Neil Pedigo, seen here wearing a white hat in the center of the first row.

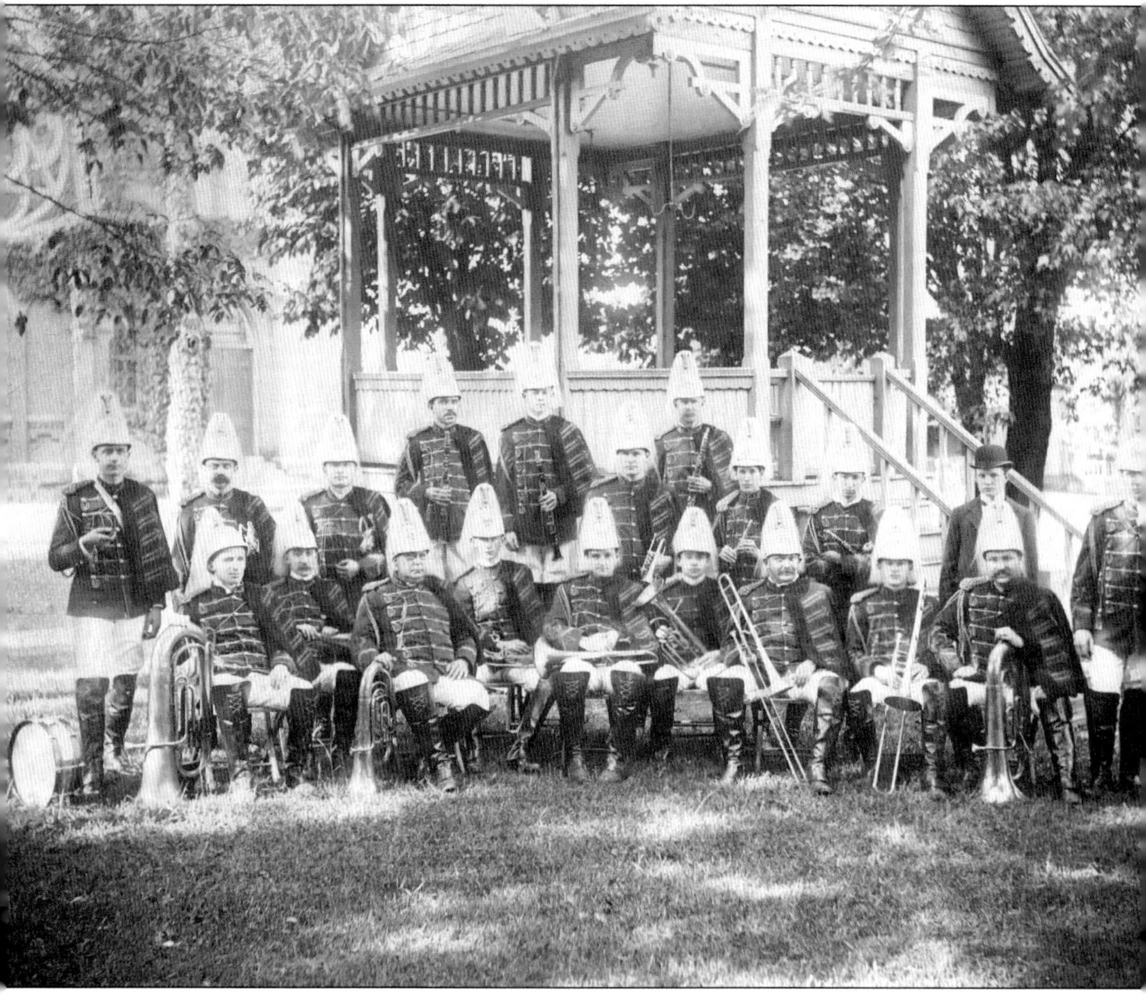

The Ashland Military Band was considered one of the best in the country from 1890 to 1924. With their white helmets and horsetail plummets, blue coats with gold braid and cord, and white corduroy trousers tucked into black patent leather boots, the band was also considered one of the best dressed. Under the direction of their only director, Jake Heitz, pictured above in the third row on left, the band was proud to play at the Republican National Convention in Philadelphia, which nominated William McKinley for president. When they weren't traveling the state or beyond, they were playing at nearly every occasion in town, including the whistle-stop speech of presidential hopeful William Jennings Bryan in 1908, as well as weekly performances at the Courthouse Park bandstand. Heitz took ill in the early 1920s, and the band dissolved, though it was soon replaced with a younger set of musicians under the direction of a young schoolteacher by the name of Louis E. Pete.

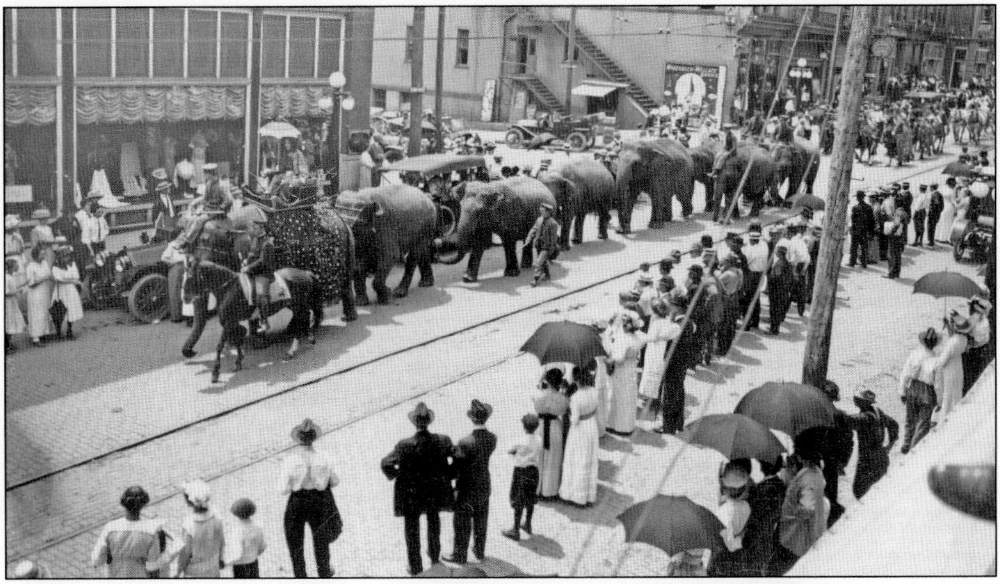

In 1879, the 5:00 a.m. arrival of the Van Amgurgh Circus from Pennsylvania brought many witnesses to the Erie depot for the appearance of the first circus to visit the town. For nearly 70 years, the circus was held at various locations throughout town, primarily at a field off Eastern Avenue. Above, elephants, caged animals, circus personnel, and equipment parade down Main Street with the 1920 Wallace and Hagenbeck Circus.

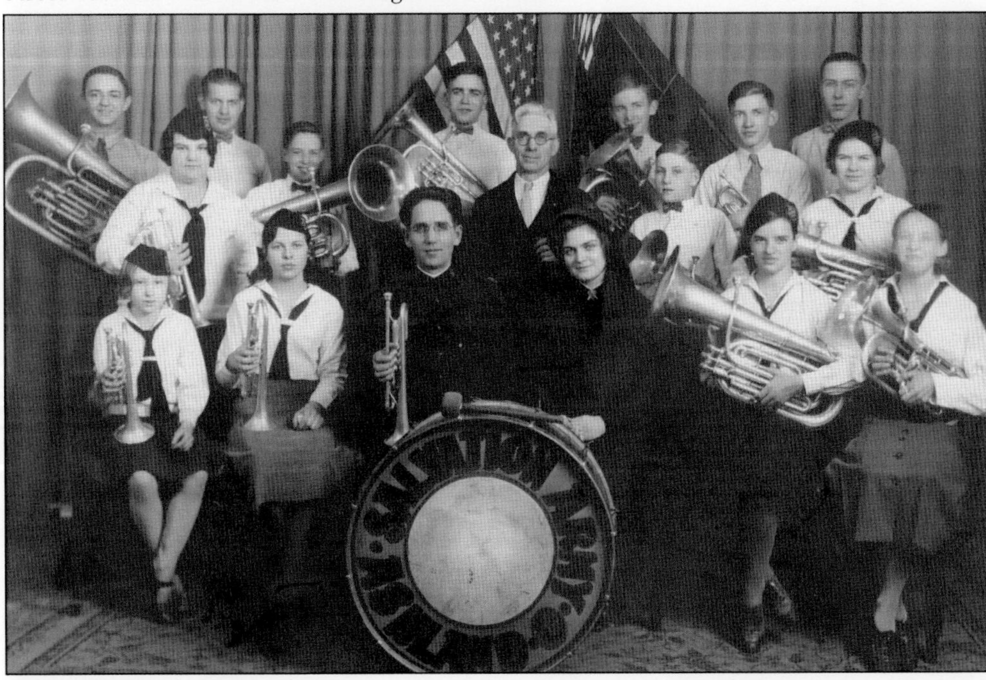

The Salvation Army Band was known for playing music at the Brookside Park Band Stand on Sunday evenings. Additionally, the band would play next to the Opera House at the corner of Main and Center Streets, when people were shopping downtown, drawing attention on Friday and Saturday nights. Charlie Jones, center under the flags, directed this Salvation Army Young People's Band during the 1930s.

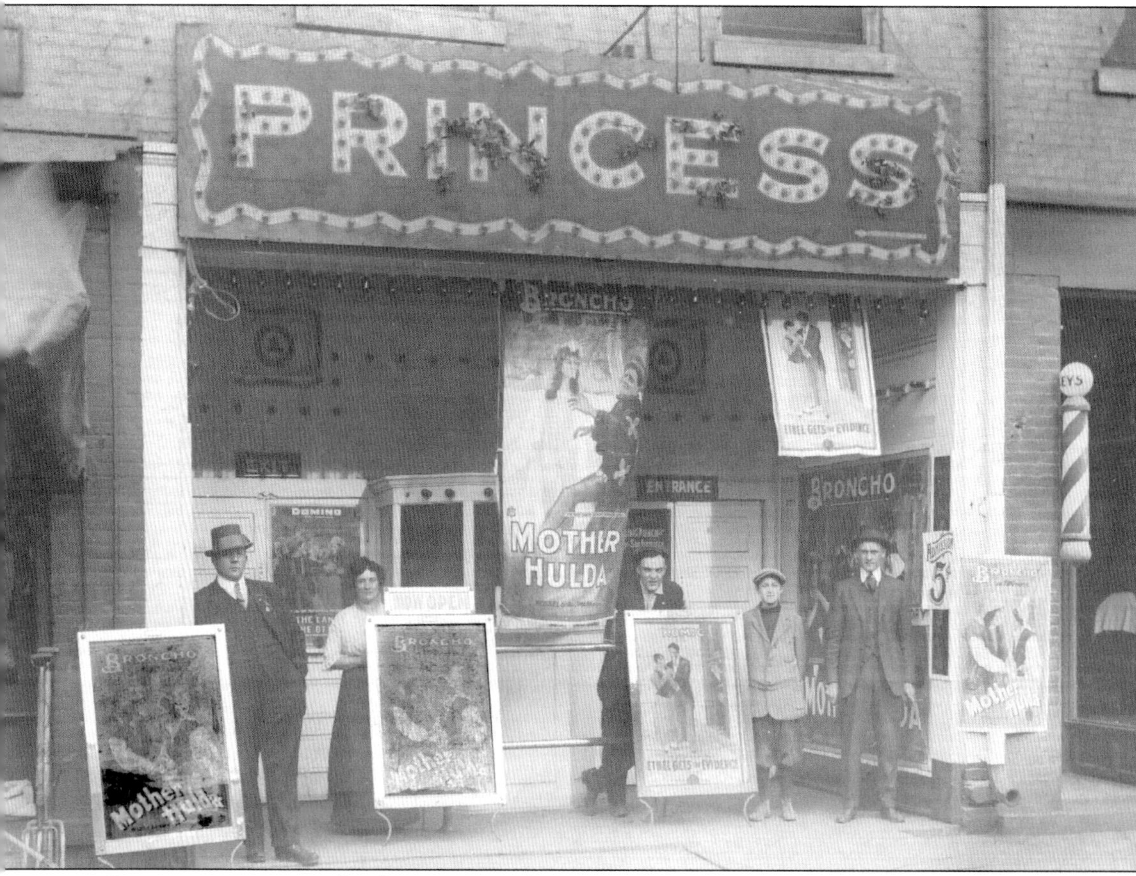

From 1911 to 1919, under the proprietorship of Roy Michael, the Princess Theatre, at 125 Main Street, showed silent movies with "High Class Photo Plays." Photoplays were books of the silent movie era, featuring images of the film's leading stars inserted amongst the text. Above, the Princess is screening *Mother Hulda*, a 1915 silent picture produced by the Bronco film company. Another popular theater located at the opposite end of Main Street was the Palace. Special features of the Palace Theatre, located at 114 East Main Street, were eight illuminated mirrors; a long, narrow lobby featuring a pond with goldfish; dialogue and announcements that flashed on the screen; and an organist that accompanied the movements of the movie being played. The Palace, one of the finest theaters in town from 1921 through 1951, boasted house seats, furniture, and drapes purchased from local merchants.

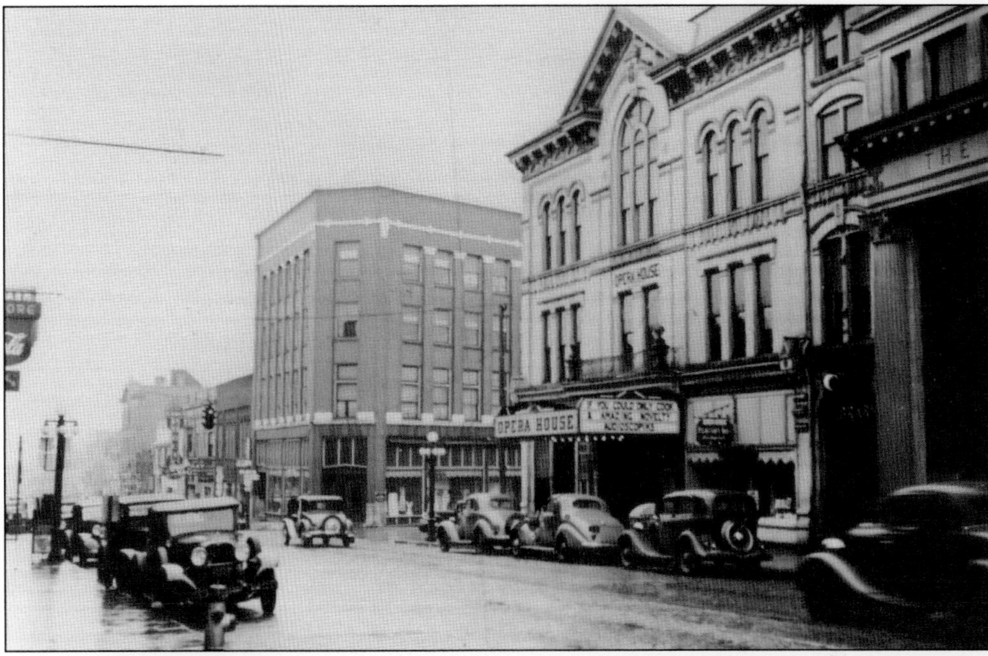

Calling itself the best theater in town, the Opera House was located at the corner of Main and Center Streets, where the 1858 town hall once stood and where a wheelwright named John Hull operated a tavern as long ago as 1822. Built in 1882, the Opera House partially burned in 1903, at which time local saloons offered whiskey to all firefighters after fighting the roaring blaze. Replaced in 1904 by a new theater, it possessed two balconies, seating for 1,000 people, and hosted various shows, including minstrels, talent shows, and commencements. The Opera House was owned by the city, and the 35¢ admission price in 1915 paid the salary of the mayor. By the late 1920s, it became a movie house. Its doors closed in 1935, and the building was razed in 1955. An undated program book from *The Fairies' Carnival* is pictured below.

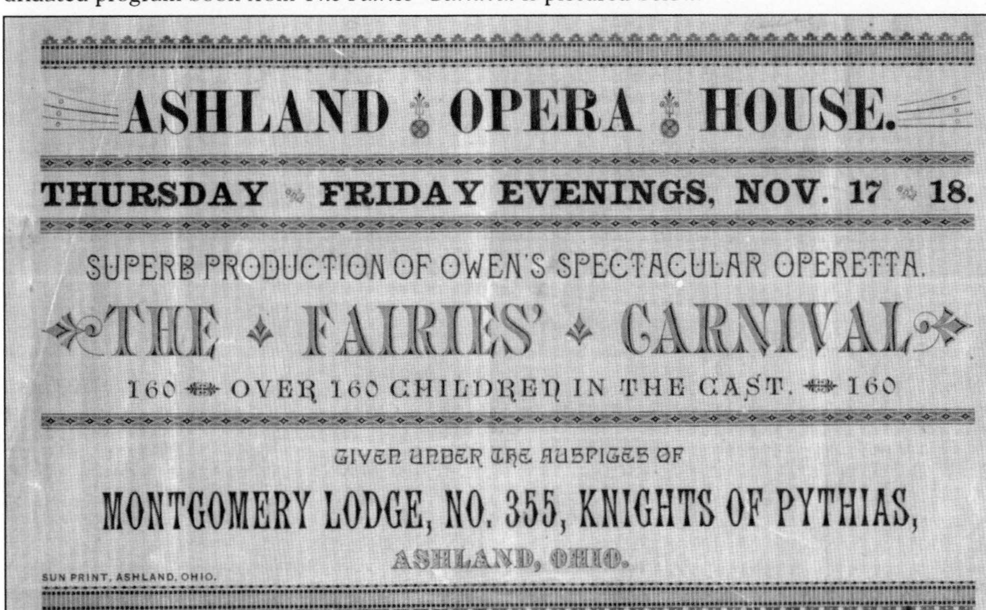

ASHLAND OPERA HOUSE.

THURSDAY & FRIDAY EVENINGS, NOV. 17 & 18.

SUPERB PRODUCTION OF OWEN'S SPECTACULAR OPERETTA.

THE FAIRIES' CARNIVAL

160 OVER 160 CHILDREN IN THE CAST. 160

GIVEN UNDER THE AUSPICES OF

MONTGOMERY LODGE, NO. 355, KNIGHTS OF PYTHIAS,

ASHLAND, OHIO.

SUN PRINT, ASHLAND, OHIO.

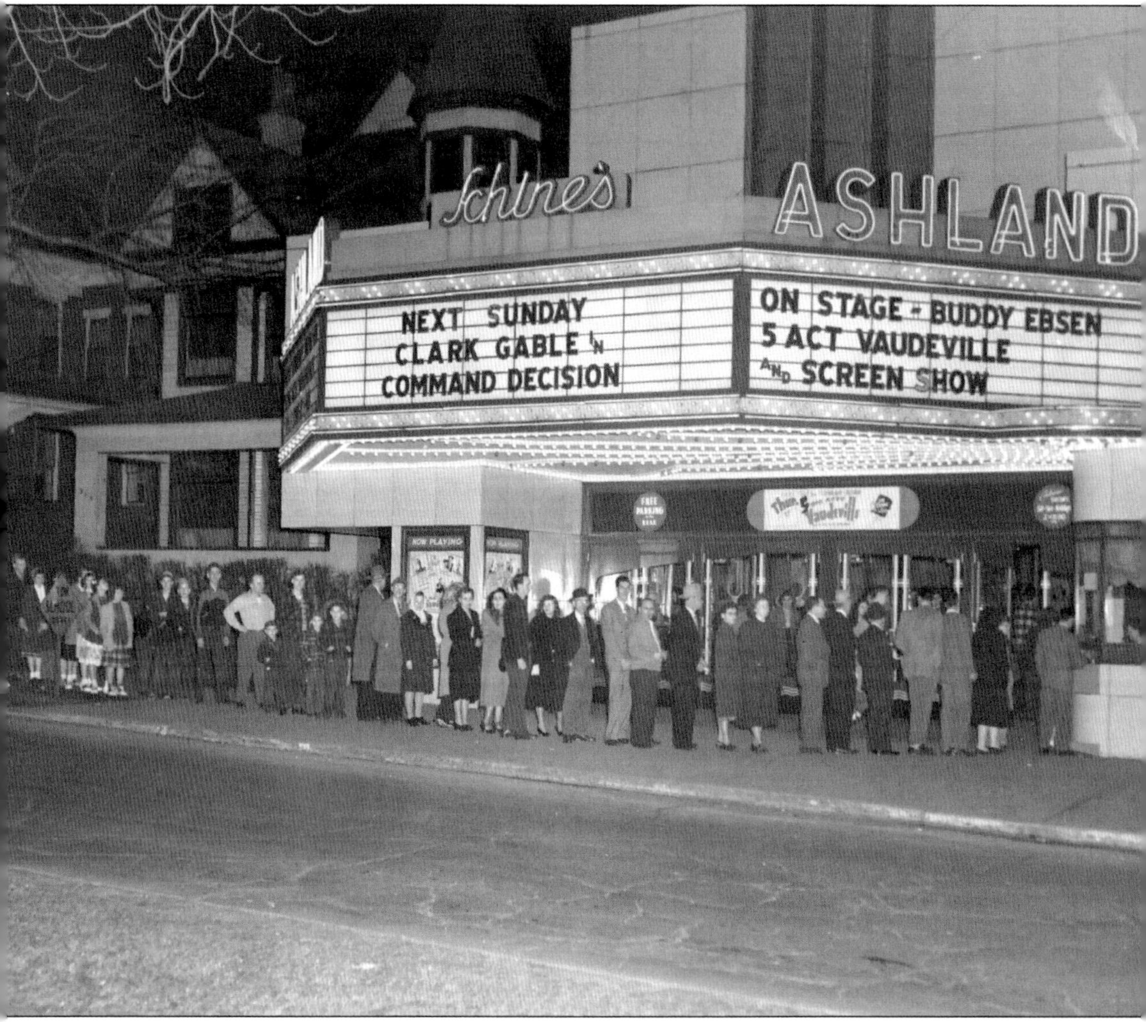

Forty cents would buy a seat to the moving picture *Rings on Her Fingers*, starring Henry Fonda, for the opening night gala of the new Schines Ashland Theatre on March 27, 1942, under the management of Wilbur Eckard. Located at 214 Center Street, at a construction cost of more than $200,000, the theater seated 1,500 and employed 18 people. Owners, J. Myer Schine and Louis W. Schine of New York designed the Ashland, as it was also known, with modern warmed and cooled air, guaranteed good seating with no "angel" glimpses, a giant screen for no eye strain, dual projectors to work in turns for no detection in the change of reel, and a large stage and dressing rooms for live acts. Being sensitive to the fact that the country was involved in World War II, dedication ceremonies were conducted by the American Legion and Veterans of Foreign Wars followed by comments from local dignitaries. The above photograph shows the popularity of the theater in 1943 when Buddy Ebsen came to town for a live performance.

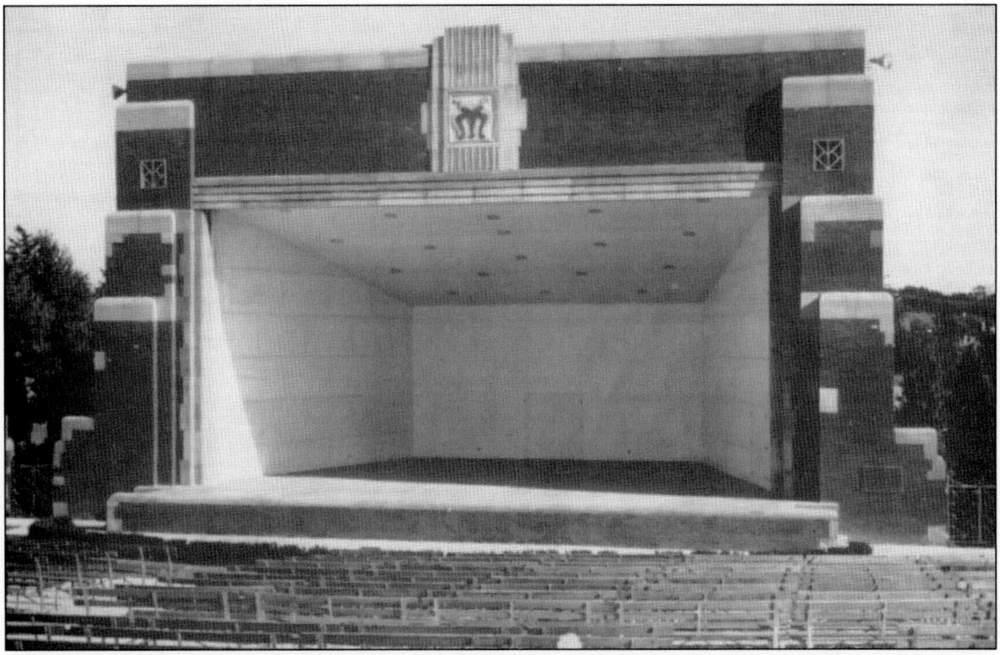

Katherine "Kate" Moore Myers, the wife of Guy C. Myers, donated $112,000 in 1949 for the construction of the Guy C. Myers Memorial Band Shell, pictured above. The completion of the band shell was the realization of a long, desired hope. Bringing the best possible music reception to its audience, with bowl seating for 2,600 people, storage space for instruments, and dressing rooms, the new amphitheater was actually a tribute to the musicians of the past, which built up music appreciation in the town. Pictured below, the Ashland Symphony Orchestra proudly plays under the direction of Dr. Louis E. Pete for a packed house on opening night of the band shell. With the growing popularity of Doc Pete's musical talents, the new band shell marked an era of new beginnings, the best in music, and the best in listening.

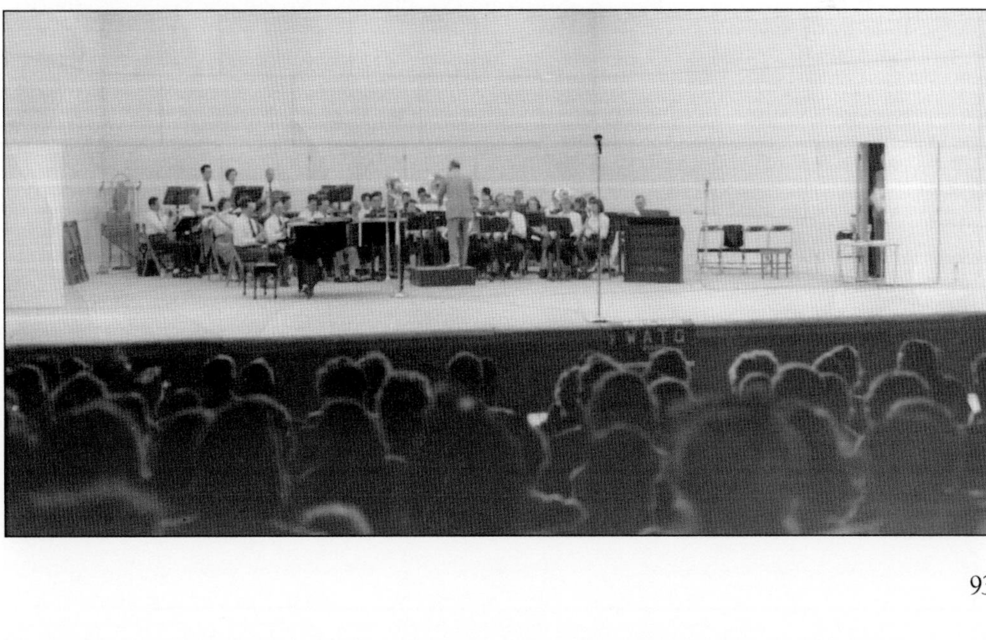

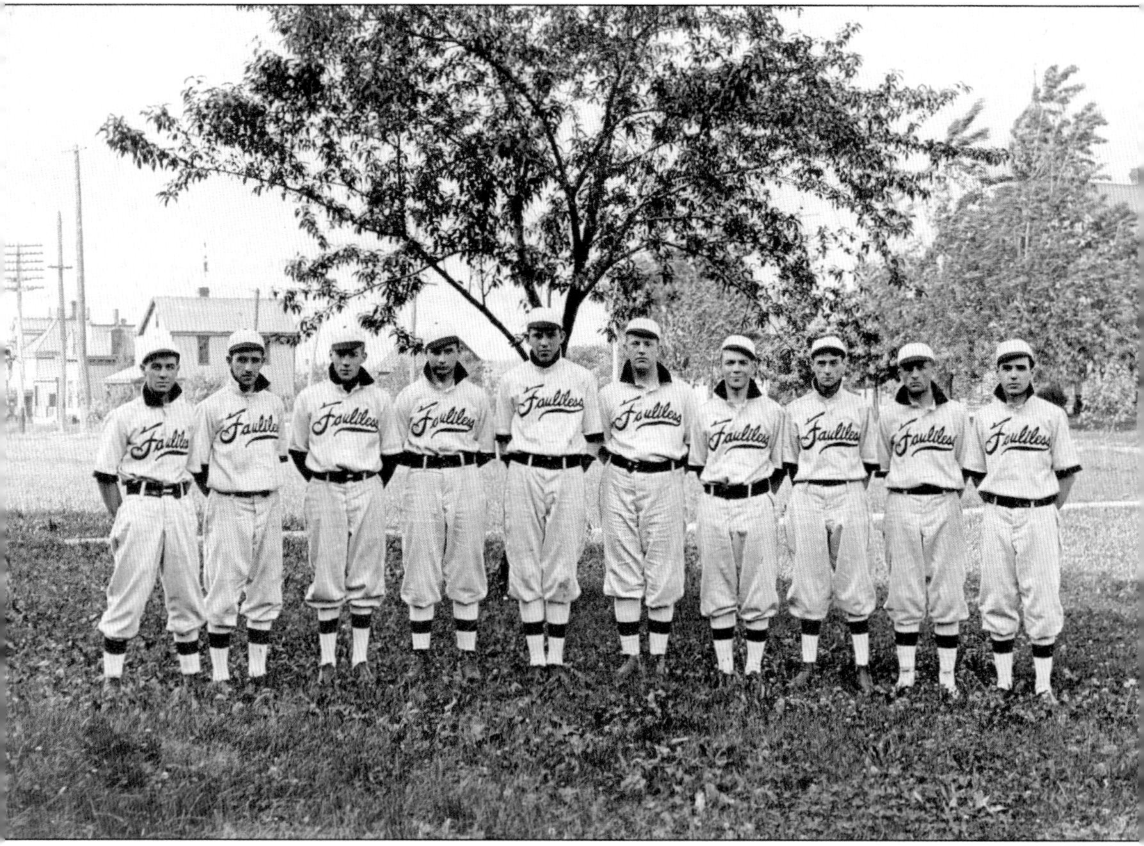

It has been said that the town was known not only for balloons, but also for fast-pitch softball. First named the Faultless Indians, as seen above in the 1940s, before becoming the Faultless Rubbermen in 1959, the team won their first state championship in 1964, additionally winning their first Amateur Softball Association (ASA) National Tournament in 1966. The Faultless Rubber fast-pitch softball team was in its heyday during the 1960s and 1980s, qualifying many times over for the national finish. T.W. Miller Jr., president of the Faultless Rubber Company from 1949 to 1968, was considered to be the founding father of men's fast-pitch softball in town, bringing some of the finest names in softball to Brookside Park. One of the most respected teams in the nation, Faultless was the pride of not only the city, but also of Ohio, boasting hall of fame players. With the success of the Rubbermen, other area teams resulted, bringing Brookside Park to the forefront of popularity. Abbott Labs-Ashland Merchants, formerly the Rubbermen, last saw action in 1998, leaving the town forever grateful for its history in fast-pitch softball.

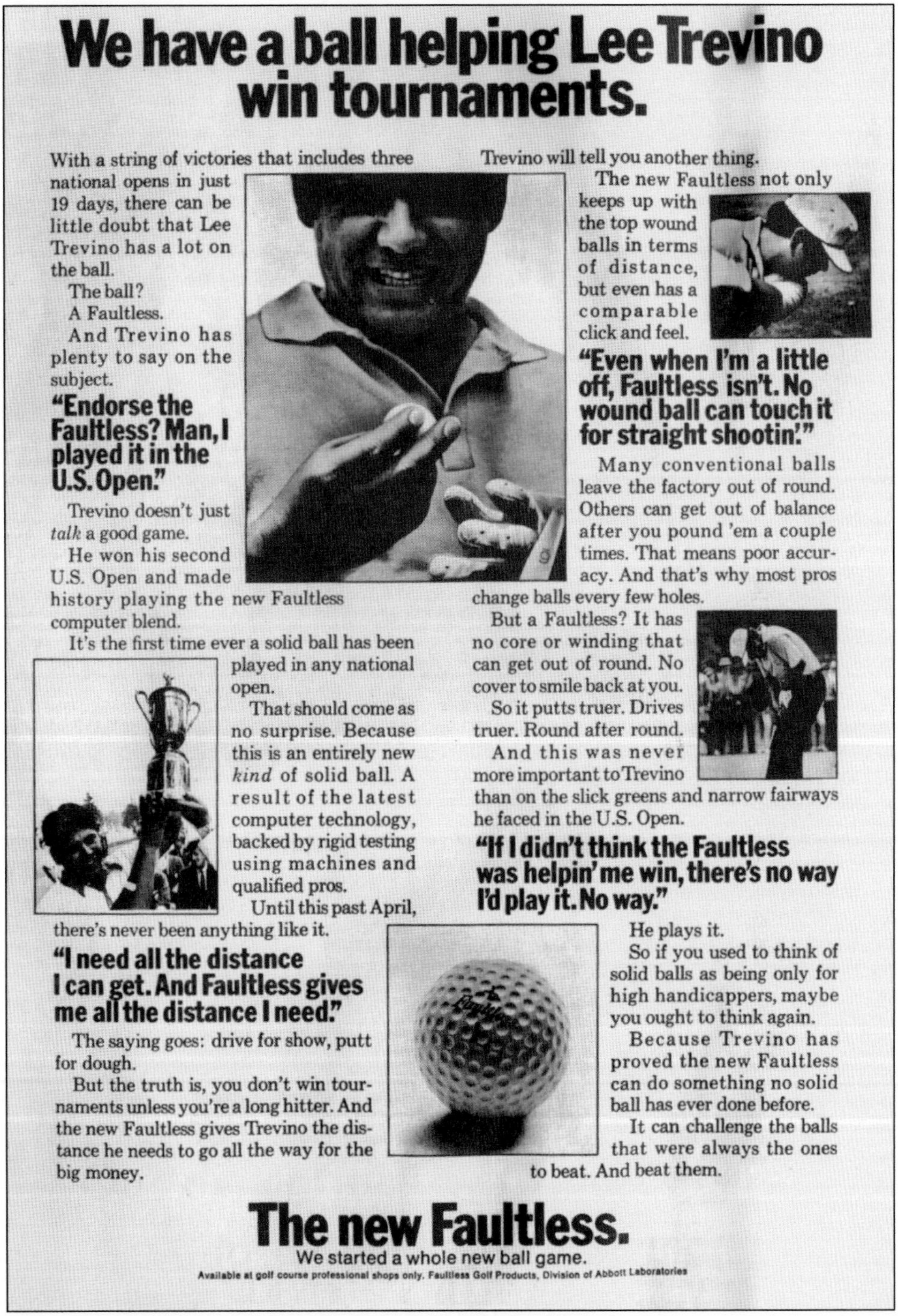

The Faultless Rubber Company had "a ball" assisting golf pro Lee Trevino with his game. In the 1970s, Faultless golf products developed a solid, one-piece golf ball, turning out more than 30,000 balls per day at a cost of 25¢ apiece. The Country Club of Ashland golfers were known to use the ball in play and for tournament giveaways. The advertisement above tells of Trevino's endorsement of the Faultless golf ball.

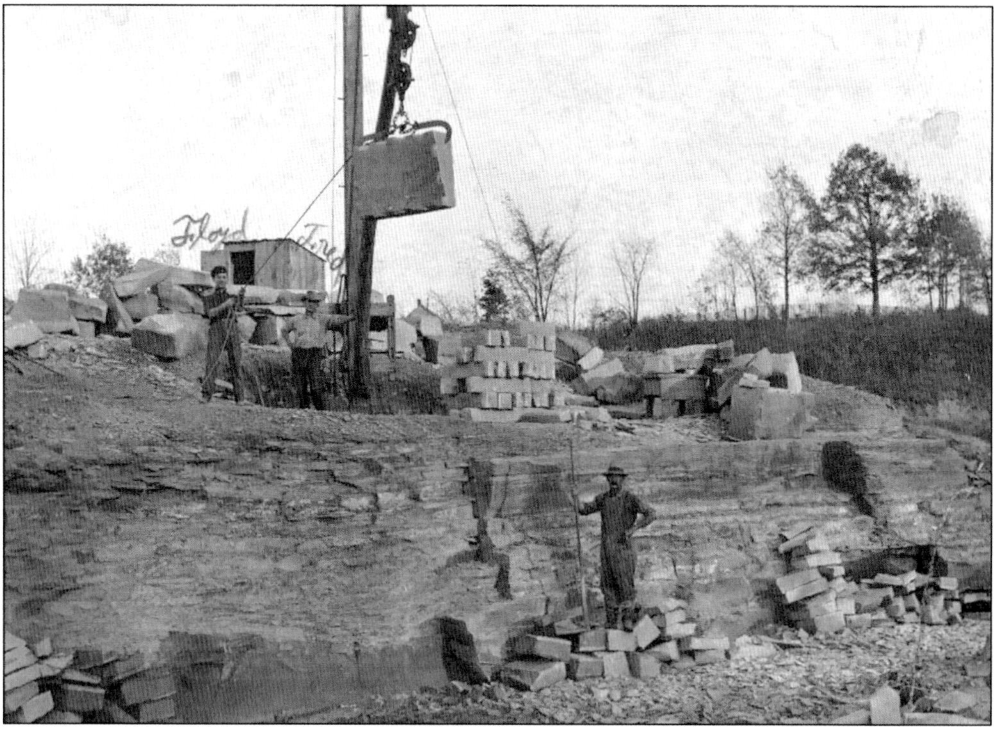

Wishes do come true, as was the case for the town in 1917 when local jeweler Frank Downs raised $6,000 to convert six acres of land and the Knapp stone quarry, shown above, into a pond and a recreational park in an area located off Lindale Avenue. The photograph below shows the pond with an island on the right and a picnic shelter on the left, which have both been removed through the years. Many changes in the park have taken place over the course of time, with the addition of a swimming pool, tennis courts, miniature golf, softball, basketball, horseshoes, shuffleboard, picnic facilities, and much more. This dream come true was only the beginning of what was to come, as Brookside Park has continued to grow to 443 acres nearly a century later. (Above, William S. Snyder collection.)

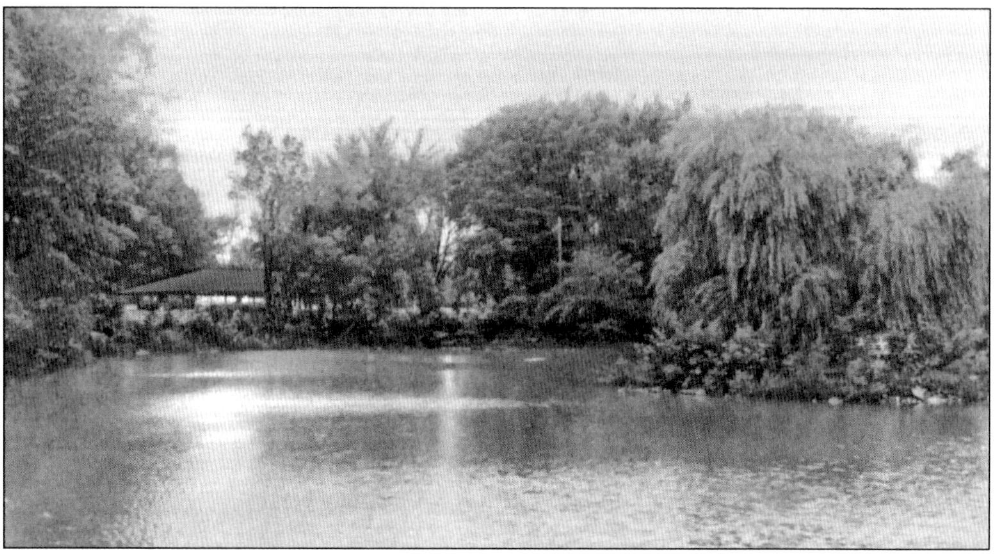

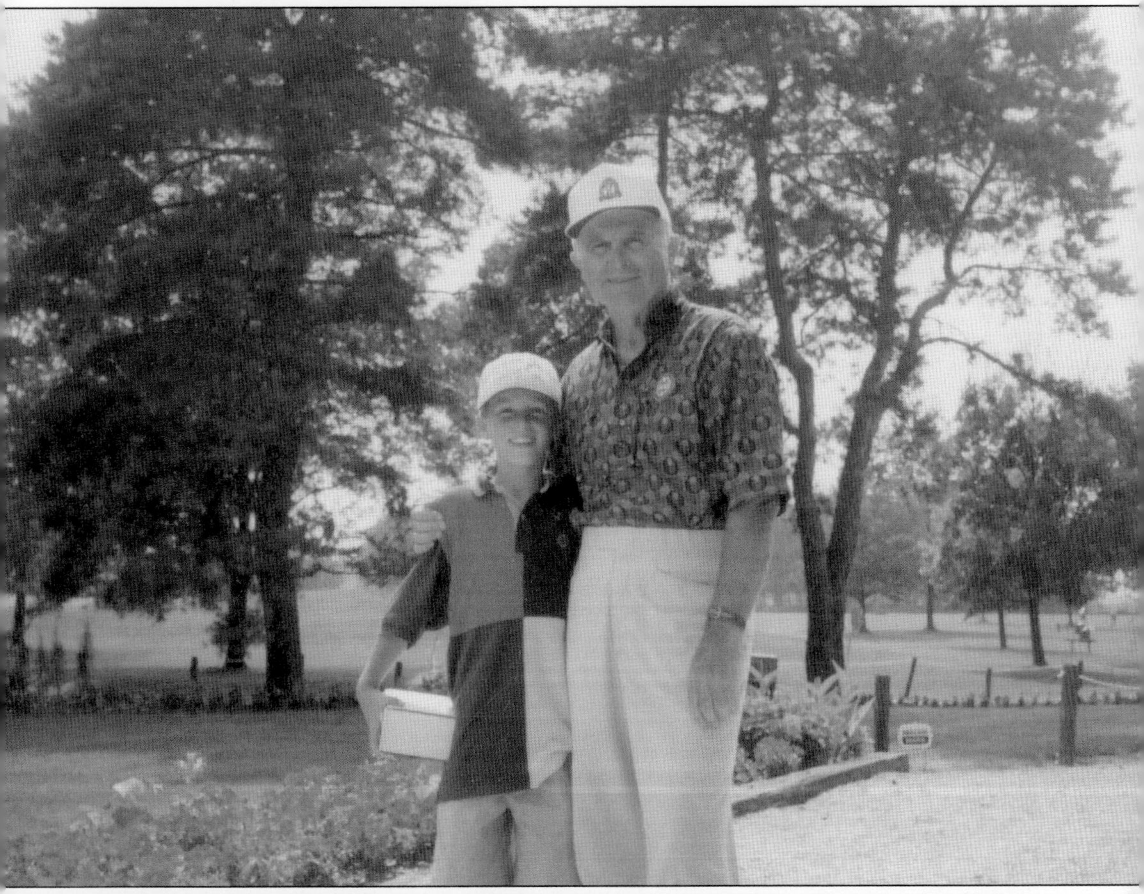

In 1968, Mayor Don Hostettler encouraged city council to purchase 97 acres of land from William Gebhart at 1299 Olivesburg Road (Sandusky Street) for the development of Brookside Golf Course, a nine-hole course to be included in the Brookside Park system. Construction of the course was completed in 1971. Seeing a vision for growth in 1977, construction began for a second nine-holes of golf, which officially opened in 1978 with Gov. James A. Rhoads hitting the first ball. Pictured above is George Valentine, Brookside's first golf pro, with one of his junior golf students. Prior to the opening of the city course, Glenwood Golf Course, located on West Main Street near Sunset Drive at the city limits, was the first and only public golf course in town. (Brookside Golf Course collection.)

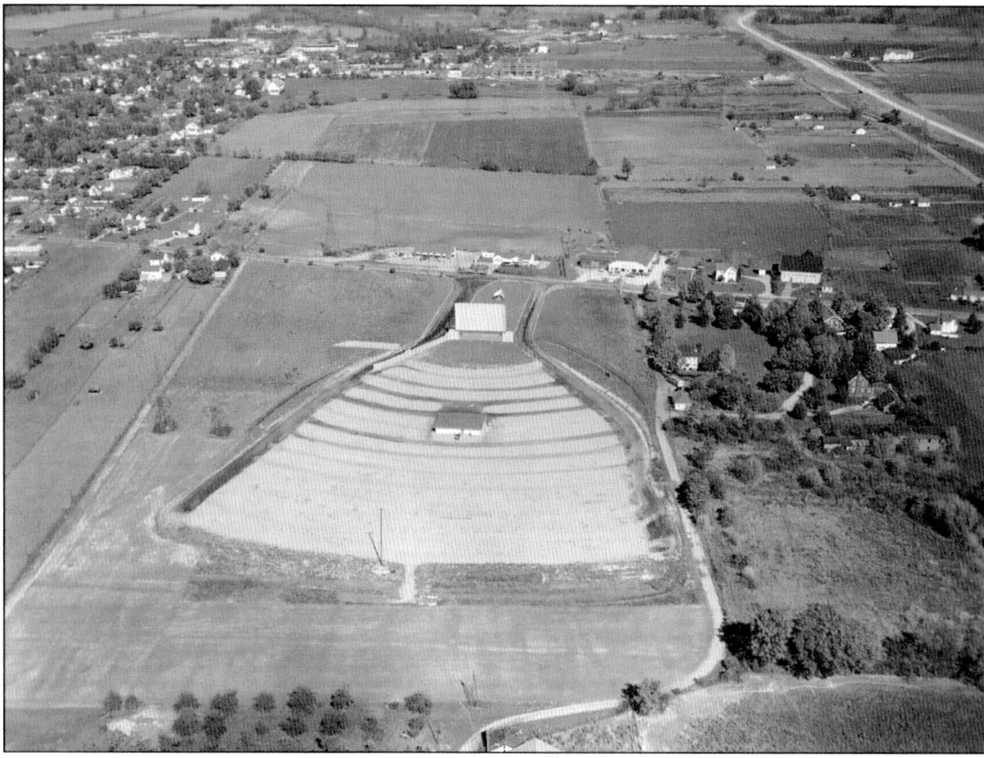

In this 1955 aerial view, two things are evident: the edge of the city limits at the left of the photograph and the V-shaped layout of Eckard's Ashland Drive-In Theatre, which placed the movie screen and concession stand in the center. Those visiting the drive-in will recall children in pajamas, a playground in front of the screen, and a hanging window speaker for sound. Owner Wilbur and Bernice Eckard opened the theater in 1953 during the era of 3-D films, but Cinemascope was also causing excitement at the theaters. The Eckard's flyer seen below promotes the release of the *The Robe*, the first movie filmed in Cinemascope—a panoramic, wide-screen motion picture format. The theater closed in 1979, and with the growth of the city, the property merged into the city limits, becoming home to the Ashland County Justice Center in 2000.

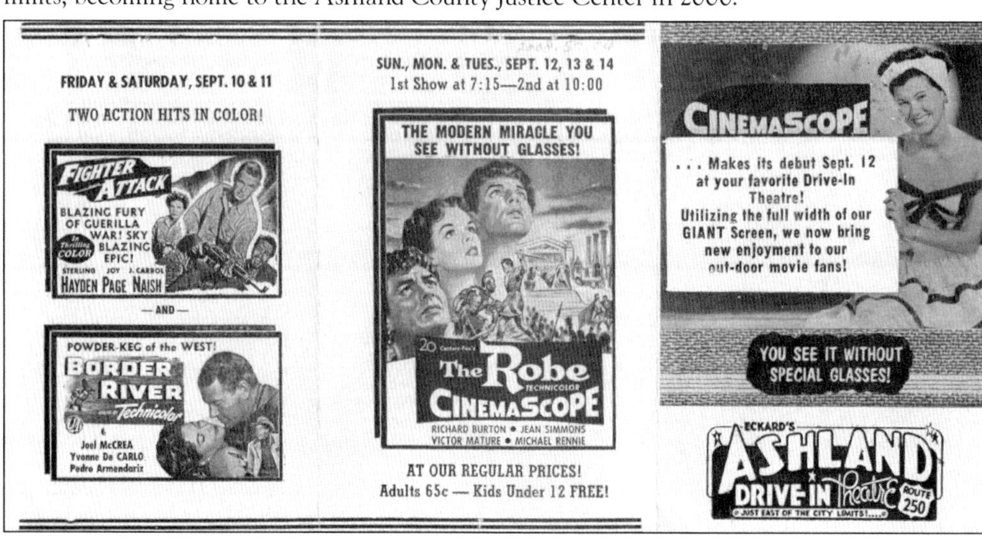

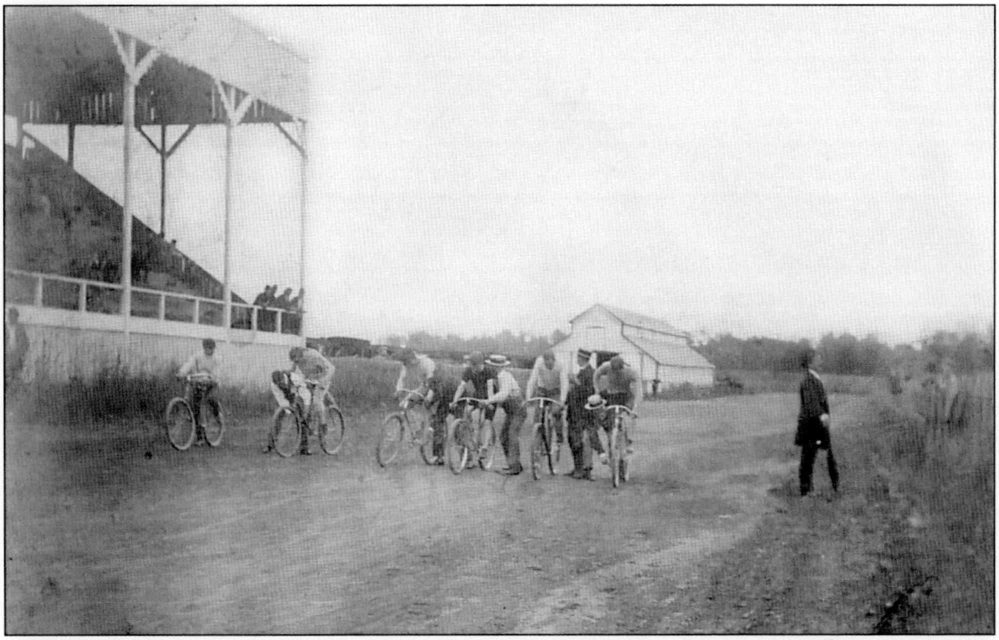

In 1845, the county fair was established in the area of Sandusky, Monroe, and Ohio Streets with the main entrance gate at the point on Sandusky, Wick, and Vine Streets. Early fairs featured horses, cattle, and the ever-popular bicycle races in front of the grandstand, as pictured above. In 1891, S.G. Wiest and William Priest of Polk built a horse stable 120 feet long and 38 feet wide. A trainer from Kentucky was hired to train horses for the track, running successful races for several years before the stable was destroyed by fire. City expansion in 1904 caused the fairgrounds to be divided into lots and sold. Twenty years later in 1924, a new county fairground was developed on the corner of the Mansfield (Claremont) and Baney Roads. A four-day pass to the 1890 fair is pictured below. (Below, Samuel G. Markel collection.)

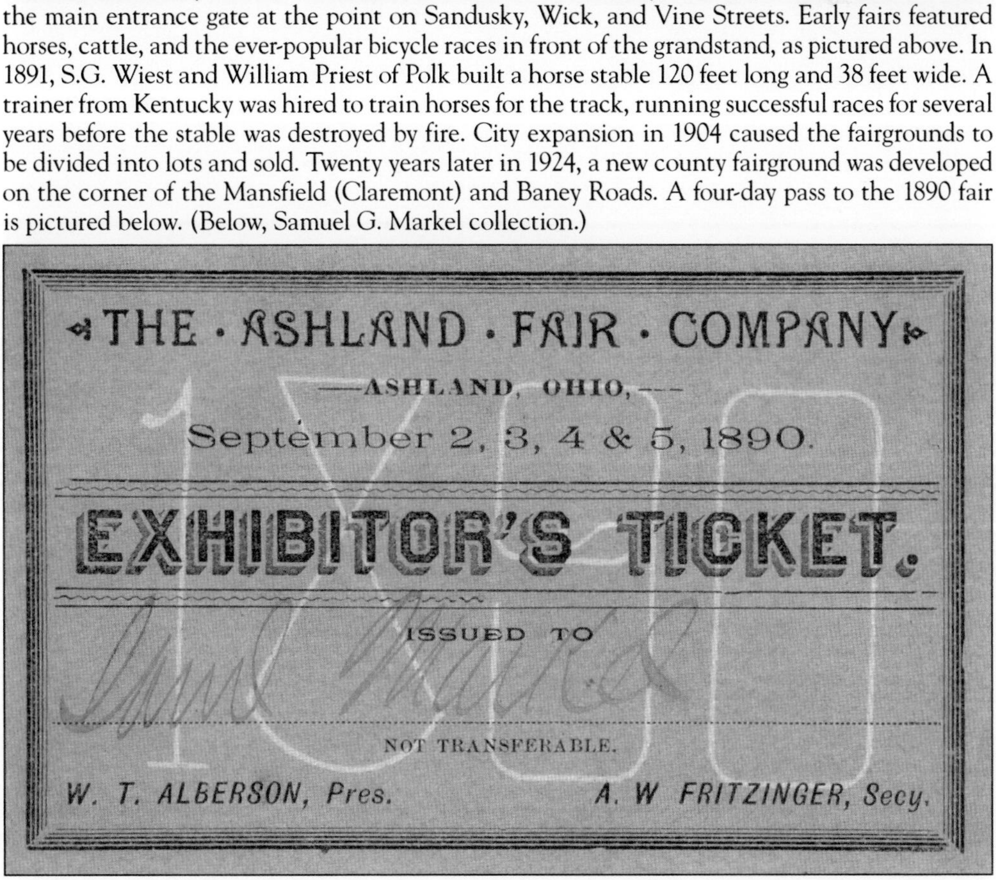

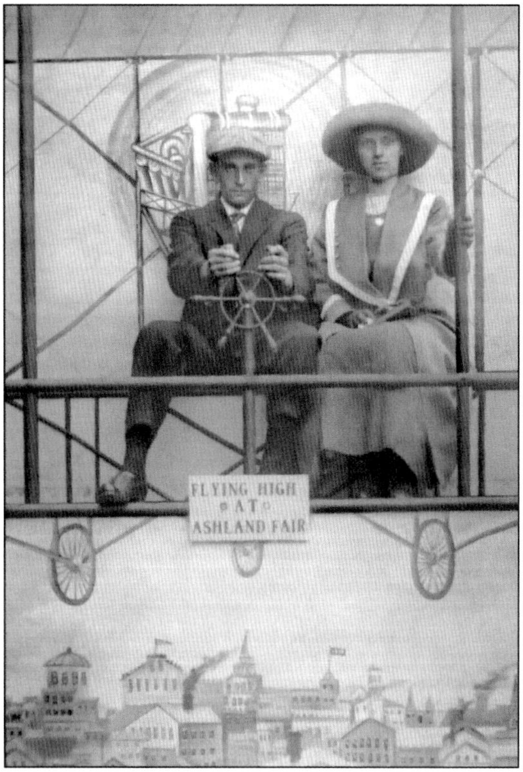

Flying High on a date are S. Harlan McGuire and Alma A. Smith in this c. 1910 photograph taken at the Ashland Street Fair. With no county fair during the early 1900s, a street fair was held on Main Street to take its place. Annually from 1907 to 1924, the center of town was filled with booths and concessions, allowing room in the middle for the cars of the Cleveland and Southwestern interurban to pass. The fair provided a variety of attractions, from exhibits on farm, poultry, and pets to household, art, and manufacturing displays. Parades, fireworks, dances, games, tumbling, and trapeze acts also took place during the five-day event. In this view below, which faces west on Main Street near Orange Street, is the 1910 Street Fair. (Left, Maxine McGuire Stafford collection.)

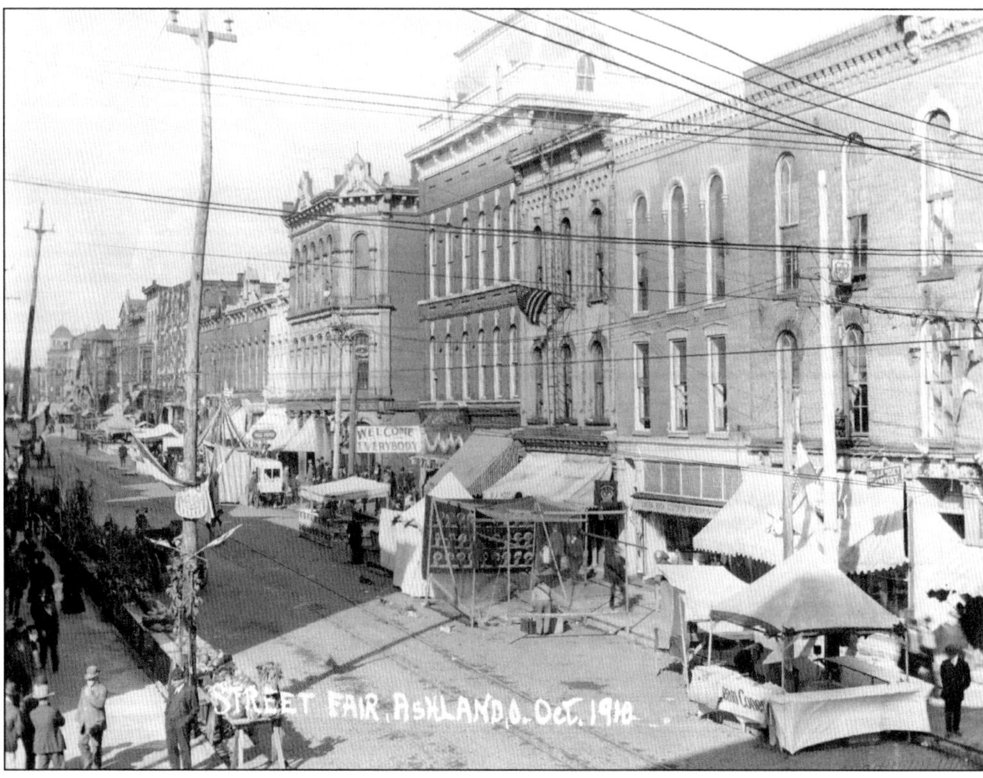

Eight

AN ERA TO REMEMBER

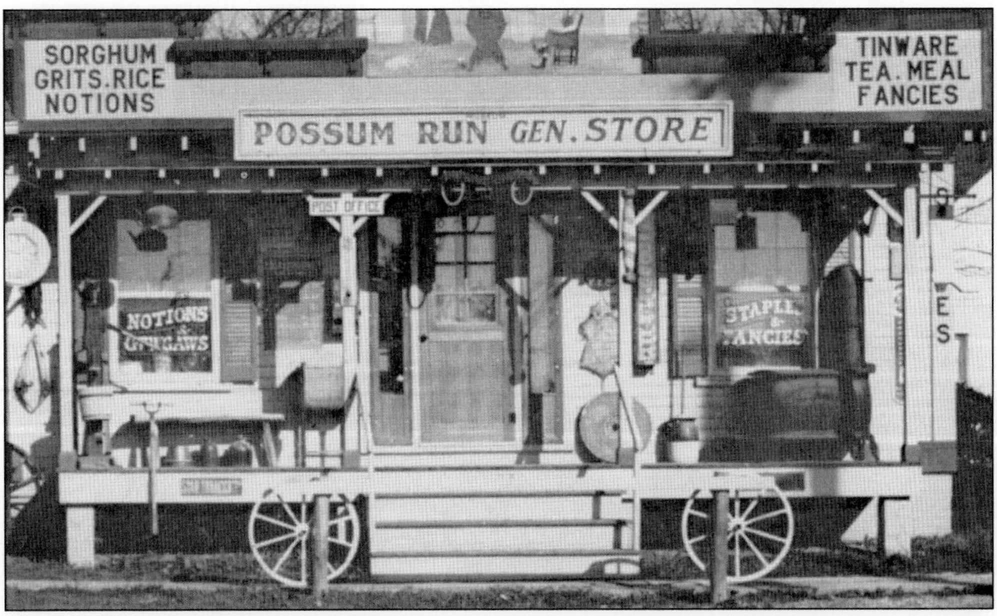

From 1931 to the 1972, Possum Run General Store was located at 1324 Cleveland Avenue. Owned by Theodore Willis, a retired city policeman, the store carried the usual general store knickknacks, antiques, and bits and pieces of hard to find items but was mainly remembered for its 128-piece candy counter. Possum Run supplied sweets favored from long ago, including 40 flavors of stick candy, a favorite of all generations. Willis estimated that 16,000 visitors frequented the store each year.

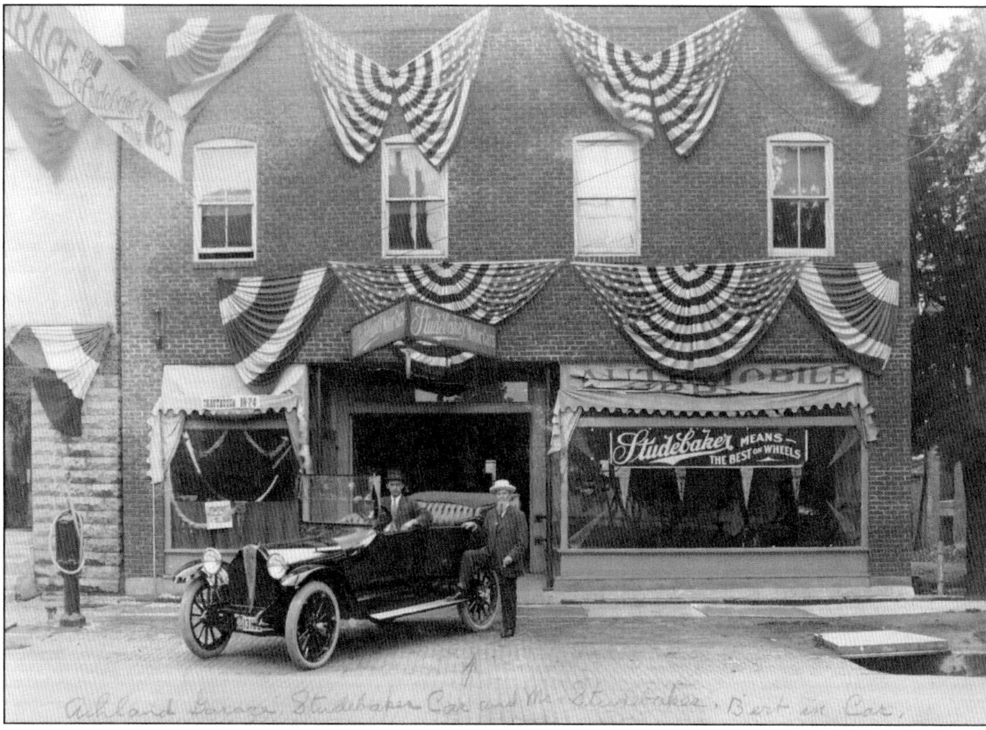

When John M. Studebaker, pictured standing above, rode into town, he received a lot of attention, especially driving his convertible Studebaker. Bert Richards is pictured above sitting in Studebaker's car in front of Richards's auto dealership at 161 Center in 1915. One of four automobile dealers in town, Richards sold Studebaker and Maxwell cars, a general line of car accessories, and offered automobile repair work. Below, pictured in front of the F.E. Myers home on Center Street, Studebaker drives for front passenger Francis E. Myers and, from left to right in the back seat, former Ashlander and Chicago circuit judge Peter Grosscup, an unidentified Studebaker grandson, and Philip A. Myers. Studebaker and his car were featured in the July 1915 auto parade, a part of the 100-year anniversary of Ashland. Formerly from Ashland, Studebaker moved to South Bend, Indiana, and eventually became the founder of the Studebaker automobile.

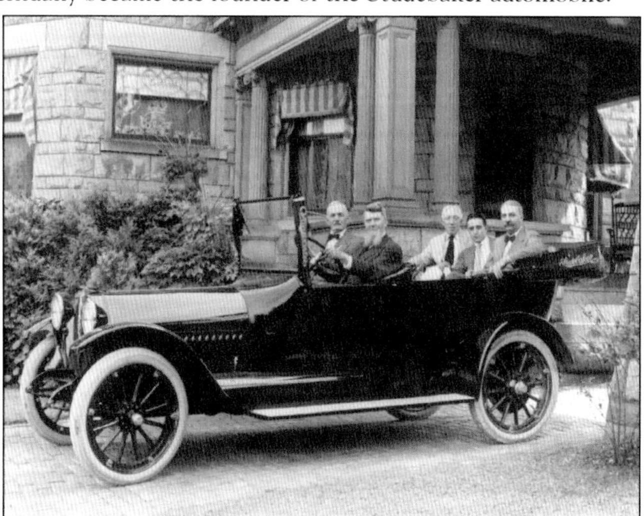

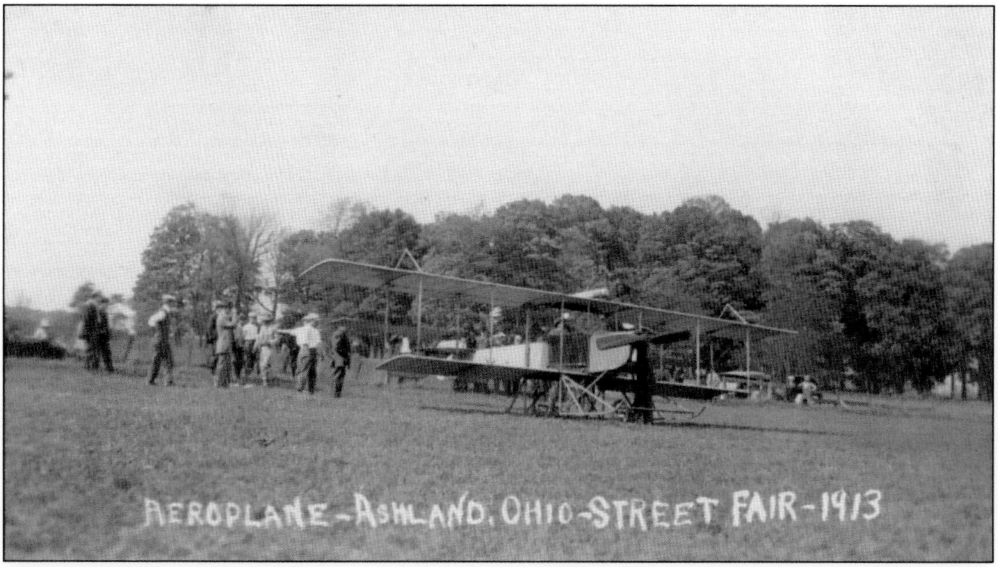

The street fair of 1913 landed a new and different attraction for its annual event with the arrival of the first "aeroplane" in town, a sight seldom seen, as it was only 10 years earlier that the Wright brothers made their first flight. The airplane was the talk of the fair, making several passes over the town before landing on the Kunkle farm at the intersection of Cleveland Avenue and Middle Rowsburg Road.

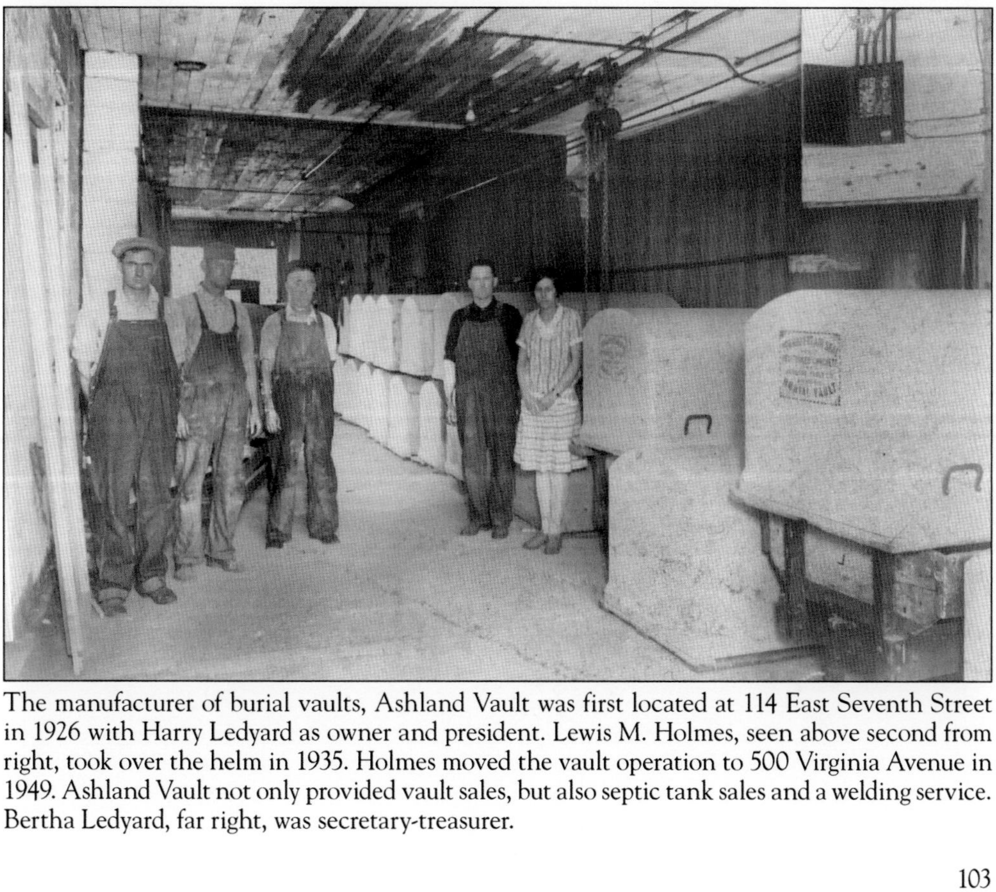

The manufacturer of burial vaults, Ashland Vault was first located at 114 East Seventh Street in 1926 with Harry Ledyard as owner and president. Lewis M. Holmes, seen above second from right, took over the helm in 1935. Holmes moved the vault operation to 500 Virginia Avenue in 1949. Ashland Vault not only provided vault sales, but also septic tank sales and a welding service. Bertha Ledyard, far right, was secretary-treasurer.

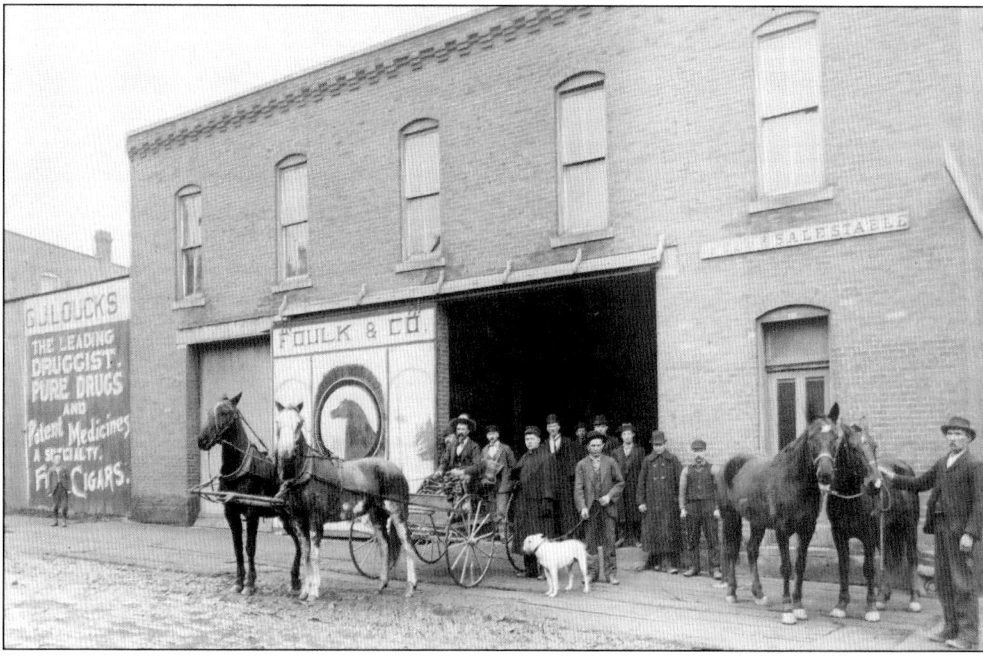

Livery stables and feed barns were once a common and necessary sight. People needing to rent a horse and buggy found their way to the livery, as did those who came to town needing a place to leave their horse and rig. With the dawn of the automobile, livery stables began to disappear after 1910. The livery pictured above was located at 34 West Second Street in 1894.

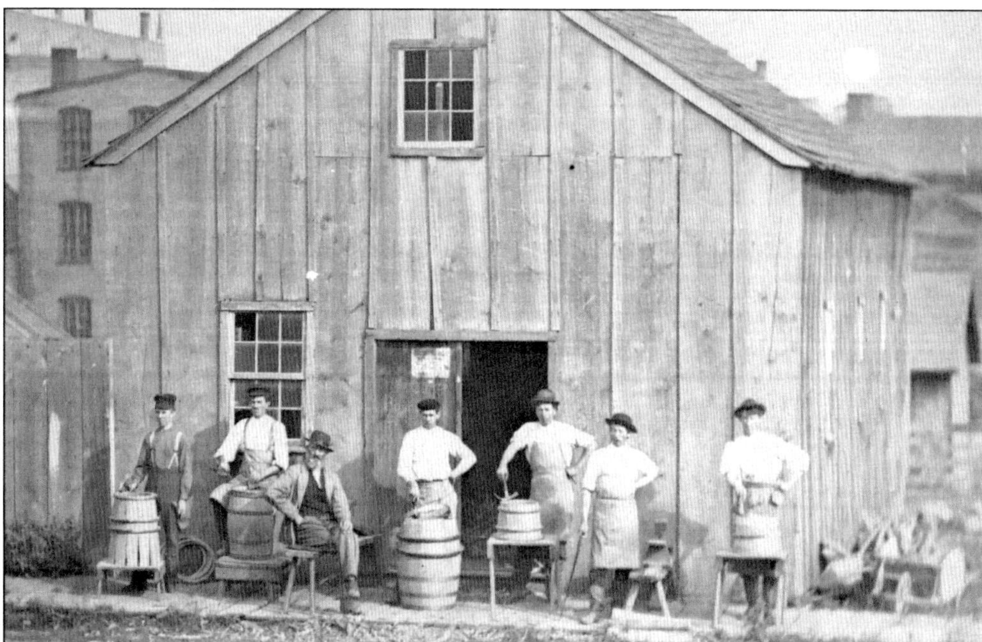

From 1863 to 1872, David Bryte owned and operated the cooper shop pictured above. A cooper was a maker of barrels of all sizes and for various purposes. Bryte's shop was likely kept busy at his location near the heart of town on the corner of Center and Maple Streets, just south of the Ashland City Mills.

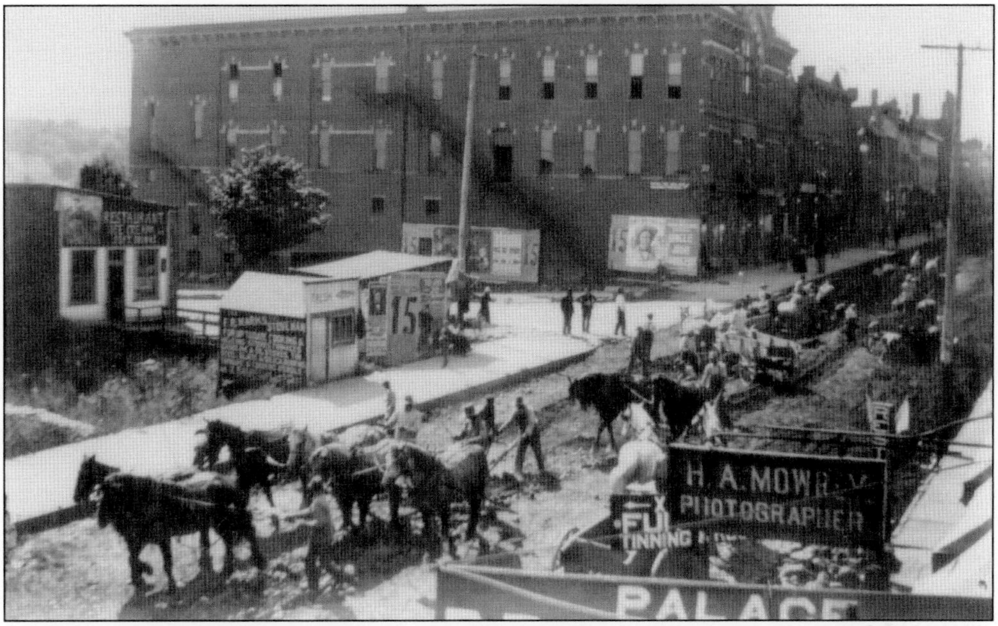

Cobblestones once lined the streets of town until 1898 when the stones were plowed up by the city street department, a crew of horses and men, in preparation for the paving of bricks. A work crew, pictured above on Main Street, prepares the street for new brick pavement near the southeast corner of Center Street, where the Home Company was built nearly 10 years later. (Home Hardware collection.)

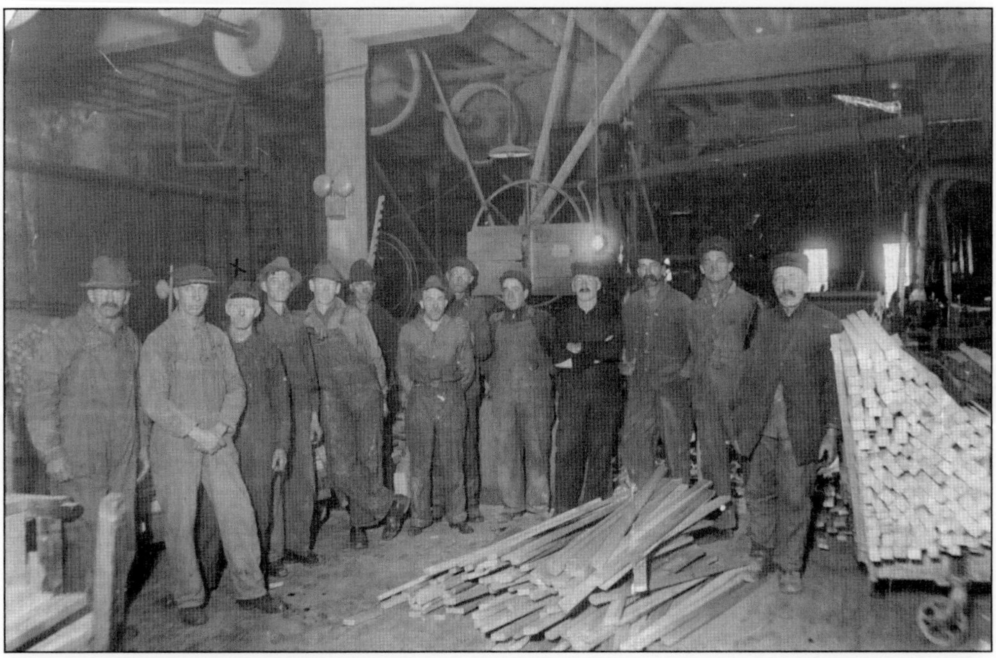

Established in 1932, the Ashland Lumber and Supply Company was located at 4 Clark Avenue. The lumberyard and sawmill was known for also providing millwork, along with selling lumber, doors, and window screens. The mill workers pictured above worked for firm president Scott H. Hanville until the company's closing in 1940. (Samuel G. Markel collection.)

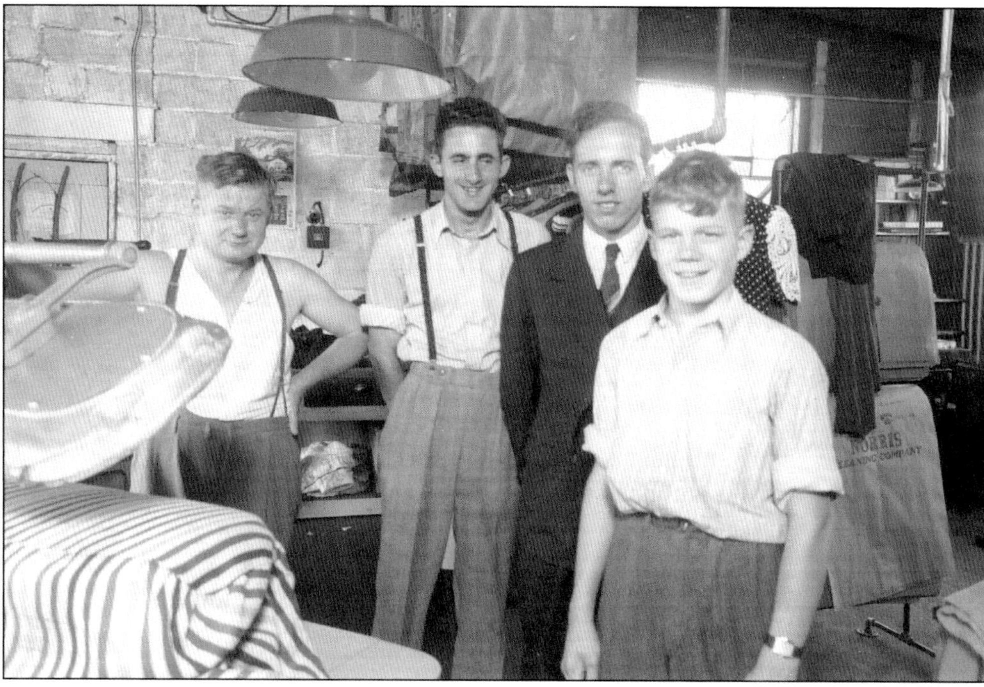

For nearly 20 years, Max Norris operated the Norris Cleaning Company, opening its doors first at 237 East Main Street in 1930 before relocating to Virginia Avenue in 1937. The Norris Company could handle all cleaning, pressing, dyeing, and repairs: "If Norris Cleans It, It's Clean." In 1948, Norris sold the cleaners to David J. Lee, who changed the name to Ashland Cleaners and Dyers.

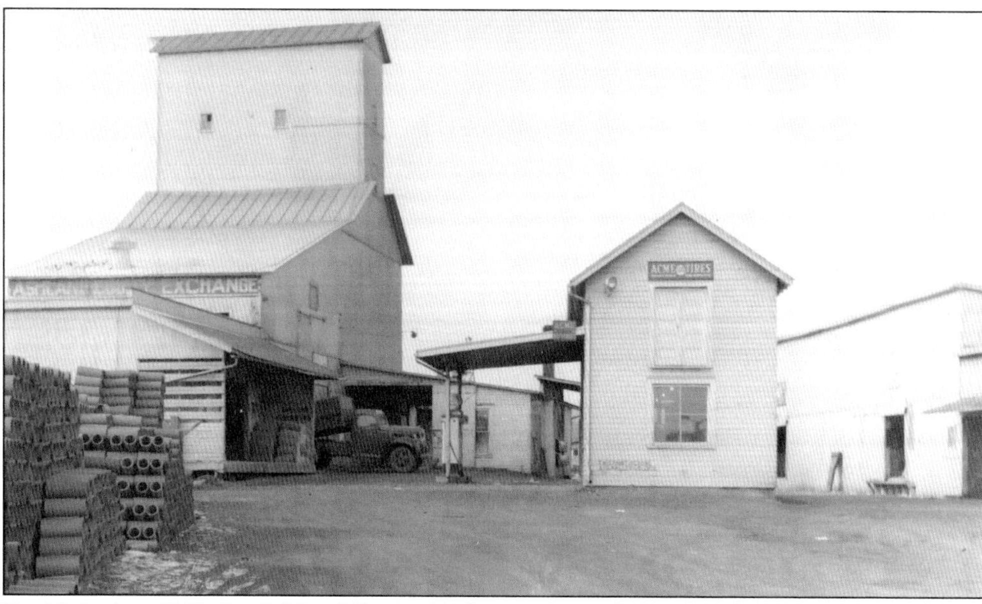

Established in 1917, the Ashland Equity Exchange, located at 612 Miller Street, carried a line of supplies for almost every person, not just farmers. The equity was a large supplier of coal, additionally selling building supplies and Sunoco gasoline along with agricultural needs such as feed, fertilizer, seed, grain, fencing supplies, and many other items.

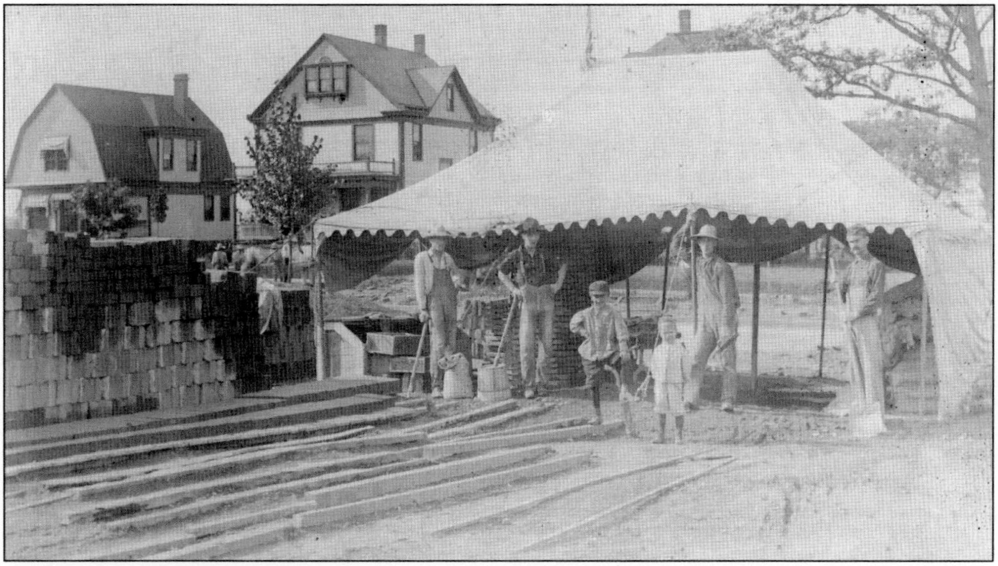

It is quite possible that Seymore Scott's block machine may have been used to make the blocks at the construction site for the Highland Avenue double home, pictured above, and at the construction site of the Brethren Church on Third Street, pictured below. Block maker H.S. Scott, located at 633 Wooster Road, produced more blocks than any maker in the city in 1906. Using the only mechanical power mixer in town, Scott and his partner, Montis Dilgard, made and sold 35,000 blocks that year. The steam-cured blocks were the only faced block in town made from stone plates taken from actual stone cut by Fred Knapp of Knapp's Quarry.

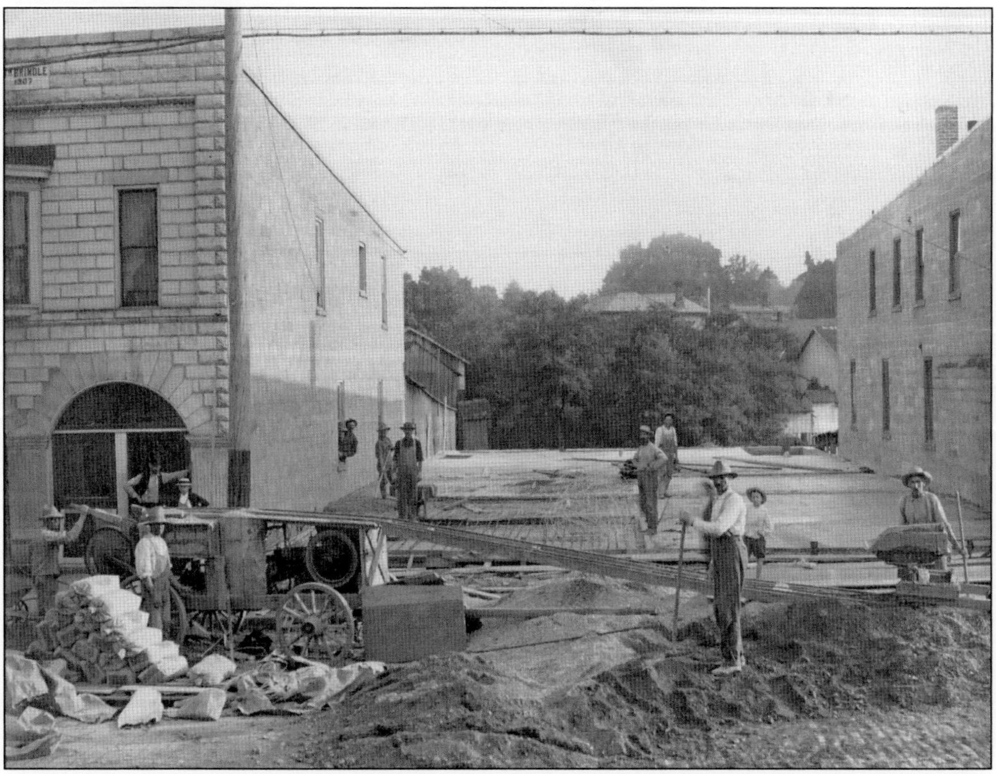

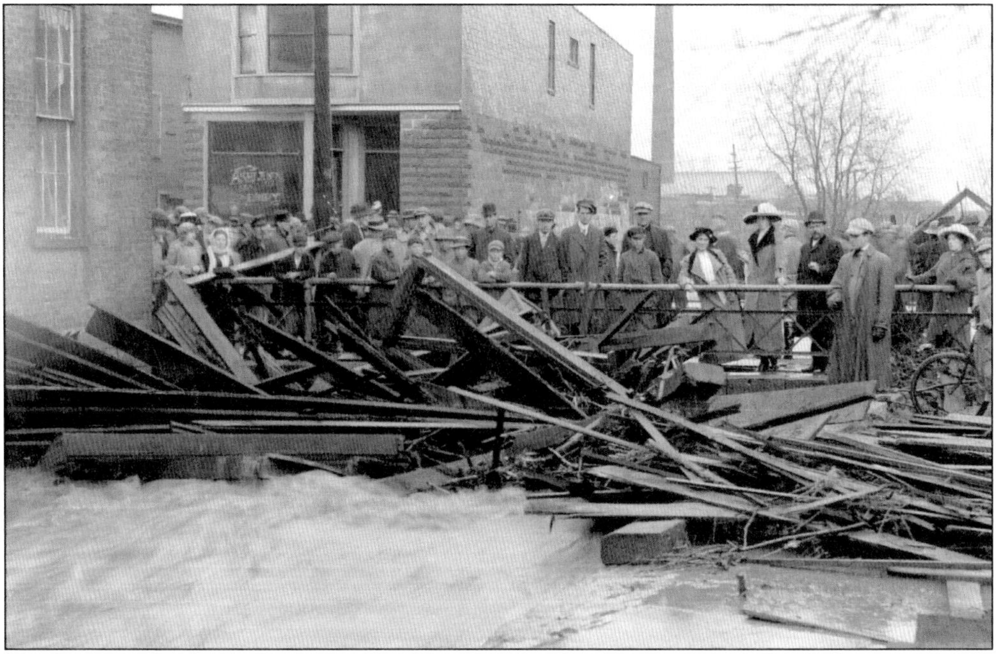

The Great Flood of March 25, 1913, caused havoc for the residents of Ashland. Basements were flooded, miles of railroad tracks were swept away, and streets became rivers. What began as a gentle rain on a Friday increased in intensity and continued nonstop until the following Tuesday afternoon. In the five-day period, approximately 10 inches of rain fell, the second highest record of rainfall in the state. One of the hardest hit areas was on Center Street at the bridge on the town creek, where chicken coops and lumber debris floated downstream in the raging water, as pictured above. With water running swiftly down both West and East Main Streets, seen below, many businesses were destroyed. Estimated damages throughout the town were $200,000 with an additional $100,000 worth of damages to the bridges alone.

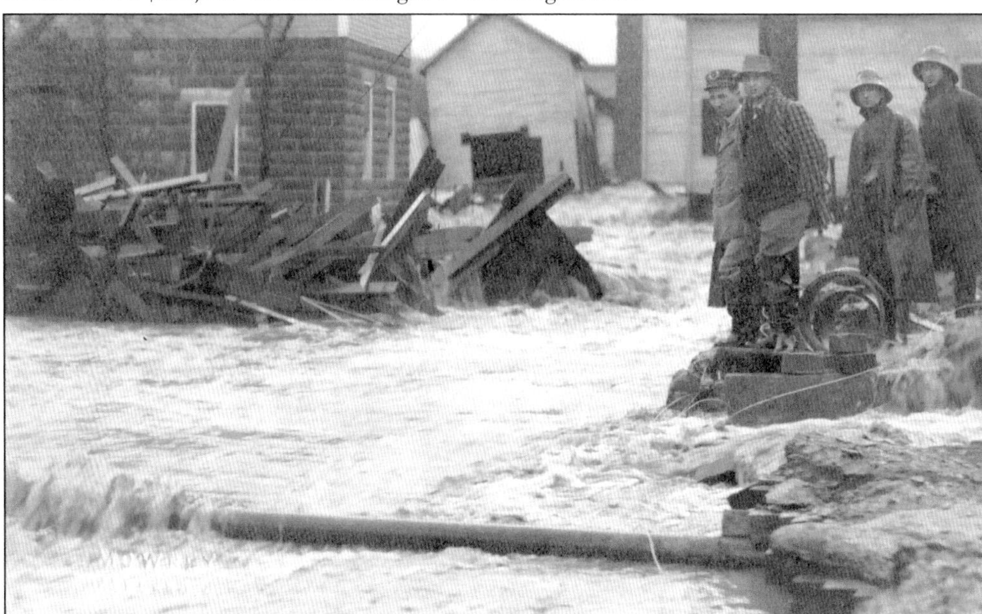

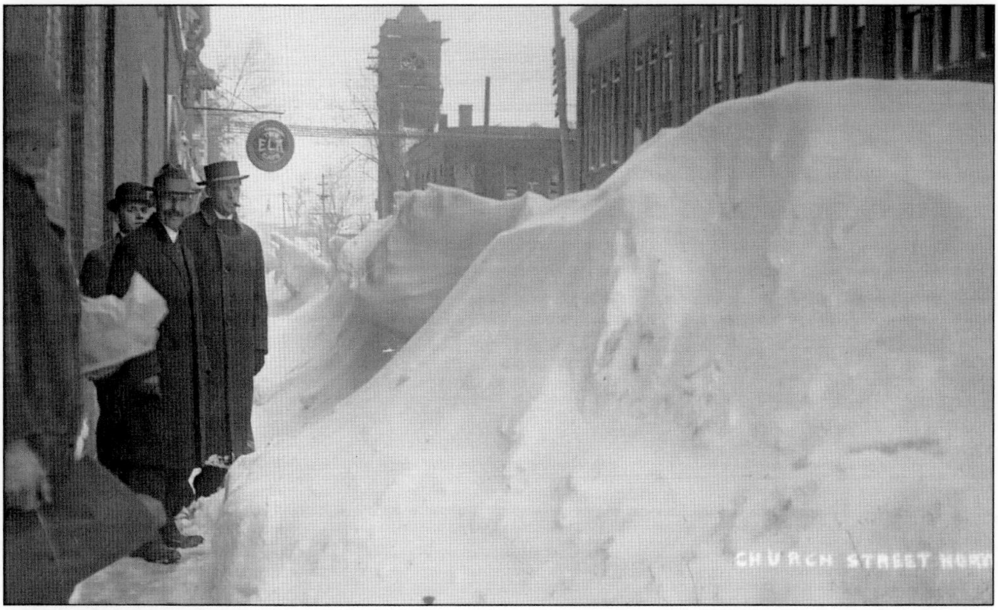

The year 1913 was an unforgettable point in time for the citizens of the town. First, the Great Flood of March 1913 was followed by the White Hurricane of November 1913, a massive snow storm that lasted four days, becoming one of the greatest in Ohio history. On November 7, an intense low-pressure system developed in the south, pushing its way into the northwest where lake effect took place, dumping several feet of snow, creating huge drifts, and immobilizing cities across the Great Lakes. The White Hurricane brought nearly two feet of snow to the town alone and was accompanied by 40-to-50-mile-per-hour winds. Snow banks stood six feet high in the streets, and the town shut down for two days. These views, both facing north, show Church Street, above, and Orange Street, below.

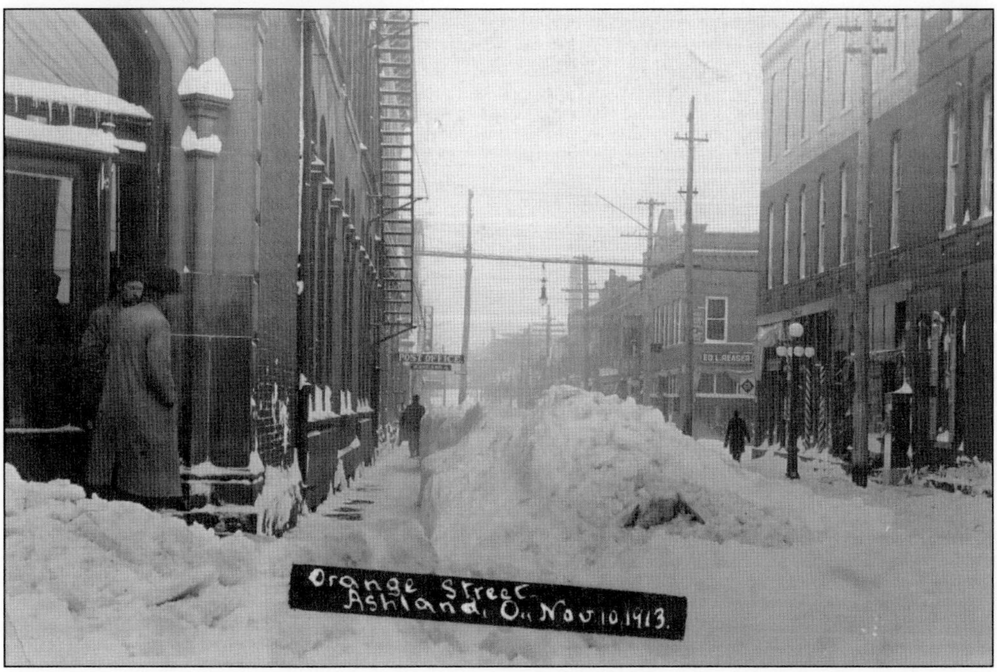

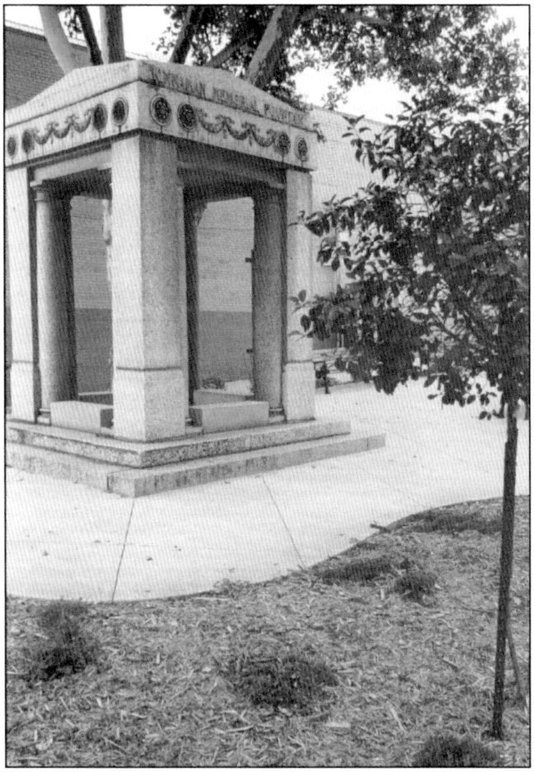

When Margaret Kinnaman died in 1928, she left a gift to the city that would keep her name alive forever—the Kinnaman Memorial Fountain, located at the corner of Main and Center Streets. Margaret, the wife of Dr. Robert Kinnaman, a leading physician and surgeon who specialized in the eye, ear, nose, and throat, left $10,000 to city for the sole purpose of constructing this fountain for public use.

Barely visible in this unidentified late-1800s Main Street saloon is a "black list" hanging alongside the bar mirror behind the bartender. The list contained names of those banned from the saloon for being a drunkard. By 1905, this list was no longer necessary as the temperance movement swept through the town, shutting down saloons with the popular dry vote. The Prohibition era closed the town's 17 saloons for nearly 30 years.

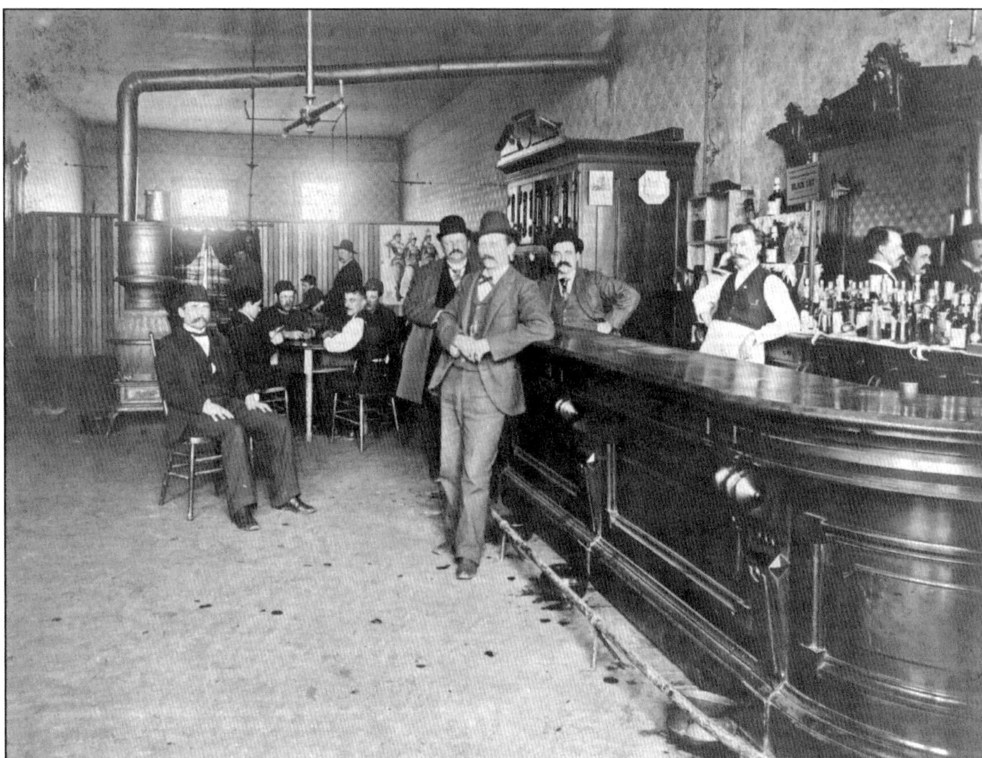

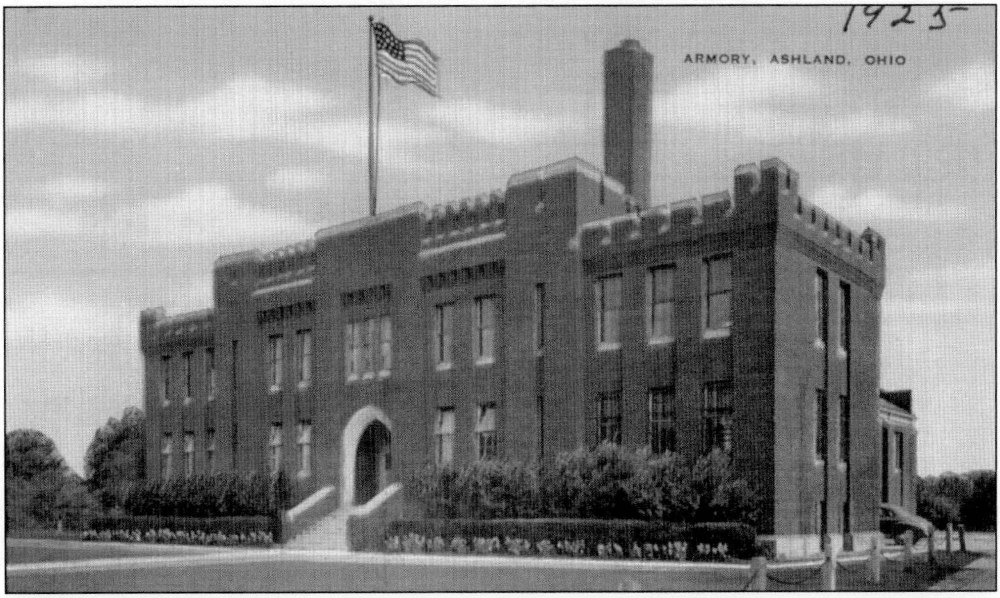

The National Guard Armory at 512 East Main Street was dedicated on May 30, 1925. The city provided the property for the armory, the state provided $75,000 for construction, and the Lions Club donated $5,000 for an expanded drill floor. The armory's large drill floor was used not only for military training, but also for civic functions. Prior to 1925, guardsmen assembled at the armory at 343 West Main Street, which was built in 1904.

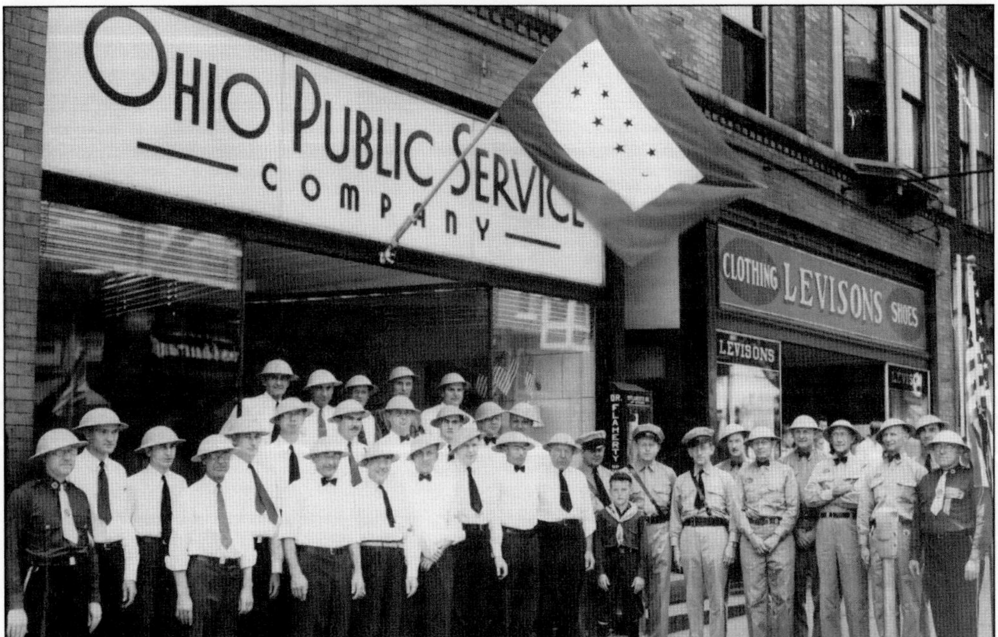

The Ohio Public Service (OPS) assisted with civil defense to the community during World War II. Organized in the 1940s, employees held weekly meetings on emergency assistance and first aid to the community. Additionally, they sold all things electrical, from light bulbs to appliances. The OPS was located at 29 East Main Street. The stars on the flag in the photograph indicate employees enlisted in the service.

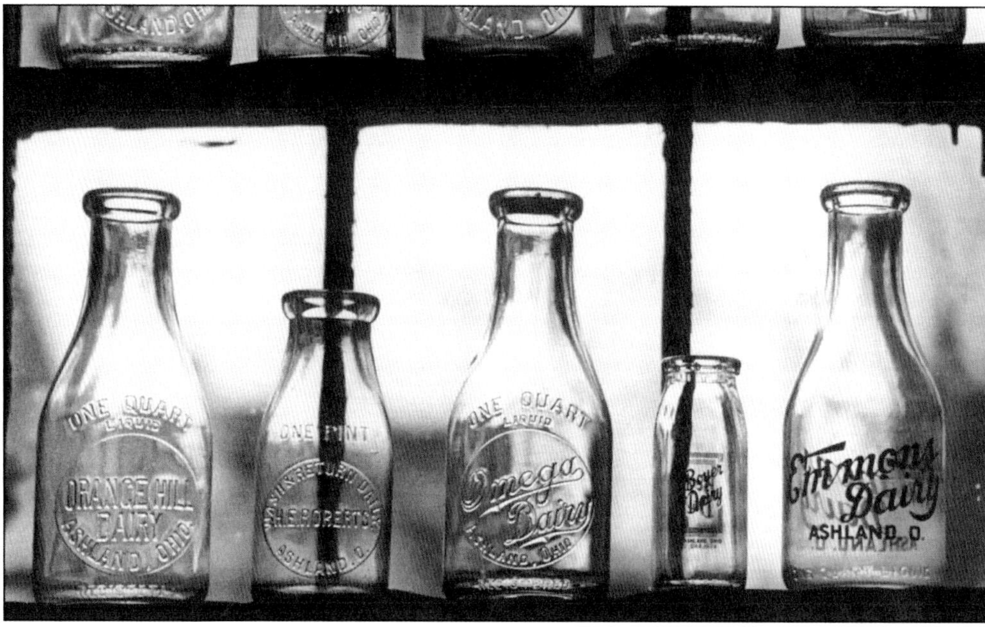

After the milk can came the creation of the milk bottle, offering a much more convenient and sanitary form of containment. The display of bottles shown above represents the various dairies that dotted the city streets in the early to mid-1900s. Of the many dairies in town, Ashland Sanitary Dairy was one of the most popular, being centrally located at 161 Center Street. This popular hangout for high schools students was also the place for families after their Saturday night of shopping downtown. The Sanitary Dairy, pictured below, closed its doors in 1965 after merging with the Boyer Dairy to form the All Star Dairy, located at 725 Clark Street. Affiliated with the Reiter and Harter All Star Dairy, which had plants in Akron and Massillon, the Ashland All Star Dairy was proud of its fleet of refrigerated trucks, which traveled routes throughout the area.

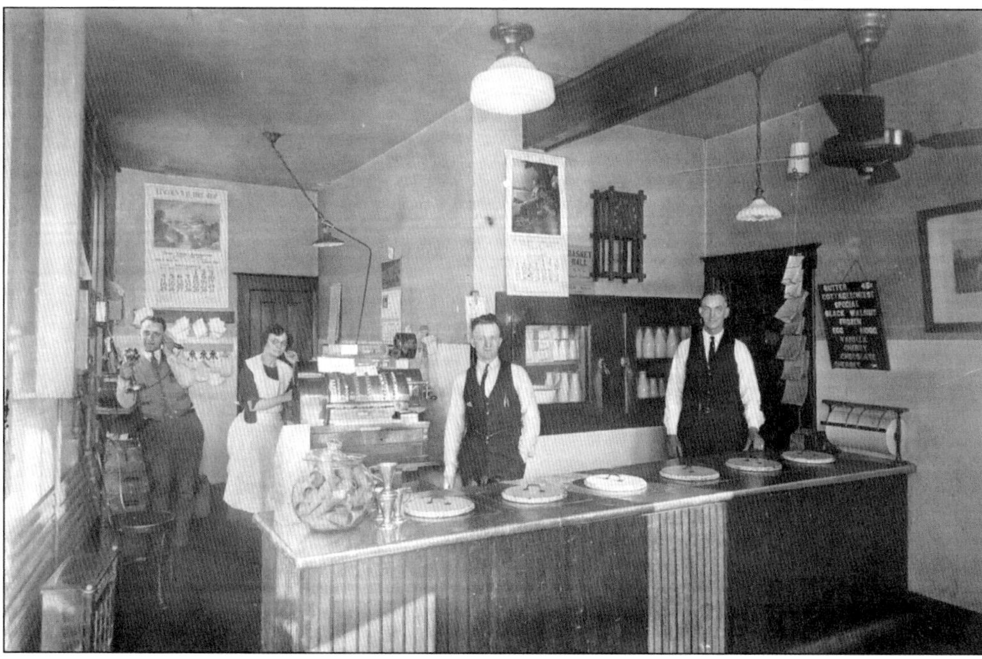

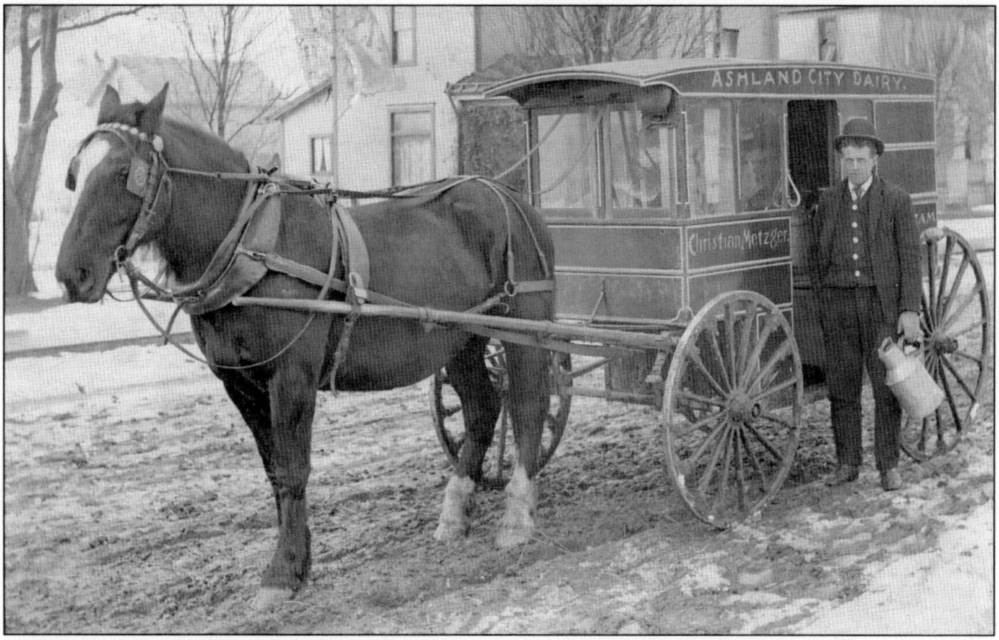

Prior to the invention of the milk bottle, dairymen used to deliver milk to customer's homes in large cans, pouring the milk into lidded pails. Christian Metzger, owner of the Ashland City Dairy, is shown above making his rounds throughout the town with his milk wagon. Because of the lack of refrigeration, the dairyman only delivered milk to nearby customers. Progress eventually brought the delivery of milk by refrigerated truck, and the milkman delivered milk to homes in glass bottles that were eventually replaced by paper cartons. Most homeowners during this time used insulated metal boxes for the placement of dairy products by the milkman. The last of his breed, milkman Larry Glenn, pictured below, dashes from his truck to make an early-morning delivery of milk and sour cream on his route through town in 1985.

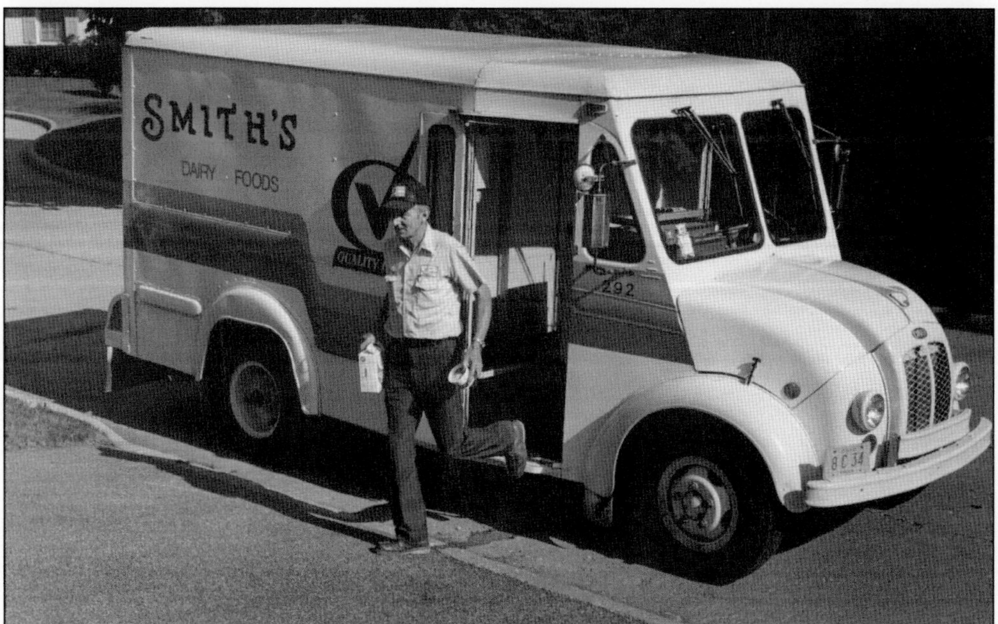

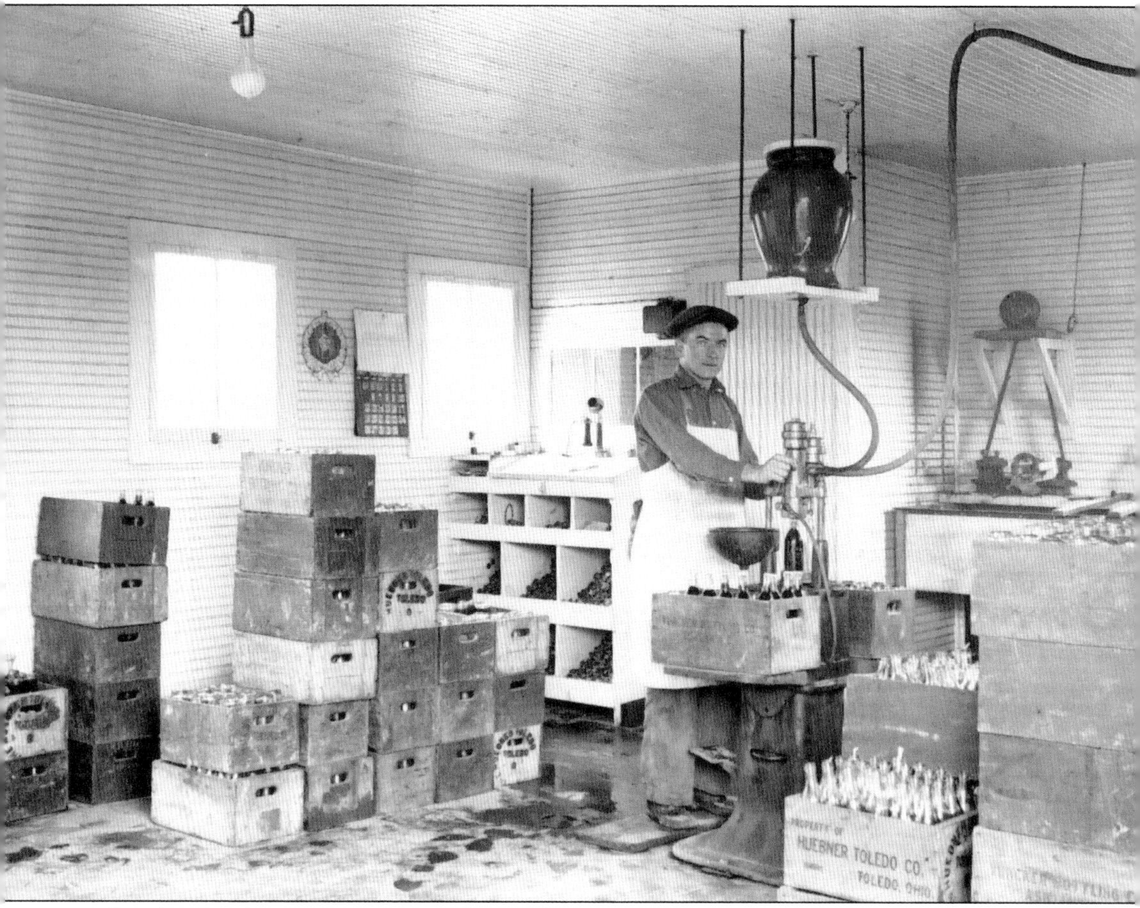

Yuncker Bottling Company manufactured and bottled soda water. City Councilman William H. Yuncker founded the company in 1903. Turning out a sweet drink of the highest quality, Yuncker's Bottling was located at 158 Main Street. Councilman Yuncker's soda found its way into the homes of Ashland and the surrounding towns. The popularity of soft drinks continued to grow during the Prohibition era. Taking advantage of this growing market, beverage-bottling companies became quite popular. Fred Moneysmith, shown above carbonating and bottling soda in his garage on Lindale Avenue, started his company in 1920. Supplies were brought to town for the bottlers by way of the interurban. With competition from the popular Nehi and Coca-Cola soft drinks, Moneysmith closed shop in 1931 but continued on by opening a restaurant at 236 Orange Street where he still made root beer and offered all one could drink for just 5¢.

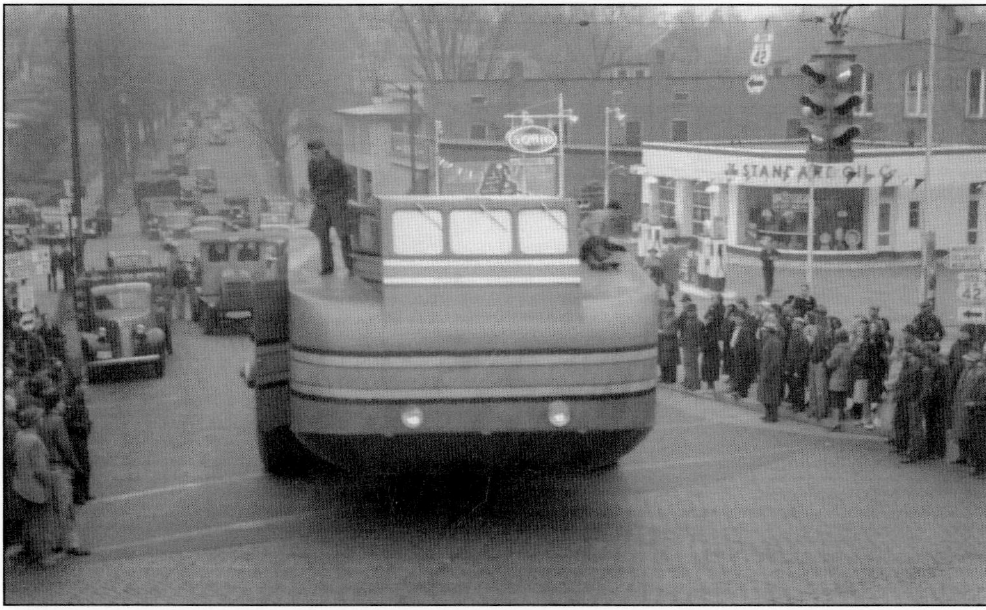

US Naval commander Richard E. Byrd led the first American Antarctic expedition in 1928. For his third Antarctic expedition, Byrd crafted a snow cruiser that measured 55 feet long, 20 feet wide, and 15 feet high. Built in Chicago in 1939, it was driven to Boston for shipment to the Great Ice Barrier. The cruiser is pictured here passing through town towards Boston at the intersection of Claremont and Main Streets, traveling at 25 miles per hour, on November 2, 1939.

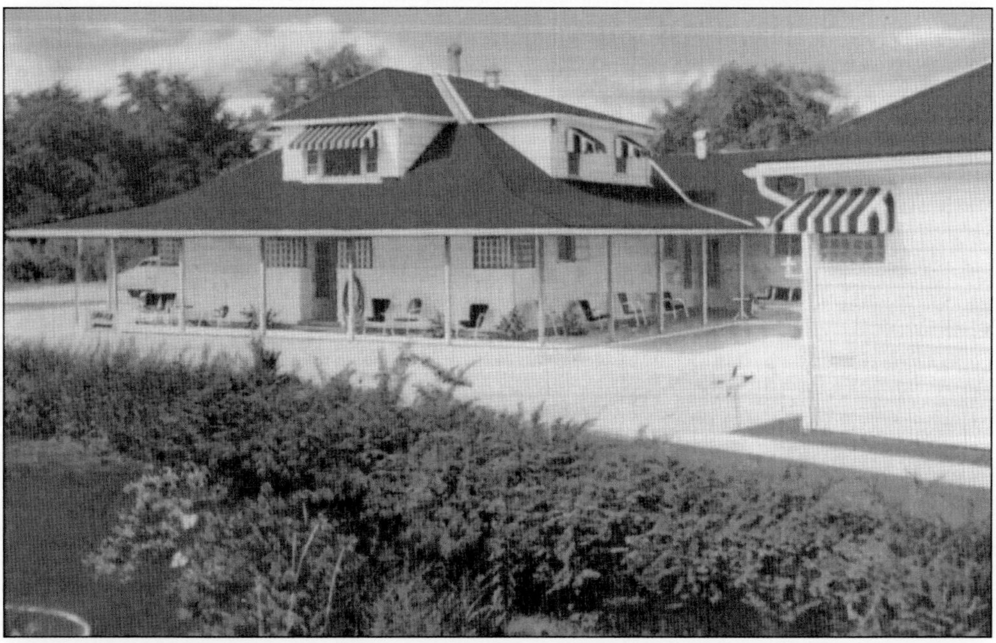

"A Fine Place for Fine People" was the slogan of Spreng's Motel, located at 601 East Main Street from 1951 to 1959, under the ownership of Don Spreng, a former county commissioner. The motel changed hands several times before Cyrus and Francis Miller owned the motel from 1962 to 2002, changing the name to the Holiday Motel. The Salvation Army bought and razed the building in 2009, using the property for operational purposes.

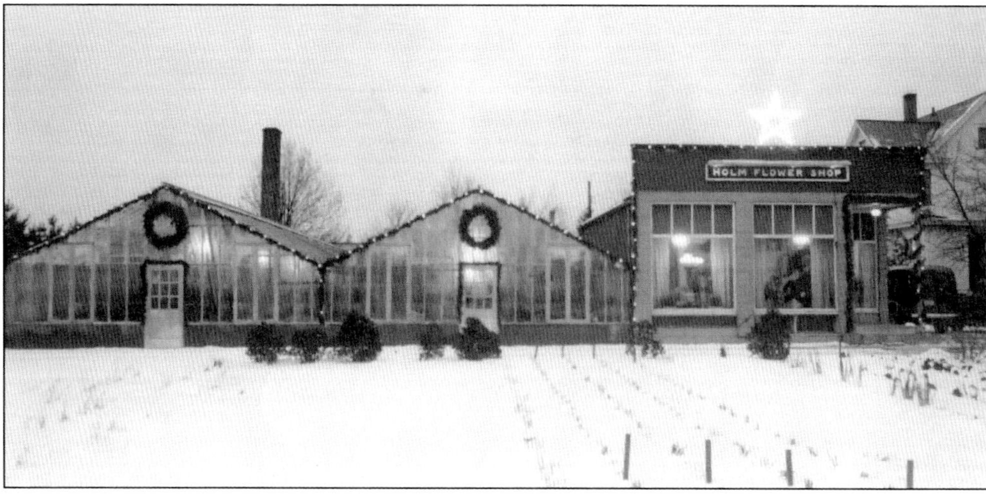

Walter Holm Sr. was an immigrant from Denmark that first settled in Minnesota before moving to town in 1918. Initially employed by florist Gus Lampbrecht, Holm established his own shop in 1924. The Holm Flower Shop, which began as a florist and nursery, was first located on East Main in the Reed-Gongwer building. Holm expanded in 1927 with the addition of a greenhouse, moving to 420 Samaritan Avenue, a narrow dirt street surrounded by pastureland with Ashland College nearby. It was at this same time that Walter Holm Jr. and his wife, Barbara, took over the florist from his parents, discontinuing the nursery division and eventually purchasing the business in 1958. The photograph above shows the shop and greenhouses on Samaritan Avenue decorated for Christmas, and below, a handsome lad contemplates his next floral delivery. (Cappie Holm Stone collection.)

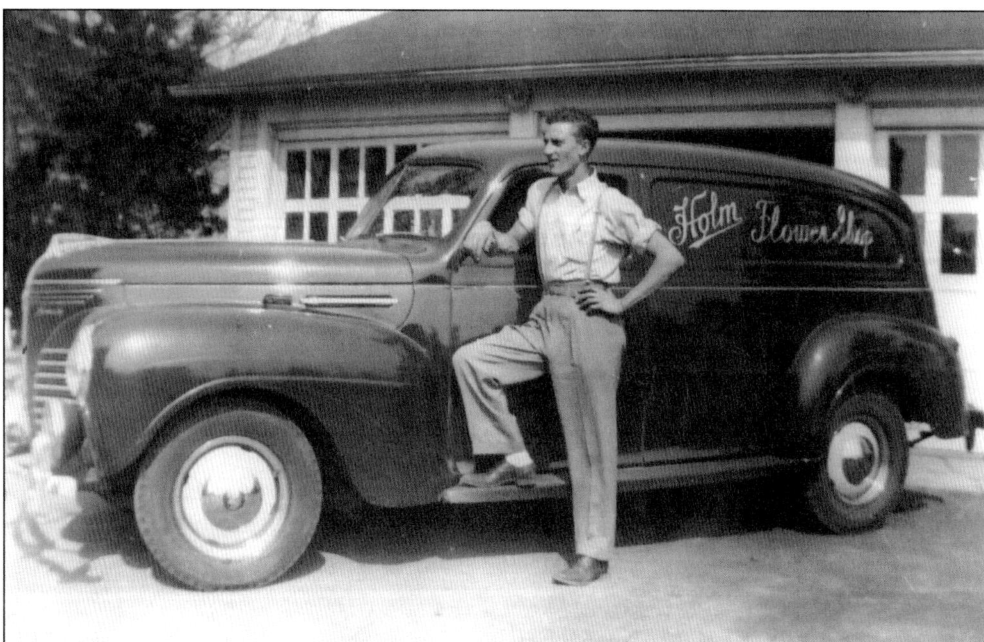

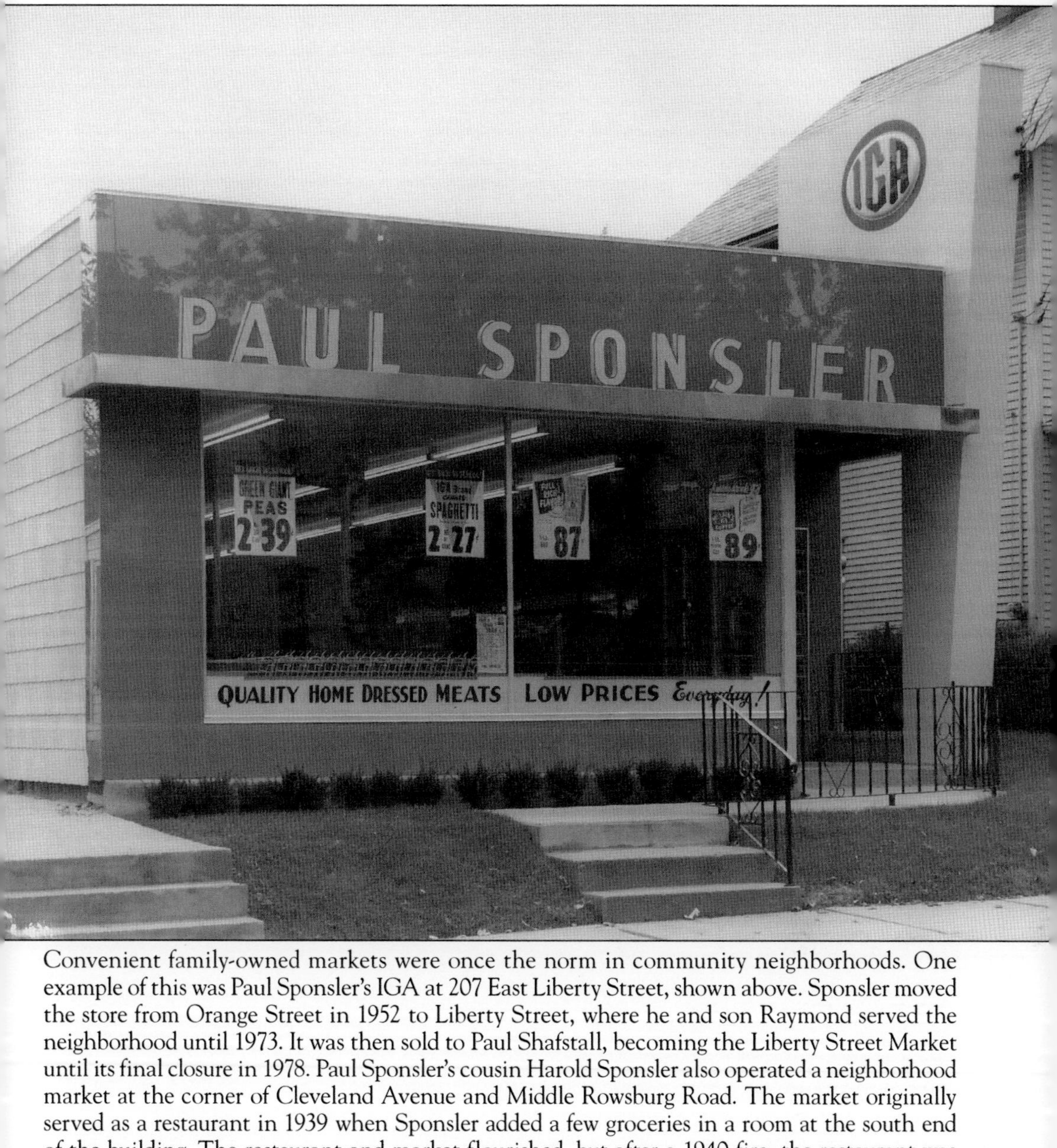

Convenient family-owned markets were once the norm in community neighborhoods. One example of this was Paul Sponsler's IGA at 207 East Liberty Street, shown above. Sponsler moved the store from Orange Street in 1952 to Liberty Street, where he and son Raymond served the neighborhood until 1973. It was then sold to Paul Shafstall, becoming the Liberty Street Market until its final closure in 1978. Paul Sponsler's cousin Harold Sponsler also operated a neighborhood market at the corner of Cleveland Avenue and Middle Rowsburg Road. The market originally served as a restaurant in 1939 when Sponsler added a few groceries in a room at the south end of the building. The restaurant and market flourished, but after a 1940 fire, the restaurant was discontinued. The grocery remained and later became part of the IGA franchise in 1951. (Brent Sponsler collection.)

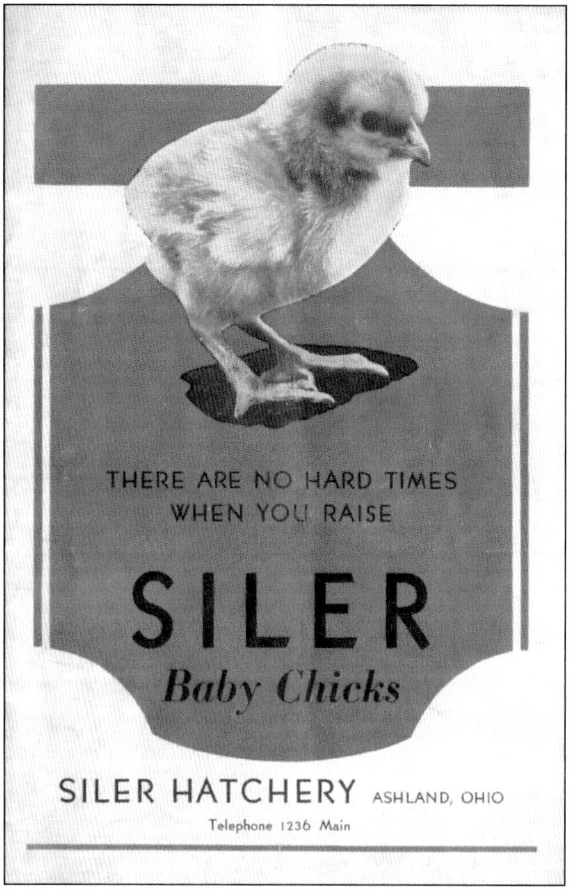

Ira Q. Siler, with the assistance of his family, owned and operated the Siler Hatchery, located on the Wooster Road, from approximately 1926 to 1948. The Siler Hatchery specialized in hatching purebred poultry, priding themselves in selection, quality, and customer service. Through a process called culling, a thorough inspection of the bird, the hatchery could determine if a bird would develop into a good layer. Because of this, Siler marketed baby chicks with higher-than-average egg-producing records. The Siler Hatchery was also known for guaranteeing 100 percent live delivery of the chicks ordered or the lost chick would be replaced free of charge. The photographs shown are from a 1934 hatchery catalog. (Ashland County Historical Preservation Alliance collection.)

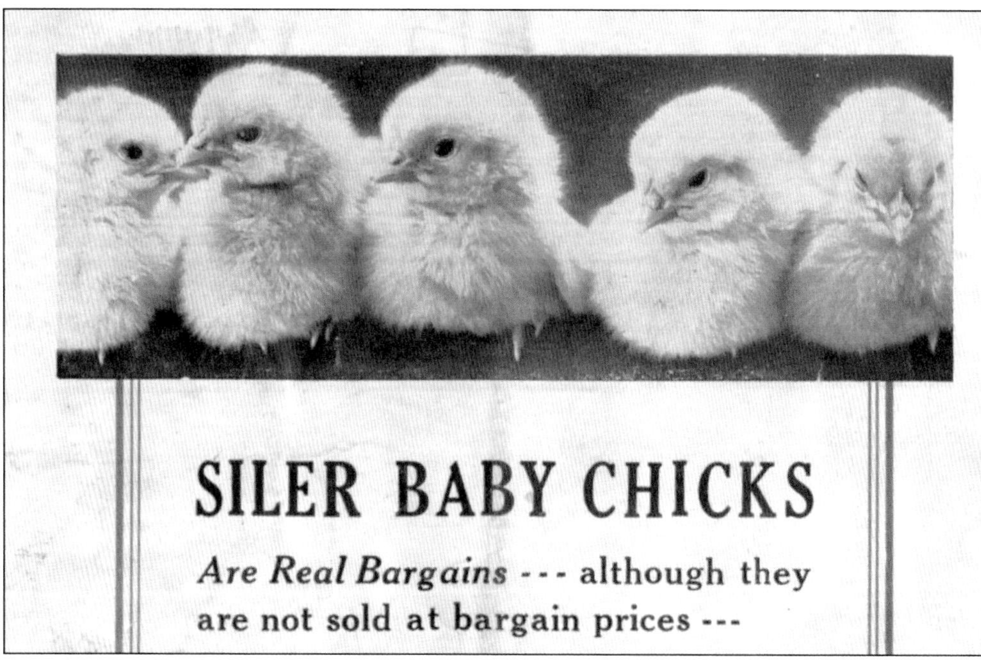

Nine

Marching through Society and Time

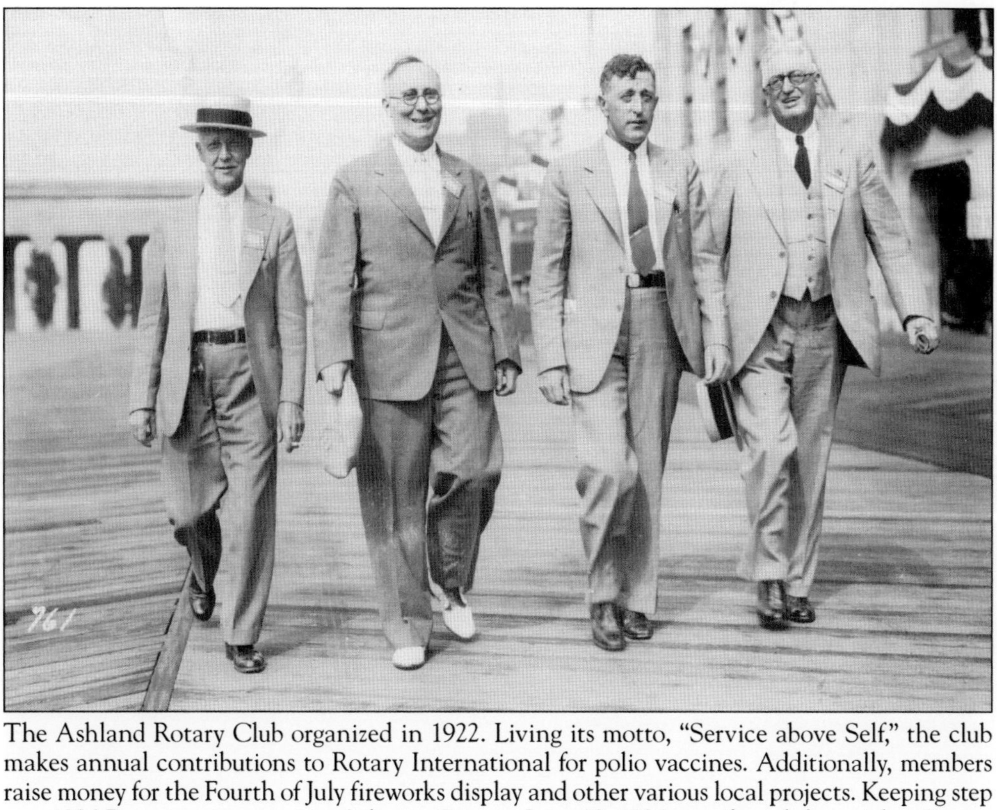

The Ashland Rotary Club organized in 1922. Living its motto, "Service above Self," the club makes annual contributions to Rotary International for polio vaccines. Additionally, members raise money for the Fourth of July fireworks display and other various local projects. Keeping step at a 1936 Rotary convention in Atlantic City on June 23, 1936, are, from left to right, George Hiner, Will Duff, Russell Moore, and Dr. William F. Emery.

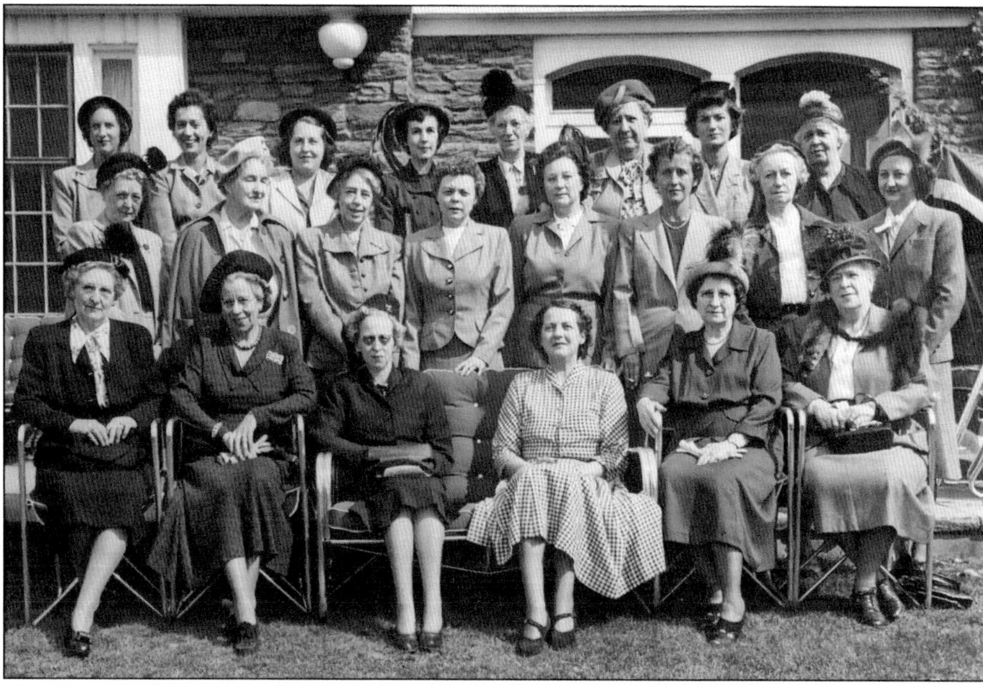

The Congenial Coterie Club, pictured above, was a social group of ladies representing distinguished leading families in society that organized their special union in 1898. The women enjoyed not only elaborate social events in their homes with, at times, 100 or more in attendance, but also traveled by way of "Alvesta," the private trolley car of F. E. Myers's wife, pictured below on Main Street in 1911. Additionally, the ladies took pleasure in studying history, art, poetry, and other topics. At a special meeting in 1918, the members invited their daughters into membership. This proposal was made in order to carry on the club as far as possible into the future, with daughters, daughters-in-laws, and granddaughters taken in at age 24. Charter members included Mrs. F.E. Myers, Mrs. Nathan Strauss, Mrs. William Gates, and Mrs. S.G. Wiest.

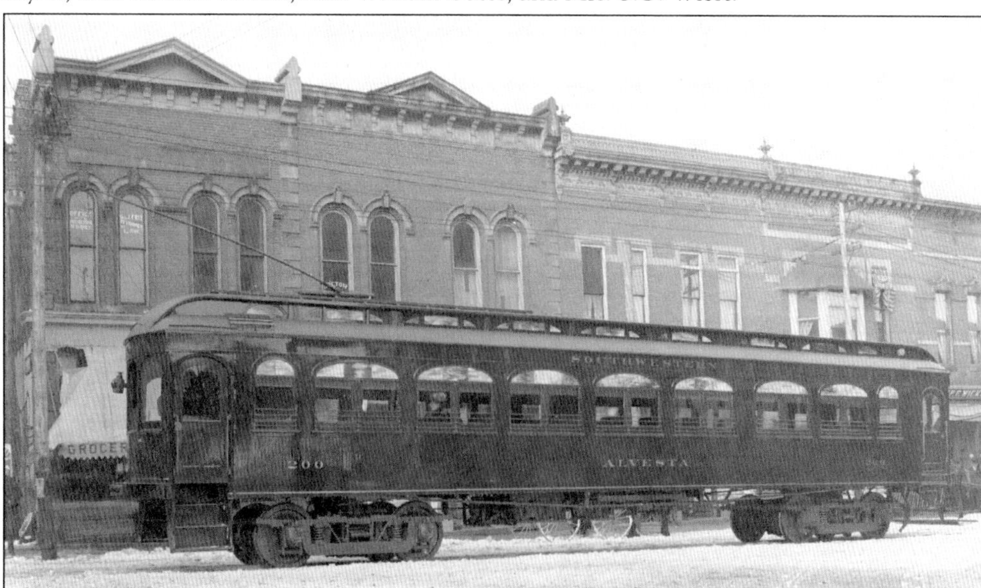

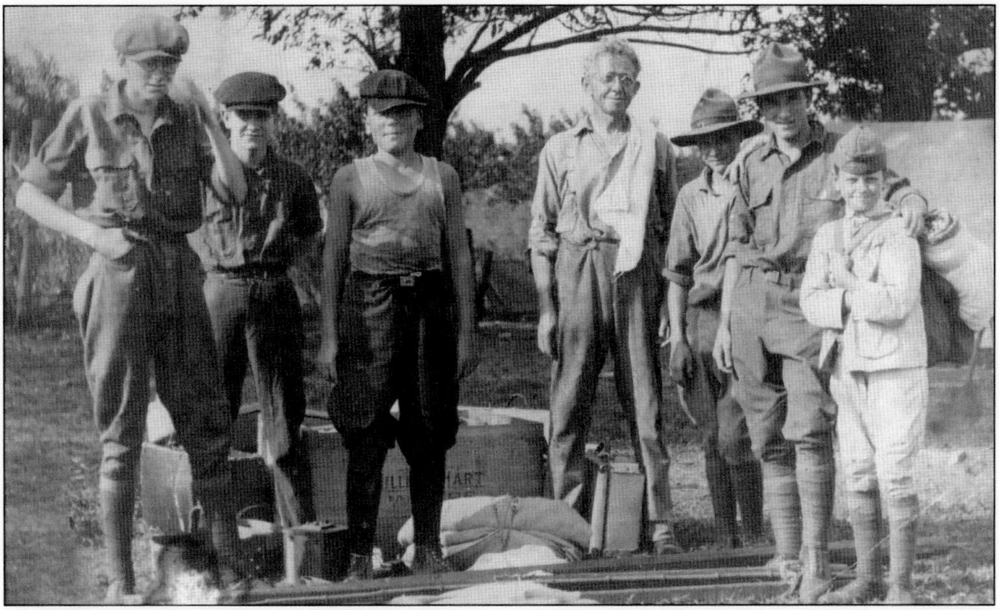

The Boy Scout program, considered a militaristic movement by some, came under heavy resistance when Ard Blackford first introduced it in 1911. Persistence paid off, and Blackford ultimately trained more than 400 scouts that worked for merit badges and annually took summer camping trips, sometimes as far away as Niagara Falls. No boy was ever refused summer camp privilege, as Blackford, pictured above in center, personally paid for those of little means. The town's first Girl Scout troop, pictured below, was formed in 1919 under the leadership of Mary Arthur but disbanded a short time later. Another formed in 1928, only to once again disband. Finally settling into existence in 1937, a council was formed with Martha Wallace as commissioner in 1942. Under this council, the Scouts acquired the Hidden Woodland camp, north of Savannah, in 1957.

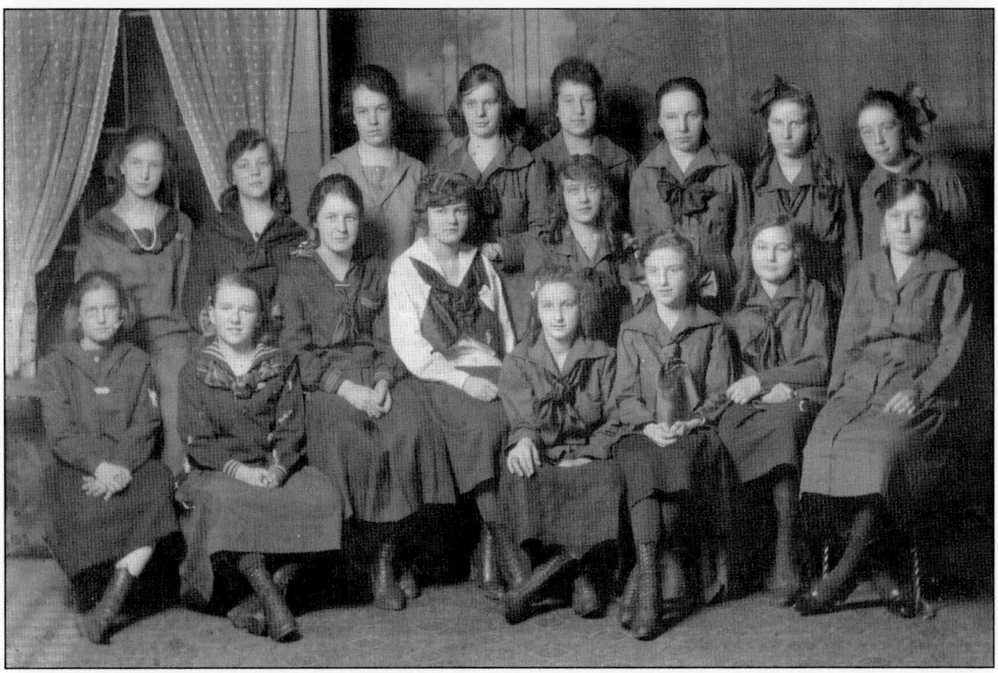

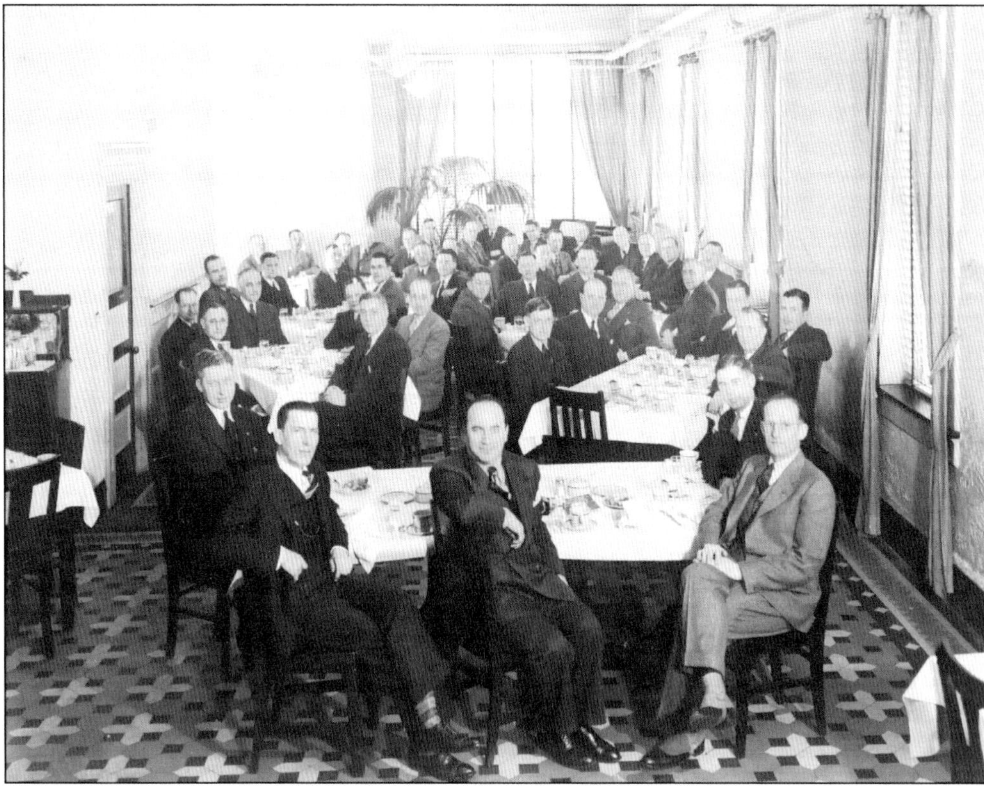

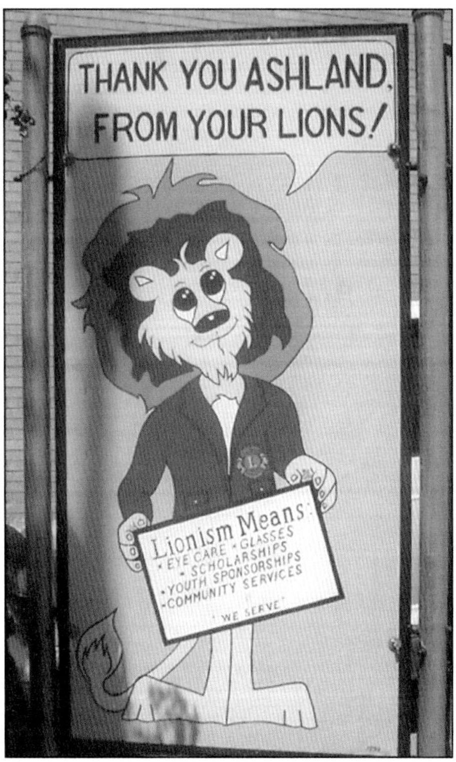

The first men's service organization in town was the Ashland Lions Club, chartered on November 16, 1920. The club, one of the oldest in the state, is pictured above, dining at Hetler's Restaurant at 22 Main Street in the early 1940s. Living up to its motto, "We Serve," members are active in sight saving and assistance to the blind, contributing to sight foundations such as Pilot Dogs, Inc., as well supporting local projects such as Hospice of North Central Ohio. The Ashland Evening Lions Club was chartered in 1963 and also supports eye care through various projects. Local projects are also important, returning monies raised back into the community to support worthy causes, such as equipment for the fire department, replacement of Myers band shell benches, and the Kinnaman Park Santa House and kiosk at the corner of Center and Main Streets. (Evening Lions collection.)

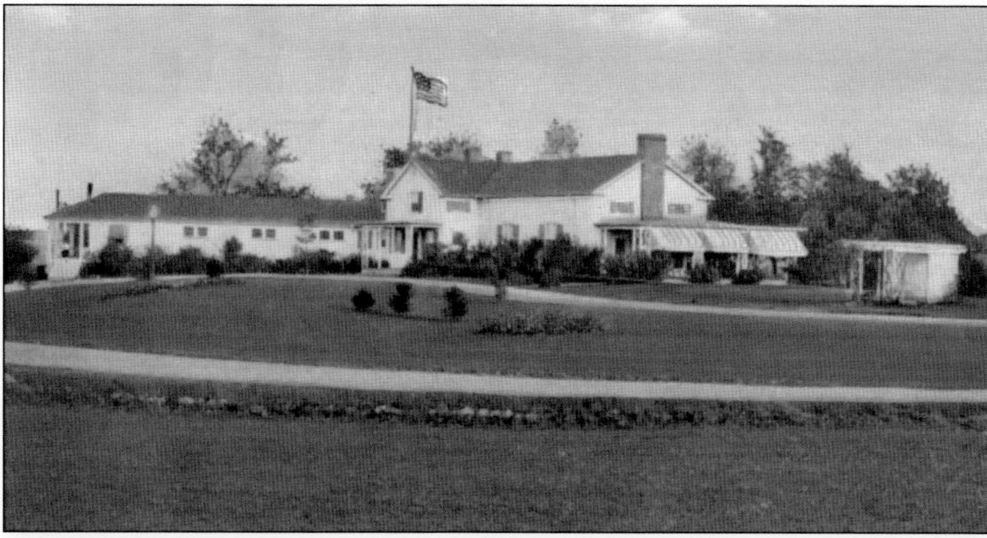

The 110-acre Eva Mohn farm, located at the end of Center Street in 1922, was the grand beginning of the Country Club of Ashland, pictured above, at a cost of $28,000. Pledges of $100 per person were made for the development of the nine-hole golf course with clubhouse and tennis courts. The photograph below is of an unidentified gathering at the new club. The club added a swimming pool in 1958 and an additional nine holes of golf in 1970. Beginning in 1961, the Amateur Two-Man Best-Ball Tournament, the longest-running tournament of its kind in Ohio, has attracted golfers from around the state and beyond, including Ed Sneed, Tom Weiskopf, and Joey Sindelar. Lee Trevino was known to appear at times with Sam Snead and Lee Edler for demonstration rounds, raising money for the Boy Scouts.

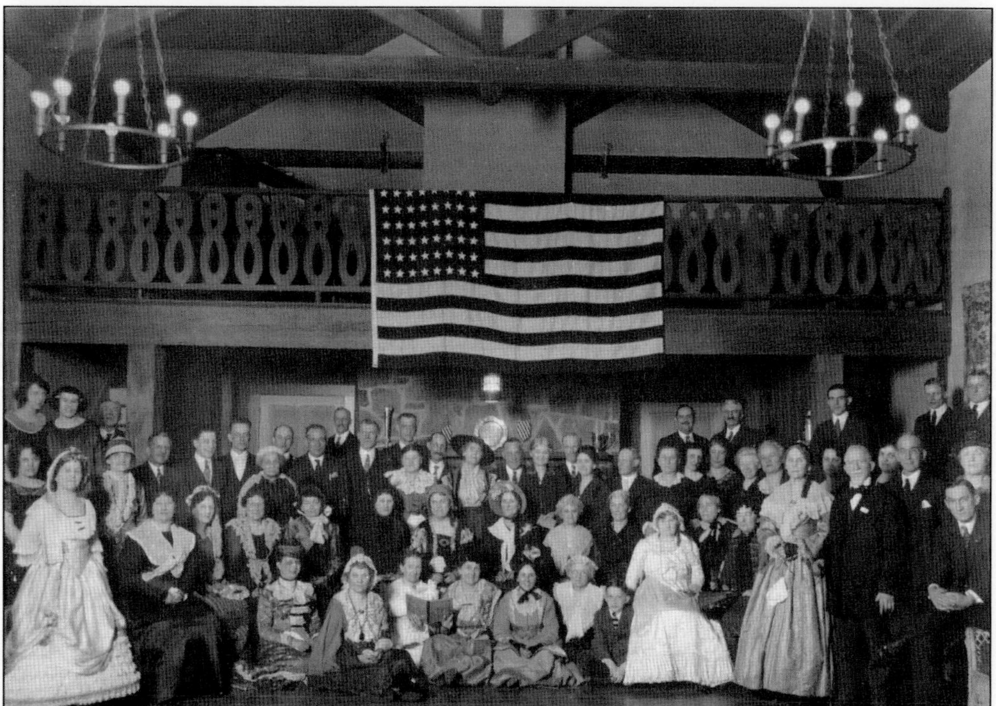

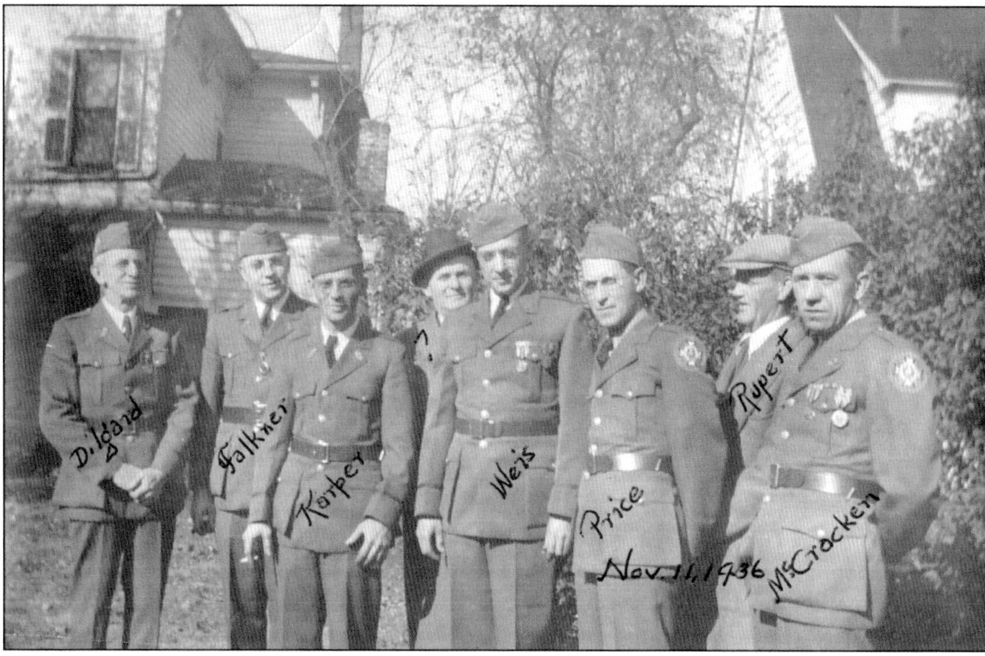

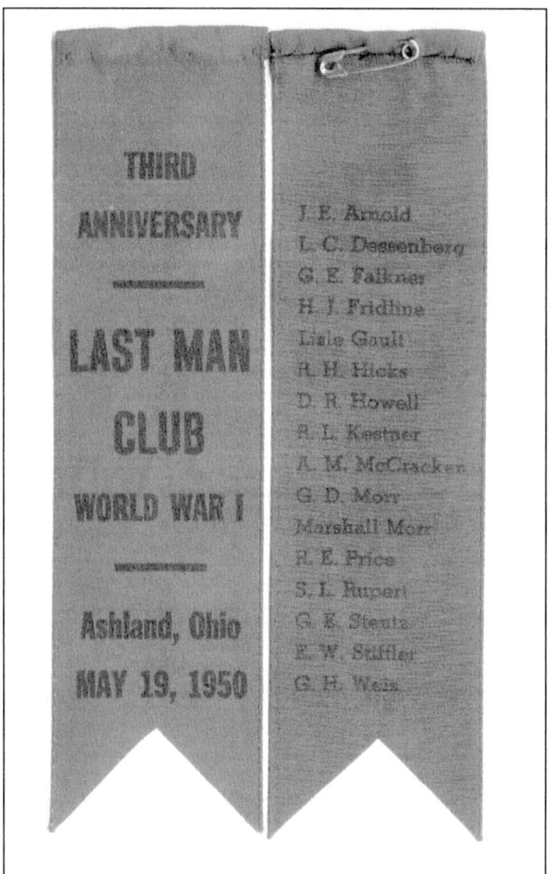

Stanton Rupert, second from right above, eventually became the "last man," as a member of the Last Man Club. In 1947, Rupert and 16 local World War I veterans formed the club, meeting monthly to carry on camaraderie. The club name was established because the last surviving man would receive the privilege of drinking a bottle of champagne that was signed by club members and entrusted through the years to the club president. Members were additionally celebrants of the first Armistice Day, or Veterans Day, on November 11, 1918. Rupert, who served with Company E of the 146th Infantry, was the last surviving member of the club, upon which he honored those gone before him by drinking the bottle of champagne with family and friends. Shown at left is a ribbon from the third anniversary gathering, which lists club members.

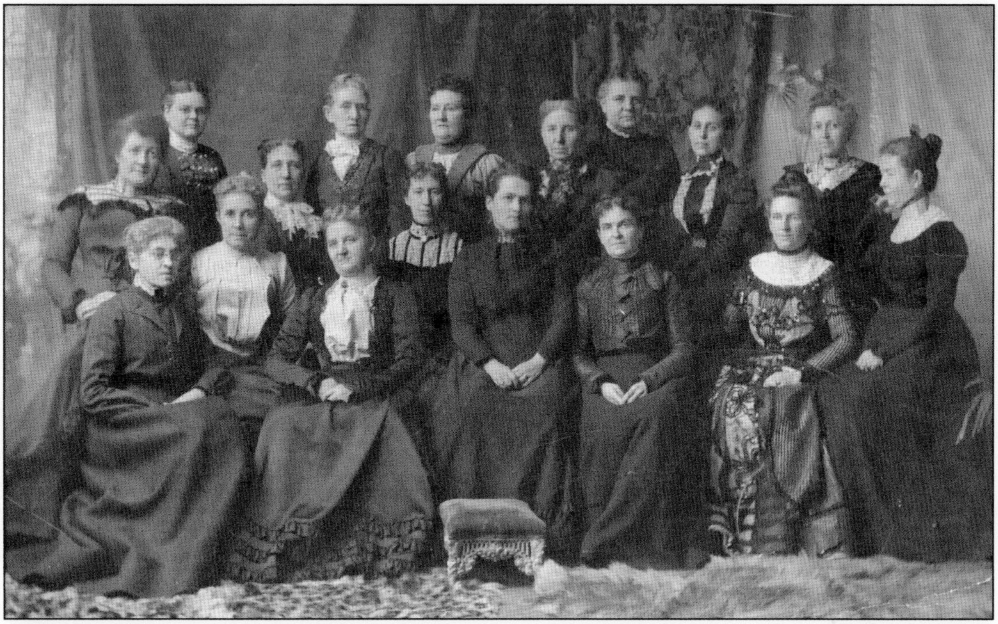

First organized in 1887 as the Chautauqua Literary and Scientific Circle, six years later, in 1893, the club name was changed to the Friday Club; it was appropriately named, as the group met weekly on Fridays. The ladies group studied different topics, such as American history, Ohio authors, and histories of various countries, but they mostly enjoyed sharing fellowship with members, as pictured above in 1897.

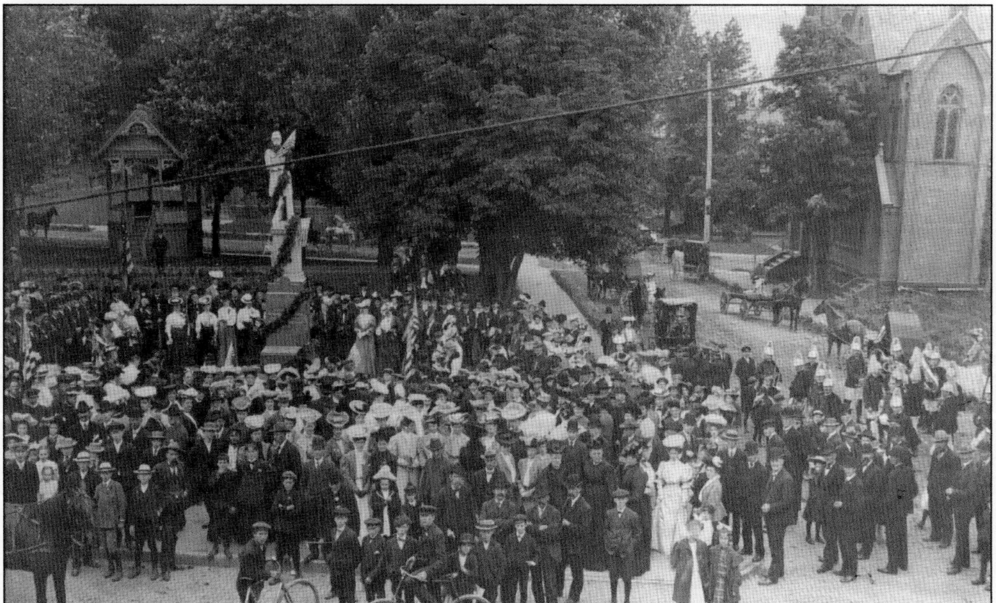

Men, women, and children of the town gather on the Courthouse Park lawn, anticipating an event to be held at the Soldiers Monument on the northwest corner of Second and Church Streets. This unidentified and undated photograph shows military band members on the far right with white hats as they prepare to play for the gathering that is believed to be a celebration on a Memorial Day in the late 1890s.

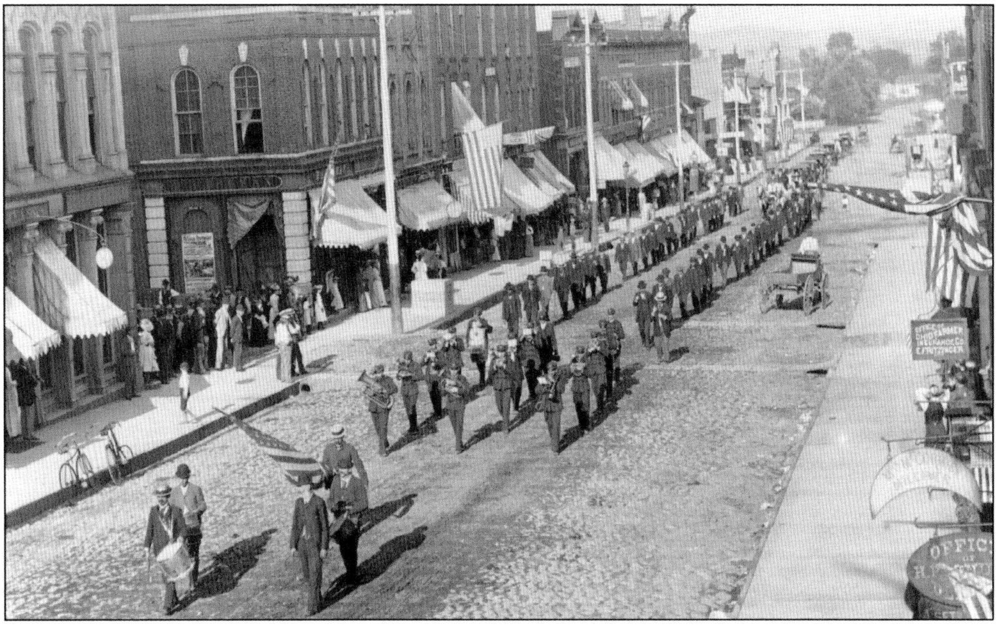

As far as the eye can see in this late 1890s photograph, a parade of music, speakers of the day, local dignitaries, and horse-drawn carriages make their way along the cobblestones west on Main Street to the cemetery as part of a Memorial Day Celebration. Prior to the parade, schoolchildren would gather flowers throughout the town, which the community made into wreaths for those to be remembered upon arrival at the cemetery.

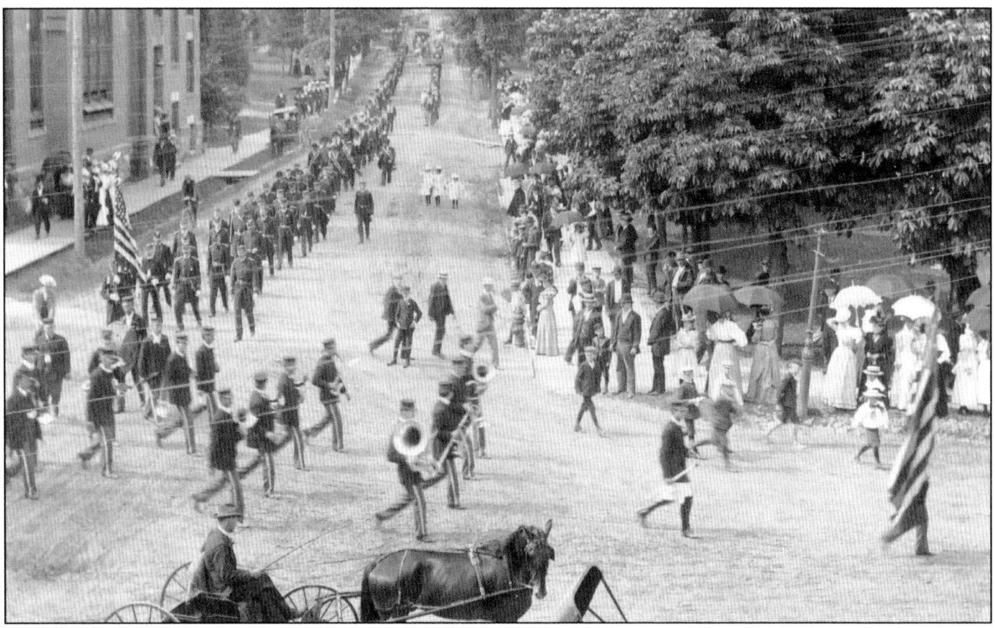

On September 28, 1897, nearly 500 former residents returned to town for the first homecoming of the community to be greeted by the above pictured parade. Welcoming committees of 30 men and women lined the sidewalks in front of the Opera House to shake the hands of those coming home to visit. The Opera House was the setting for welcoming ceremonies. Former citizens, such as Clem Studebaker, shared family success stories.

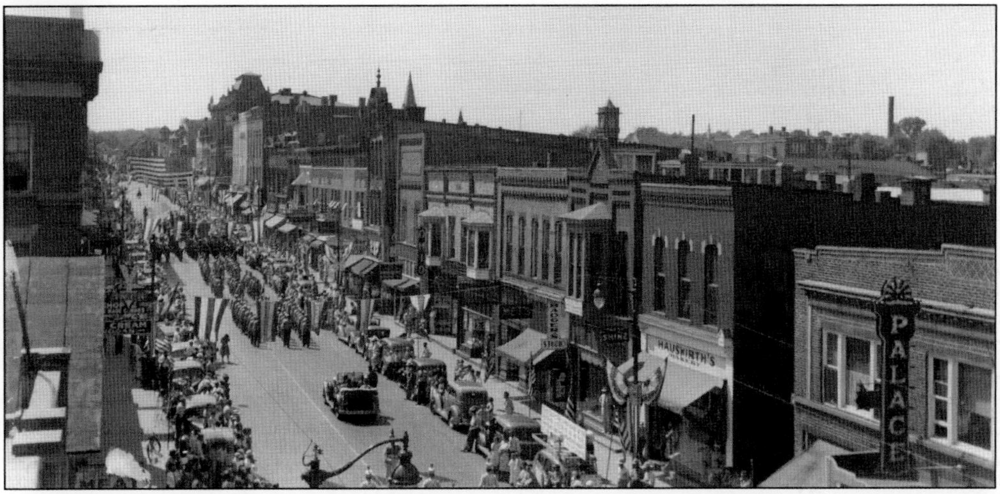

In 1940, one highlight of the 125th anniversary celebration of the town was the two-hour parade that marched from Main Street to Brookside Park. Coined the Cen-Quar celebration, the community was pleased to present their 125-year-old city to those coming home, proud of how much their community had grown. In 1965, the 150th sesquicentennial anniversary of the town was observed. The four-day affair featured events such as local industrial tours, world championship softball games, and band shell concerts. At that time, Ashland was referred to as the balloon capital of the world and the hub of industrial Ohio. Today, the community marches on, quite proud of what the little city with big vision has achieved. Pictured below are sesquicentennial parade organizers, from left to right, Hazel Bowers, Georgia Boyd, Sid Boyd, and chairman John Gongwer, as they look forward to Ashland's future.

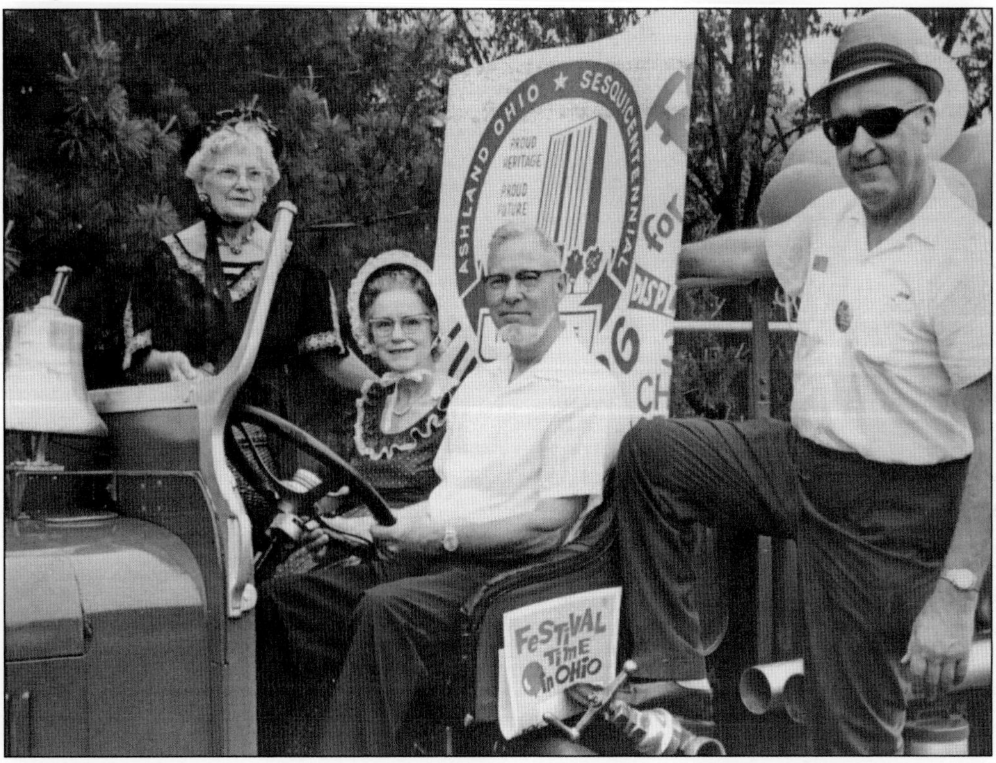

Consistent with our mission to preserve history on a local level, this book was printed in South Carolina on American-made paper and manufactured entirely in the United States. Products carrying the accredited Forest Stewardship Council (FSC) label are printed on 100 percent FSC-certified paper.

MADE IN THE USA